Agape and *Hesed-Ahava*

POSTMODERN ETHICS SERIES

Postmodernism and deconstruction are usually associated with a destruction of ethical values. The volumes in the Postmodern Ethics series demonstrate that such views are mistaken because they ignore the religious element that is at the heart of existential-postmodern philosophy. This series aims to provide a space for thinking about questions of ethics in our times. When many voices are speaking together from unlimited perspectives within the postmodern labyrinth, what sort of ethics can there be for those who believe there is a way through the dark night of technology and nihilism beyond exclusively humanistic offerings? The series invites any careful exploration of the postmodern and the ethical.

Series Editors:

Marko Zlomislić (Conestoga College)

David Goicoechea (Brock University)

Other Volumes in the Series:

Cross and Khôra: Deconstruction and Christianity in the Work of John D. Caputo edited by Neal DeRoo and Marko Zlomislić

Agape and Personhood with Kierkegaard, Mother, and Paul (A Logic of Reconciliation from the Shamans to Today) by David Goicoechea

The Poverty of Radical Orthodoxy edited by Lisa Isherwood and Marko Zlomislić

Theologies of Liberation in Palestine: Contextual, Indigenous and Postcolonial Perspectives edited by Nur Masalha and Lisa Isherwood

Agape and the Four Loves with Nietzche, Father, and Q (A Physiology of Reconciliation from the Greeks to Today) by David Goicoechea

Fundamentalism and Gender: Scripture—Body—Community edited by Ulrike Auga, Christina von Braun, Claudia Bruns, and Jana Husmann

Future Volumes:

David Goicoechea is producing "Millennial Meditations on 2000 Years of Christian Love: A Postmodern Summa—Agape as Reconciliation," of which the present volume is the third of nine.

- IV *Agape and Bhakti with Bataille and Mark, at Loyola-St. Francis (A Mysticology of Reconciliation based on Hindu Karma from Arjuna to Augustine)*
- V *Agape and Karuna with Foucault and Luke, at Brock Philosophy Department (A Therapeutology of Reconciliation based on Buddhist No-Self from Buddha to Francis)*
- VI *Agape and Rahim with Deleuze, Brock Philosophy Society, and John (An Atheology of Reconciliation based on Islamic Sharia from Muhammad to Luther)*
- VII *Agape and Zen with Kristeva, Wilhelmina, and Catholic School (A Semiology of Reconciliation based on Japanese No-Drama from Nishida to John XXIII)*
- VIII *Agape and Jen with Cixous, Carolyn, and Pauline School (A Phenomenology of Reconciliation based on the Confucianist Family from Tu Wei-Ming to John Paul II)*
- IX *Agape and Tao with Irigaray, Johanna, and the Johannine School (An Eschatology of Reconciliation based on Taoist Gendering from Moeller to Benedict XVI)*

VOLUME THREE

Agape and *Hesed-Ahava*

*With Levinas-Derrida and Matthew
at Mt. Angel and St. Thomas*
(A Doxology of Reconciliation)

DAVID L. GOICOECHEA

POSTMODERN ETHICS SERIES 7

☙PICKWICK *Publications* • Eugene, Oregon

AGAPE AND HESED-*AHAVA*
with Levinas-Derrida and Matthew at Mt. Angel and St. Thomas (A Doxology of Reconciliation)

Postmodern Ethics 7

Copyright © 2015 David L. Goicoechea. All rights reserved. Except for brief quotations in critical publications or reviews, no part of this book may be reproduced in any manner without prior written permission from the publisher. Write: Permissions, Wipf and Stock Publishers, 199 W. 8th Ave., Suite 3, Eugene, OR 97401.

Pickwick Publications
An Imprint of Wipf and Stock Publishers
199 W. 8th Ave., Suite 3
Eugene, OR 97401

www.wipfandstock.com

ISBN 13: 978-1-62564-621-7

Cataloging-in-Publication data:

Goicoechea, David L.

Agape and hesed-*ahava* : with Levinas-Derrida and Matthew at Mt. Angel and St. Thomas (a doxology of reconciliation) / David L. Goicoechea.

Postmodern Ethics 7

xx + 356 p.; 23 cm—Includes bibliographical references.

ISBN 13: 978-1-62564-621-7

1. Lévinas, Emmanuel. 2. Derrida, Jacques. 3. Bible. Matthew. 4. Reconciliation—Religious aspects. I. Title. II. Series.

B2430 D484 G55 2014

Manufactured in the USA.

For my Seminary Communities
with whom I still pray daily

Father Ambrose
My Confessor

Father Bernard
Our Rector

Father Louis
Our Phys. Ed. Director

Contents

List of Images | viii
Detailed Line of the Argument | ix
Introduction | 1

Part One: Experiencing Problems
At Mt. Angel | 20
With Levinas and Derrida | 47
In *Hesed* and *Ahava* | 74
With Matthew | 102

Part Two: Seeking Their Causes
With Benedictine Spirituality | 134
With Jewish Postmodernists | 161
With *Hesed* and *Ahava* | 188
With Matthew's *Agape* | 215

Part Three: Receiving Solutions
With Sulpician Spirituality | 246
With Levinas and Derrida | 273
Through *Hesed* and *Ahava* | 300
Through Matthew's *Agape* | 327

Bibliography | 355

Images

Father Ambrose | v
Father Bernard | v
Father Louis | v
The Idaho Seminarians with Father Bernard | 101
The Major Seminary Community in Kenmore Washington | 101
When We Were Freshmen with the Sophomores | 129
Our Junior Class | 129
Running the Hurdles | 130
The Tennis Court and Willamette Valley | 130
Mount Angel Hill Top | 131
The Grotto at Mount Angel | 131
The Monastery Church | 132
At Mount Angel in the Play *Christ in the Concrete City* | 132
Father Sullivan | 242
The Entrance to St. Thomas Seminary | 242
The Seminary Chapel at St. Thomas | 243
The Major Seminary Community in Kenmore Washington | 244
St. Thomas Seminary Dedicated | x

Detailed Line of the Argument

Part One: Experiencing Problems

I At Mt. Angel

I, 1 Mt. Angel's Spiritual, Intellectual, Vital, Physical Values
I, 1.1 Our Alma Mater's Spiritual Nourishing
I, 1.2 Our Alma Mater's Intellectual Nourishing
I, 1.3 Our Alma Mater's Vital Nourishing
I, 1.4 Our Alma Mater's Physical Nourishing
I, 1.5 Father Bernard and the Spiritual
I, 1.6 Father Ambrose and the Intellectual
I, 1.7 Father Anthony and the Vital
I, 1.8 Father Louis and the Physical
I, 1.9 From Money—to Death—to Sex—to Religion

I, 2 Growing Spiritually in That Seminary Seed Bed
I, 2.1 Nourishing *Agape* for All Persons with the Liturgy
I, 2.2 Nourishing *Agapeic* Affection with the Liturgy of the Word
I, 2.3 Nourishing *Agapeic* Friendship with the Word's History
I, 2.4 Nourishing *Agapeic* Eros in the Word's Present
I, 2.5 Nourishing *Agapeic* Mourning in the Word's Future
I, 2.6 Nourishing *Agapeic* Affection in the Liturgy of the Eucharist
I, 2.7 Nourishing *Agapeic* Friendship with the Eucharist's History
I, 2.8 Nourishing *Agapeic* Eros in the Eucharist's Present
I, 2.9 Nourishing *Agapeic* Mourning in the Eucharist's Future

I, 3 Growing Intellectually in That Seminary Seedbed
I, 3.1 Nourishing *Agape* with the Trivium
I, 3.2 Nourishing *Agapeic* Affection with Grammar
I, 3.3 Nourishing *Agapeic* Eros with Rhetoric
I, 3.4 Nourishing *Agapeic* Friendship with Logic
I, 2.5 Nourishing *Agape* with the Quadrivium

I, 2.6	Nourishing *Agapeic* Affection with Mathematics	
I, 3.7	Nourishing *Agapeic* Eros with Music	
I, 3.8	Nourishing *Agapeic* Friendship with Science	
I, 3.9	Nourishing *Agapeic* Mourning with History	

I, 4   **Growing Vitally in that Seminary Seed-Bed**
I, 4.1   Nourishing *Agape* with Poverty, Chastity and Obedience
I, 4.2   Nourishing *Agapeic* Affection with Poverty
I, 4.3   Nourishing *Agapeic* Eros with Chastity
I, 4.4   Nourishing *Agapeic* Friendship with Obedience
I, 4.5   Nourishing *Agape* with the Moral Virtues
I, 4.6   Nourishing *Agapeic* Affection with Justice
I, 4.7   Nourishing *Agapeic* Eros with Temperance
I, 4.8   Nourishing *Agapeic* Friendship with Prudence
I, 4.9   Nourishing *Agapeic* Mourning with Fortitude

I, 5   **Growing Physically in that Seminary Seed-Bed**
I, 5.1   Nourishing *Agapeic* Health, Happiness, Wisdom, Holiness
I, 5.2   Nourishing *Agapeic* Health with Physical Exercises
I, 5.3   Nourishing *Agapeic* Health with Physical Work
I, 5.4   Nourishing *Agapeic* Health with Physical Play
I, 5.5   Nourishing *Agapeic* Health with Team Sport
I, 5.6   Nourishing *Agapeic* Health with Track and Tennis
I, 5.7   Nourishing *Agapeic* Health with Right Diet
I, 5.8   Nourishing *Agapeic* Health with Right Hygiene
I, 5.9   Nourishing *Agapeic* Health with Right Sleep

I, 6   **Growing in Excellence with the Liberal Arts**
I, 6.1   Growing in 1st Commandment Obedience with Better Reading
I, 6.2   Growing in 2nd Commandment Obedience with Better Writing
I, 6.3   Growing in 3rd Commandment Obedience with Better Speaking
I, 6.4   Growing in 4th Commandment Obedience with Better Listening
I, 6.5   Growing in 5th Commandment Obedience with Better Dreaming
I, 6.6   Growing in 6th Commandment Obedience with Better Thinking
I, 6.7   Growing in 7th Commandment Obedience with Better Wonder
I, 6.8   Growing in 8th Commandment Obedience with Better Gratitude
I, 6.9   Growing in 9-10th Commandment Obedience with Better Empathy

I, 7	**Faith seeking understanding at St. Thomas**
I. 7.1	Father Gustafson taught us the history of philosophy
I, 7.2	Growing in love with the Greek's love of wisdom
I, 7.3	Growing in faith with the Medieval's wisdom of love
I, 7.4	And he taught us systematic philosophy
I, 7.5	Helping Jesus be in our mind with metaphysics
I, 7.6	Helping Jesus be in our heart with psychology
I, 7.7	Helping Jesus be on our lips with epistemology
I, 7.8	So that he might be in our hands for others
I, 7.9	And always in our vision with his logic of love
I, 8	**Believing that We Might Understand in the Seminary**
I, 8.1	How modernity separated faith and reason
I, 8.2	With the Reformers Choosing Faith Alone
I, 8.3	And the enlightenment thinkers reason alone
I, 8.4	Contemporary philosophy puts them together again
I, 8.5	The Dying Face of Stephen Reveals a New Ethics
I, 8.6	By Revealing the Vision of the Dying Face of Jesus
I, 8.7	And the Logic of a New Cosmology
I, 8.8	By Revealing the Loving Face of God
I, 8.9	And the Logic of Its New Natural Theology
II.	**With Levinas and Derrida**
II, 1	**Levinas' Ethics as First Philosophy**
II, 1.1	Levinas Grew up with the Jewish Religious Ethics
II, 1.2	Philosophy's Love of Wisdom and the Wisdom of Love
II, 1.3	By Letting my Totality Welcome your Infinity
II, 1.4	With a "*me voici*" Beyond Buber's "I and Thou"
II, 1.5	And a Transcendence Beyond Plato's Divine Madness
II, 1.6	And an Infinity Beyond Descartes' Infinite
II, 1.7	And a Face Beyond Heidegger's Ontology
II, 1.8	And a Responsibility Beyond Kierkegaard's Subjectivity
II, 1.9	And beyond Nietzsche's Philosophizing with a Hammer

II, 2	**Derrida's Deconstruction of *Totality* and *Infinity***	
II, 2.1	With a Jewish Aporetic Ethics that Deconstructs	
II, 2.2	Levinas' Logic of Exclusive Opposites	
II, 2.3	And Levinas' Deconstruction of Buber's *I and Thou*	
II, 2.4	And Levinas' Deconstruction of Husserl's Phenomenology	
II, 2.5	And Levinas' Deconstruction of the Heidegger's Ontology	
II, 2.6	And Levinas Destruction of Plato's Metaphysics	
II, 2.7	And Levinas' Destruction of Aristotle's Metaphysics	
II, 2.8	And Levinas' Destruction of Descartes' Infinite	
II, 2.9	And Levinas' Destruction of Kierkegaard and Nietzsche	
II, 3	**The Wisdom of Love in *Otherwise Than Being***	
II, 3.1	How the Notion of the Third Opens Levinas	
II, 3.2	To the Double Responsibility of Love and Justice	
II, 3.3	With a Wisdom of Love at the Service of Love	
II, 3.4	Which Goes from Loving Widows, Orphans and Aliens	
II, 3.5	To being the Suffering Servant	
II, 3.6	Who Loves the Enemy in a Proximity	
II, 3.7	That Lets me Lovingly Substitute for Him	
II, 3.8	With a Glory that Manifests the Unmanifest	
II, 3.9	Even in its Unmanifestness	
II, 4	**Derrida's Ethics as First Philosophy Demands**	
II, 4.1	Improving Demonstrations with deconstruction	
II, 4.2	Improving Definitions with Dissemination	
II, 4.3	Improving Distinctions with Differance	
II, 4.4	Improving Dialectics with a Double Dissymmetry	
II, 4.5	Improving Decisions with Indecidability	
II, 4.6	Improving Desires with Donation	
II, 4.7	Improving the Death of Debt with Divine Redemption	
II, 4.8	Improving Delirium with Dream Work	
II, 4.9	Improving Destiny with *Densite*	
II, 5	**What it Means that Love as Pure Giving is Impossible**	
II, 5.1	Jewish Altruism seeks to give the Pure Gift	
II, 5.2	Which can be Traumatic and Joyful Folly at Once	
II, 5.3	The Pure Gift of Giving our Time is Impossible	
II, 5.4	As is the Pure Gift of Giving our Life	
II, 5.5	As is the Pure Gift of Giving our Death	

II, 5.6   How Derrida does not Catch Up with Kierkegaard
II, 5.7   And How Levinas Deconstructs Derrida
II, 5.8   With a Justice of the Third Beyond Deconstructive Justice
II, 5.9   So that the Impossible Pure Giving is not Necessary

II, 6   **How Kierkegaard might Deconstruct Derrida**
II, 6.1   Who Deconstructs him by Ignoring *Agape*
II, 6.2   Which Hates Preferential Love
II, 6.3   In Order to Absolutely Love the Absolute
II, 6.4   And then Relatively Love the Relative
II, 6.5   That he Loves a Self-Love that is not Pure
II, 6.6   In Primarily Loving all Others and Secondarily his Own
II, 6.7   Because Unlike Abraham God did Sacrifice his Son
II, 6.8   Out of Love for Us
II, 6.9   Which Gives us a Pure Love that is Possible

II, 7   **Derrida's *Praeparatio Evangelica***
II, 7.1   With a Messianicity without the Messiah
II, 7.2   With a Responsibility without Celibacy
II, 7.3   With a Postmodernity without Modernity
II, 7.4   With a Spirituality without Organized Religion
II, 7.5   With a Logic of Mixed Opposites without Exclusive Opposites
II, 7.6   With the Sacrifice of Economy without Heavenly Reward
II, 7.7   With a Just War Politics without Non-Resistance
II, 7.8   With a Psychology of Loving ours Without Loving All
II, 7.9   With a Metaphysical Rescue of my Cat but not all Flesh

II, 8   **Levinas' Praeparatio Evangelica**
II, 8.1   With the Third Without the Trinity
II, 8.2   With the Wisdom of Love Without The Love of Wisdom
II, 8.3   With a Postmodernity Without Modernity
II, 8.4   With a Holiness Without the Sacred
II, 8.5   With an Ethics Without Ontology
II, 8.6   With an Authority Without Force
II, 8.7   With a Peace Without Price
II, 8.8   With a Manifestation of Infinity Without Manifestation
II, 8.9   With a Transcendence Without Imminence

II, 9	**Levinas and Derrida Enlighten Us Concerning *Agape***
II, 9.1	For Levinas Loves the Jewish Love of *Hesed* and *Ahava*
II, 9.2	And Expresses its Beauty, Goodness, Truth and Holiness.
II, 9.3	And Derrida's Aporia Reveals the Mystery of Revelation.
II, 9.4	And Redoes the Approach to Western Philosophy.
II, 9.5	So even though Derrida and Levinas have a Messianicity.
II, 9.6	Without Jesus, the Messiah, and his *Agape*.
II, 9.7	Their *Hesed* and *Ahava* Prepares for that *Agape*.
II, 9.8	So that God can be *Agapeic Hesed* and *Ahava*.
II, 9.9	And we can have Gratitude for the Salvation of All.
III, 1	**Glueck's Treatment of *Hesed* as Mutual Love**
III, 1.1	*Hesed* as Secular, Religious and Divine Conduct
III, 1.2	A Secular Covenant Bond with Lasting Loyalty
III, 1.3	A Religious Bond with Justice and Law
III, 1.4	*Hesed* as Divine Conduct with Nine New Traits
III, 1.5	The *Hesed* of the David Promise
III, 1.6	The Trusting Faith and Mercy of Davidic *Hesed*
III, 1.7	And Its Peace for those who Fear the Lord
III, 1.8	God's *Hesed* gives the Hasadim Knowledge and Confidence
III, 1.9	For Even though He Punishes there is Salvation
III, 2	**Correcting Glueck's Understanding of *Hesed***
III, 2.1	Masing Rejects the Pattern of Mutual Reciprocity
III, 2.2	Masing Rejects Glueck's Universal *Hesed*
III, 2.3	Masing Questions the Idea of a Davidic Covenant
III, 2.4	Hills Shows how *Hesed* is Done by the Superior Party
III, 2.5	And is Distinct from Judicial or Legal Action
III, 2.6	*Hesed* is Action with Special Moral Qualities
III, 2.7	Hills Shows how *Hesed* Responds to an Essential Need
III, 2.8	Hill's *Hesed* has its Source in God
III, 2.9	Stoebe Claims that *Hesed* was Introduced by J

III, 3	**Sakenfeld Doob Sakenfeld's Treatment of *Hesed***
III, 3.1	Also Studies "Secular", "Theological" and "Religious" Usages
III, 3.2	The Primacy of the Theological Davidic *Hesed*
III, 3.3	Does God's Revelation of *Hesed* Prepare for the Secular?
III, 3.4	Does Theological *Hesed* Support Religious *Hesed*?
III, 3.5	The Modification of *Hesed* in Religious Usage
III, 3.6	*Hesed* is Primarily not Covenantal
III, 3.7	*Hesed* is Primarily not Reciprocal
III, 3.8	*Hesed* is Primarily not Related to Justice
III, 3.9	*Hesed* is like a Mother's Love for her Child
III, 4	**The *Ahava* of the Shema**
III, 4.1	What is this *Ahava* with which we should Love Yahweh?
III, 4.2	It is Related to Fifteen Kinds of *Ahava*
III, 4.3	Wallis Explains the Secular Uses of *Ahava*
III, 4.4	And the Theological Uses
III, 4.5	The Deuteronomist and God's *Ahava* for Israel
III, 4.6	Which should be Reciprocated by Isreal's *Ahava*
III, 4.7	So all Fifteen Dimensions of *Ahava* are Commanded
III, 4.8	And can be Learned by Attentive Listening
III, 4.9	Which Ponders God's *Ahava* always in the Heart
III, 5	**The Command of *Ahava* for One's Neighbor**
III, 5.1	Jews are Commanded to Love One's Neighbor
III, 5.2	And this is the Source of Jewish Ethics
III, 5.3	Together with *Hesed* as the Other Source
III, 5.4	The Prophet's Ethical Criticism of the Cult
III, 5.5	Shows how Hard it is to Love Others Equally
III, 5.6	But that is what True Ethical Altruism Demands
III, 5.7	And to have *Ahava* for the Stranger as for Oneself
III, 5.8	And *Ahava* for the Enemy as Oneself
III, 5.9	These Neighbors, Strangers and Enemies are Jewish

III, 6   Jewish *Ahava* for Yahweh and *The Song of Songs*

III, 6.1   Where Each Image Expresses a Quality of *Ahava*
III, 6.2   For his Banner over me is *Ahava*
III, 6.3   And I am Sick with *Ahava*
III, 6.4   For *Ahava* is Stronger than Death
III, 6.5   And Many Waters Cannot Quench *Ahava*
III, 6.6   For Yahweh's Conversation is Sweetness Itself
III, 6.7   And we Belong to each Other
III, 6.8   And my Love's Desire is for Me
III, 6.9   And all my Desire is for Him

III, 7   *Hesed* and *Ahava* in Hosea

III, 7.1   Can we Compare, Contrast and Relate them?
III, 7.2   Yahweh's *Ahava* for Israel
III, 7.3   And her Responsible *Hesed* to Him
III, 7.4   And His Responsible *Hesed* for her
III, 7.5   But she Goes a Whoring with a False *Ahava*
III, 7.7   For even Though Israel Betray *Ahava*
III, 7.8   And then Betray *Hesed*
III, 7.9   Yahweh's *Hesed* will Bring her Back to *Ahava*

III, 8   How do *Hesed* and *Ahava* Relate in the Psalms?

III, 8.2   Is *Ahava* Primarily Man's Love for God (Psalm 33)
III, 8.3   Even Though Hosea Reverses this Pattern
III, 8.4   *Hesed* is Primarily God's Love for us (Psalm 51)
III, 8.5   And we must Love our Neighbor with *Hesed* (Psalm 69)
III, 8.6   But *Ahava* must be our Primary Love for God (Psalm 117)
III, 8.7   And we must Love our Neighbor with *Ahava* (Psalm 119)
III, 8.8   And Come to See God's *Ahava* for us (Psalm 119)
III, 8.9   Which He Shows us with His *Hesed* (Psalm 119)

III, 9	**How do *Hesed* and *Ahava* Lead up to *Agape*?**
III, 9.1	Do the Jews have Four Opinions on Everything?
III, 9.2	The Septuagint Usually Translates *Ahava* as *Agape*.
III, 9.3	But how New is the Meaning of *Agape* in Matthew?
III, 9.4	And How does Matthew Relate *Hesed* to *Agape*?
III, 9.5	A Preview of Matthew's *Agape*
III, 9.6	A Preview of Matthew's Many Voices
III, 9.7	Does the Christ Expand a Davidic *Hesed*?
III, 9.8	And Does Jesus Expand a Mosaic *Ahava*?
III, 9.9	Are There Four Ways of Doing the Expanding?
IV, 1	**The *Agape* of Matthew's Infancy Narrative**
IV, 1.1	Can be seen in terms of The Sermon on the Mount
IV, 1.2	For its New *Ahava-Agape* for the Enemy
IV, 1.3	Lets us see the Infancy Story's New *Hesed-Agape*
IV, 1.4	Especially in Four of Mary's Predecessors
IV, 1.5	And in God's Love in the five Dreams
IV, 1.6	And in Fulfilling the five Prophecies
IV, 1.7	And God's *Hesed* let the Magi Adore with *Ahava*
IV, 1.8	As these Aliens Manifest the New Universal Love
IV, 1.9	Of *Agape* that Governs *The Infancy Narrative*
IV, 2	***Agape* in Matthew's three Q Texts**
IV, 2.1	The *Agape* of the Historical Jesus of Q1
IV, 2.2	Fits in with Matthew's Doctrine of Reconciliation
IV, 2.3	But the Jesus of Q2 is a Punisher
IV, 2.4	With whom Matthew Himself Agrees
IV, 2.5	For while He is Sympathetic to Judaism
IV, 2.6	He is Highly Critical of the Jewish Leaders
IV, 2.7	And He is Closer to Q2 than to Q3
IV, 2.8	Does Matthew Alter many Prophecies?
IV, 2.9	And know Jewish Leaders will Object?

IV, 3		***Agape* in Matthew's use of Mark**
IV, 3.1		Mark's *Agape* appears in Matthew's First Part
IV, 3.2		Markan *Agape* introduces Matthew's Second Part
IV, 3.3		The Kingdom of Heaven is Preached
IV, 3.4		Matthew Builds on Mark's *Agape* for God's Kingdom
IV, 3.5		And on Mark's Preaching of the Good News
IV, 3.6		And of Mark's Casting out of Devils
IV, 3.7		And on Mark's Healing of the Sick
IV, 3.8		And on Mark's Forgiveness of Sin
IV, 3.9		Especially by the Suffering Servant
IV, 4		**Matthew's *Agape* Seeks First the Kingdom of Heaven**
IV, 4.1		As the Son Reveals its Mystery in the Father
IV, 4.2		By Teaching it Directly to the Disciples
IV, 4.3		But Through Parables to the People
IV, 4.4		With Hope that they will Understand
IV, 4.5		And be Converted and Healed
IV, 4.6		For this Mystery of the Kingdom is Joyful
IV, 4.7		Even Though it is Sorrowful
IV, 4.8		For it is Glorious
IV, 4.9		In Manifesting the Unmanifest in its Unmanifestness
IV, 5		**And His Righteousness**
IV, 5.1		Matthew alone Stresses Seeking God's Righteousness
IV, 5.2		For Partial Obedience will not Suffice
IV, 5.3		Either in Jewish Ethics
IV, 5.4		Or in Jewish Good Works
IV, 5.5		Or in their Code, Creed, Cult and Canon
IV, 5.6		And Jesus Embodies Righteousness
IV, 5.7		For Righteousness is Love in Action
IV, 5.8		And it Helps Others in Reconciliation
IV, 5.9		By Being Humble like a Little Child

IV, 6   **And thus makes Affection Righteous**
IV, 6.1   For Affection can be Self-centered
IV, 6.2   But *Agape* can Orient it to the Other
IV, 6.3   And Matthew's Child has Righteous Affection
IV, 6.4   That lets Everyone be Brother and Sister
IV, 6.5   And lets Humble Little Ones be the Greatest
IV, 6.6   For They are Dependent on Others
IV, 6.7   And thus Live out *Agapeic* Praise
IV, 6.8   And *Agapeic* Affectionate Gratitude
IV, 6.9   And *Agapeic* Affectionate Petition

IV, 7   **And *Eros* Righteous**
IV, 7.1   *Eros* too can be Self-Centered
IV, 7.2   As Was the Case with King David
IV, 7.3   And it Can Cause Great Family Hatred
IV, 7.4   But Jesus' *Agape* can Redeem *Eros*.
IV, 7.5   For Self-sacrificing Celibacy can take Us
IV, 7.6   Into the Mystery of the Three Great Secret Things
IV, 7.7   And the Women Loved the Celibate Jesus
IV, 7.8   For His *Agape* can Heal Broken Erotic Hearts
IV, 7.9   With His Reconciliation of which Matthew Writes

IV, 8   **And Friendship Righteousness**
IV, 8.1   Friendship too can be Self-centered
IV, 8.2   But David and Jonathan
IV, 8.4   And Jesus' *Agape* makes that Possible
IV, 8.3   Wanted it to Reconcile their Families
IV, 8.5   For his Disciples were Friends
IV, 8.6   Working with an Angelic Celibacy for All
IV, 8.7   And Righteously Obeying Him
IV, 8.8   By going out to baptize all the nations
IV, 8.9   And Bring them all Reconciliation

IV, 9   **And Septuagint *Agape* Righteousness**
IV, 9.1   By Fulfilling *Ahava* with Eternity
IV, 9.2   By Fulfilling *Ahava* with Universality
IV, 9.3   By Fulfilling *Ahava* with Altruism
IV, 9.4   By Fulfilling *Ahava* with Unconditionality
IV, 9.5   By Fulfilling *Ahava* with Childlikeness
IV, 9.6   By Fulfilling *Ahava* with Celibacy
IV, 9.7   By Fulfilling *Ahava* with Missionary Love
IV, 9.8   By Fulfilling *Ahava* with Purgatorial Love
IV, 9.9   By Fulfilling *Ahava* with the Loving of Love

Introduction

For nine years with the Benedictines of Mt. Angel
and the Sulpicians of St. Thomas-Seattle
I learned of *agape* as fulfilling *hesed-ahava*.
With their wise teaching and loving example
they taught me that if we love the Lord our God
with our whole heart, mind, and soul
and our neighbor as ourselves with *ahava*
and because God loves us with his *hesed*,
or his everlasting love, we can discover
the glory of Jesus' reconciling *agape*.
As Derrida and Levinas pushed each other
further and further into the loving wisdom
of their Jewish tradition in their postmodern ways
Levinas came to define glory
as the manifesting of the unmanifest
even in its unmanifestness.
The two thousand years of the Jewish tradition
before Christ was a progressive revealing
of the glory of Yahweh, or Elohim.
The Jewish people came to know
more and more the mystery of God
as Yahweh revealed his *hesed* to David
and as they practiced
love for God and each other.
Matthew, by showing how Jesus revealed
agape as fulfilling *hesed* and *ahava*,
clarified its nine unique traits.
Agape as altruistic, universal, and eternal,
as childlike, unconditional, and celibate,
as missionary, purgatorial, and loving of love
gives us a faith and hope in *agape* that
the family of humankind can be reconciled.

Agape and *Hesed*

The Minor Seminary—The Major Seminary
From the time I was fourteen until twenty
I studied with the Benedictine Monks of Mt. Angel.
Their special spirituality of "*ora et labora*"
nourished me in the habit of prayer and work.
The monks lived in the atmosphere of *agape*
as they chanted the eight hours
of the Divine Office each day,
prayed a private mass and
a common chanted mass each day
and each said his daily Rosary.
Then they worked for hours each day,
be it physical work or intellectual,
or often a combination of both.
We seminarians were nourished
by our Alma Mater in the heart's love,
the mind's wisdom, the soul's moral virtue,
and the body's physical strength through
constant physical, moral, intellectual, and
spiritual exercises that became habitual.
What could be more loving than prayer?
Prayer is a making of love with God.
Our Abba Father leads us to prayer
with his grace, inspiration, love, and mercy
and as we respond our hearts can grow
daily in love and as we pray for
our loved ones we love them more each day.
We awakened each morning at five-thirty
and after years that became a habit
that let us rise and shine for prayer
and then for work throughout the day,
and that habit still lives with me today.

Introduction

Often at mass we would pray and sing
the *Gloria in Excelsis Deo*
(the *Glory to God in the Highest* and
on Earth Peace to People of Good Will).
The monks and the seminarians both
wanted to give glory to God and for that
we would live in poverty, celibacy, and obedience.
We believe that God is love
and that our purpose in living is
to make God and his love more manifest
so that all can love God and
grow in the peace of a good will.
Often each day in the Divine Office
and at mass and with the Rosary
we would pray and ponder:

> Glory be to the Father and the Son
> and the Holy Spirit as it was
> in the beginning, is now and ever
> shall be world without end. Amen.

At Mt. Angel we received
a wonderful liberal arts
education so that we would be free to
learn anything we wanted.
By studying Latin for six years
we came to appreciate literature and
history and to develop especially our
memory so that we came to love
reciting beautiful poetry by heart.
I discovered the three great secret things
of sex, death, and religion
and with Father Ambrose as my confessor
I was able to be pure and
not have to confess masturbation.

Agape and *Hesed*

For three years and three months I studied
with the Sulpician Fathers at St. Thomas
Major Seminary near Seattle, Washington.
The Sulpicians were founded in order to
educate men to become secular priests.
Sulpician spirituality centered on the face
of Jesus and seeing his face and showing
his face to all the peoples of the earth.
The Sulpician priests taught me to have
Jesus in my mind and in my heart
and in my hands and on my lips
and to help all see the glory of his love.
The priest would have Jesus in his hands
as he brought the Eucharist to his people.
At ordination he is given the special
sacramental power to transform the bread
and wine into the body and blood of Jesus.
His mind and heart would be centered
on that joyful, sorrowful, glorious Jesus
as he did his spiritual reading and
as he prayed the Mass, his Rosary, and
the eight hours of the Divine Office.
It was his task to speak of Jesus
to others with Jesus always on his lips.
As he went out among people his
black suit and Roman collar would
call those people to be reminded of Jesus.
They could have a range of feeling
for him from empathy and sympathy
even to antipathy, just as they would
toward Jesus, and in our secular society
he would be a reminder of the *agape* of Jesus.

Introduction

At St. Thomas each of us could choose
our confessor and I liked Father Gustafson,
my philosophy professor, so much that
I chose him, and each week I would
kneel beside him and confess my sins.
Strangely my impurity returned and he
told me that he just did not understand me.
He said that he never had such problems.
Sex really became a great secret thing
for as I tried to be celibate for nine years
many mysterious things continued to happen.
Perhaps celibacy can develop a kind of
feminine spirituality within the male
and perhaps the feminine became more lovely.
After my ninth year I fell in love with Jane
and experienced the sublimation that Plato
describes in his *Phaedrus* with the myth
of the charioteer and I came to know of
erotic inspiration, enthusiasm, and divine madness.
Father Gus taught me ten philosophy courses
and I learned all about medieval philosophy
and Augustinian, Thomistic, and Franciscan
varieties of the love of wisdom and the wisdom of love.
In my year and a third of theology
two Scripture scholars introduced me
to biblical studies in the old and new way.
Every three years at daily Mass we had
readings that covered the whole of the Hebrew Bible.
I loved the philosophy and theology that I
learned at St. Thomas so much that I wanted
to do it for the rest of my life and
thank God, I am still doing it even now.

Agape and *Hesed*

Levinas and Derrida

For many years I had read Kierkegaard and Nietzsche
as existentialists but it was Levinas and Derrida
who first taught me the meaning of postmodernity.
Levinas as a Rabbi had a deep understanding
of the Hebrew Scriptures and Jewish worldview.
For him ethics had to be first philosophy
and he heard from the infinite face of the other
the call to serve widows, orphans, and aliens.
Derrida as a Jewish Philosopher of great knowledge
agreed with Levinas about ethics as first philosophy
but as he wrote on Levinas's book *Totality and Infinity*
he showed how Levinas was still using a logic
of exclusive opposites and thus excluded not only
Buber but also Kierkegaard and Nietzsche.
Derrida showed how the infinite face of the other
implied a metaphysics of excess that in turn
would imply a logic of mixed opposites.
Derrida's deconstruction of *Totality and Infinity*
made sense to Levinas and he went on to write
Otherwise Than Being, which agreed with Derrida
but went on to show how the epistemology
of postmodernity had to be a nominalism.
Levinas developed a new model of ethics
as first philosophy with the Suffering Servant.
Levinas went on to the passages in Second Isaiah,
which had the Suffering Servant as suffering
to the point of death out of love for others.
The Gospels also used these images to show
how Jesus fulfilled this Suffering Servant philosophy.
This Suffering Servant as Levinas saw him
already loved his enemy and would suffer for him.

Introduction

Derrida knows the history of philosophy
very well and especially works with Kierkegaard
and Nietzsche as he develops his own philosophy.
Classical philosophy was based upon the four D's
of demonstrating a thesis with proper definitions,
key distinctions, and a dialectical answering
of objections to those first three procedures.
As Derrida thought about ethics as first philosophy
he saw with Kierkegaard that we cannot get
objective certainty about religious ethical decisions.
Rather those decisions made over the abyss
of indecidability will bring us to Derrida's four D's
of deconstructing demonstrations, by showing
the dissemination of definitions and the differance
of all distinctions that takes dialectics into
the realm of an existential uncertainty about decision.
Derrida's aporetic faith lead from pride to humility
as he discovered a logic of the paradox and
its mixed opposites that governed each decision
that we make over the abyss of indecidability.
It moved him from pretension to honesty
as the question of responsibility about the
dissemination of all knowledge and definition
led him to a metaphysics of excess.
It led him from being ponderous to being humorous
with a psychology of the decentered self
because of the differancing of all distinctions.
It led him from being pompous to being healthy
because of his new epistemology of embracing
uncertainty as he saw justice as deconstruction.
With this Derrida made clear for me
the meaning of a postmodern philosophy.

Agape and *Hesed*

None of the modernists from Luther and Descartes
to Calvin and Hobbes, to Henry VIII and Locke,
to Newton and Rousseau, to Hume and Kant
and to Hegel, Marx, and Adam Smith got to
this postmodern view that Levinas and Derrida
spell out with such philosophical clarity.
One could show that their postmodernity
goes back to the premodernity of the Franciscans
as their thought culminated in the metaphysics
of excess with Scotus's haecceity and then
the consequent nominalism of Ockham's epistemology.
With this help from Derrida I came to see
how Kierkegaard had first clearly spelled out
the logic of mixed opposites as he built his
philosophy around the paradox of the God-man.
Levinas's definition of glory as a manifesting
of the unmanifest even in its unmanifestness
clearly expressed the paradox of giving glory
and this helped me to understand Kierkegaard's
Works of Love, which would give that glory
and the Drama of Zarathustra, which revealed
more and more glory with each act of the Drama.
Any act of love that we perform, be it of
Nietzschean *amor fati* or Kierkegaardian works of love,
does make the God of love more manifest.
But Levinas and Derrida remain Jewish
and do not make the leap of love that
would let them love Jesus as the Messiah.
Derrida argues for a messianicity
without a Messiah and Levinas does not
see any fulfillment of *hesed* and *ahava*
in an *agape* that would take them further.

Introduction

Levinas and Derrida can greatly help us
to understand *hesed* and *ahava* and how
far they can go in the direction of *agape*.
Derrida could be seen as developing a
preparation for the gospel, which makes clear
how far he will and will not go in loving.
He does develop a psychology of loving ours
without loving all and of rescuing his cats
but not of loving all flesh as eternal.
Levinas thinks carefully and often about
the difference between Jewish and Christian love.
He does develop the idea of a third but
without thinking of God as a Trinity of Persons.
Derrida and Levinas both think deeply
about glory and the glory of love and at Brock
we had a conference on *Derrida's Glorious Glas*.
As Kenneth Itzkowitz says in his article
in the proceedings of that conference *Glas*
might be thought of as *The Tolling Knell,*
The Mournful Knell and the Tolling-Mournful Knell.
It has to do with the mourning process
and with turning sorrow into joy through glory.
If one goes through the mourning process
in a successful way one can be healed of
one's grief and even get in touch with
the spirit world as did the Shamans.
So the question that Derrida and Levinas
raise is about the difference between
Jewish love and glory and Christian love and glory.
We can now consider love in the Hebrew Bible
and love in Matthew and see how Jewish
love prepared the way for the good news of *agape*.

Agape and *Hesed*

Hesed and *Ahava*

Nelson Glueck's wonderful book, *Hesed in the Bible*, which was published in 1927, is so helpful in clarifying the kinds of love in the Bible. In the 1967 edition there is an introductory essay by Gerald A. Larue that treats eighteen responses to Glueck and that are very enriching. Glueck shows how there are three basic kinds of *hesed* in the Hebrew Bible for as loving conduct it can have secular, religious, or divine meanings. Its main importance as a forerunner of *agape* is the divine meaning that begins with God's promise of an everlasting love to David and his house, which appears in 2 Sam 7:14–16:

> I will be his father and he shall be my son. When he commits iniquity, I will chasten him with the rod of men, with the stripes of the sons of men; but I will not take away my *hesed* from him, as I took it from Saul, whom I put away from before you. And your house and your kingdom shall be made sure forever before me; your throne shall be established forever.

In the New Testament Jesus is seen as the son of David and his kingdom of love or *agape* is seen as the fulfillment of this kingdom of *hesed*. Matthew sees Jesus' altruistic *agape* as extending this *hesed* to the entire human family and the followers of Jesus are to be missionaries who bring the Good News of God's love to everyone. This promise makes sense of suffering, which can be seen as punishment bringing us to God.

Introduction

Ahava is quite different from *hesed*
as we see in Deuteronomy 6:5

> Listen, Israel: Yahweh our God is the one,
> the only Yahweh. You must love Yahweh
> your God with all your heart, with all
> your soul, with all your strength.

Ahava is very different from *hesed* in that
hesed is a duty to do good to the other whereas
ahava is a felt desire to be with and is
what we mean by the various kinds of love
such as affection, friendship, *eros*, and *agape*.
The root *ahava* is used well over 200 times
in the Hebrew Bible and is an emotional feeling
that is contrasted with any sort of hatred.
Ahava has to do with our love for God
and our love for our neighbor and thus
ahava is the source of the Jewish ethics.
The Song of Songs gives a beautiful description
of *ahava* in which each image expresses
a quality of *ahava* and its lovely love,
for his banner over me is *ahava*
and I am sick with *ahava*
for *Ahava* is stronger than death
and many waters cannot quench *ahava*
for Yahweh's conversation is sweetness itself
and we belong to each other
and my love's desire is for me
and all my desire is for him.
So *hesed* is a promise of love from God
if we do our duty to him and others.
Ahava is the yearning to be close to
and a love for each other with our very veryness.

Agape and *Hesed*

As we can see in the Psalms there is
a variety of ways to understand *hesed*
and *ahava* for in Psalm 5 we wonder
if *hesed* is primarily God's love for man
and in Psalm 69 it is indicated that
we must love our neighbor with *hesed*.
Psalm 119 tells us
that we come to see God's *ahava* for us
which he shows us with his *hesed*.
So in the Psalms these terms get
opposite meanings and in the prophet Hosea
that opposite usage is very evident,
for according to Hosea
Yahweh has *ahava* for Israel
and she should have
a responsible *hesed* to him.
She goes a whoring with a false *ahava*
but God's Davidic *hesed* will save her.
For even though Israel betray *ahava*
and then betray *hesed*
Yahweh's *hesed* will bring her back to *Ahava*.
This last statement seems to be
an excellent understanding of *hesed* and *ahava*
but what goes before seems confused.
In any case the Hebrew view is that
because God first loved the Jews they
are God's chosen people and they will
be able to love God and each other.
And if they do not God will be merciful
and bring them even through punishment to love.

Introduction

As we ponder how the *agape* of Matthew's Jesus
will fulfill the *hesed* and *ahava* of the Jews
we might in general terms think of *Ahava*
as belonging to the Mosaic covenant theology
and *hesed* as belonging to the Davidic
promise theology with its emphasis on duty.
The command to love with *Ahava* tells us
that we should have as our main task
to nourish a loving heart that can feel
great affection for God and for our neighbor.
God's promise of an everlasting *hesed* to David
can be associated with his grace
that will help us to grow in piety and do
the right thing and if not we will be punished.
But that punishment is a type of grace itself
and it can help David and the children of David
do their duty and be loyal to Yahweh.
The Hasidic Jew who is faithful to
the covenant will go beyond what
the law requires and strive to be selfless.
The promise to David shows an
unconditional loyalty of God's *hesed*
toward the family of David forever.
Agape's traits of eternal love and
unconditional love are already there
in *hesed* and it is this Davidic promise,
which is given to Abraham, that
he will have land, nation, and name.
And in the Davidic promise of *hesed* there
is even something of universal love,
for Abraham is promised that his name
will be a blessing for all peoples of the earth.

Agape and *Hesed*

Matthew's *Agape* Fulfills *Hesed-Ahava*
In the Sermon on the Mount we hear how
the *agape* of Jesus fulfills *hesed* and *ahava*
for at Matthew 5:43–47 we read

> You have learned how it was said:
> you must love your neighbor
> and hate your enemy.
> But I say to you: love your enemies
> and pray for those who persecute you.
> In this way you will be
> sons of your Father in Heaven,
> for he causes his sun to rise
> on bad men as well as good,
> and his rain to fall on honest
> and dishonest men alike.
> For if you love those who love you,
> what right have you
> to claim any credit?

If we go beyond Jewish *ahava* to an *agape*
that loves everyone even our enemies
we will have an *agape* like God's *hesed*
that sends sun and rain to all.
Our love should be like God's love
so that his kingdom of love might come
and his will be done on earth
as it is in heaven, and this is the main
point of the Gospel of Matthew, which
shows how Jesus' *agape* fulfills *hesed*
by showing us that all belong to the house
of David and all will receive his promise.
It fulfills *ahava* by showing us how
we should love all, even our enemies.

Introduction

One might wonder why Matthew's Gospel
is placed first in the New Testament
as if it were written before Mark's
upon which it depends so much.
But, Matthew's Gospel is not only synoptic
in that it builds upon Mark, but
it also contains an Infancy Narrative,
the sayings of Jesus in Q 1, 2, and 3,
and Matthew's own special material.
The Q 1 sayings and the Infancy Narrative
are earlier than anything in Mark so
it is justified to see Matthew as first.
Once we read the Sermon on the Mount
which is part of the Q 1 sayings
and learn about God loving non-Jews
and sinners then we can understand
how he always loved that way and
we can see this in the Infancy Narrative.
This special *hesed* can be seen in relation
to the four of Mary's predecessors:
Tamar, Rahab, Ruth, and Bathsheba.
In the Infancy Narrative we also see
a new *hesed—agape* in the fulfilling
of the five dreams and then in
the fulfilling of the five prophecies.
However, the main message about *agape*
in Matthew is found in his own perspective
in terms of which he sees *agape*
as fulfilling *hesed* and *ahava* in
terms of nine new dimensions that
let *agape* build upon Jewish love but
go beyond it by fulfilling it.

Agape and *Hesed*

According to Matthew we should obey Jesus
and live righteously as did he
to bring about the kingdom of love.
Matthew shows how Jesus revealed
nine new dimensions of his kingdom.

1) It will be an eternal kingdom
2) The chosen people will include all.
3) It will be a kingdom of altruistic love,
4) which will especially love enemies.
5) It will be for childlike believers.
6) The closest disciples will be celibate,
7) that they might bring all to the kingdom.
8) Purgatory will let us all be reconciled
9) and we should love *agape* more than anything.

So, *agape* as Jesus revealed it is

1) an eternal love   2) a universal love
3) an altruistic love   4) an unconditional love
5) a childlike love   6) a celibate love
7) a missionary love   8) a purgatorial love
9) and a love that loves love above all.

Matthew shows us how the disciples
both men and women followed Jesus
and worked more and more for
the mysterious kingdom of heaven.
But they often failed to obey him
as did Peter and yet *agape* reveals
how Peter is a saintly sinner.
So this kingdom of *agape* is glorious
and the whole task of *agapeic* lovers
is to give glory to God by manifesting
more and more his mysterious love
so that all might begin to see it.

Introduction

The only mention of reconciliation
in the Four Gospels is at Matt 5:23–24
where Jesus says:

> If you are bringing your offering
> to the altar and there remember
> that your brother has something
> against you, leave your offering
> there before the altar, go and be
> reconciled with your brother first,
> and then come back and present
> your offering.

This can be understood as having to do
with the entire family of humankind.
Kierkegaard has shown us the logic
of this reconciliation and with Nietzsche
we can understand its physiology, but
with Levinas and Derrida we can
better understand how glorifying God
can help bring about this reconciliation.
Jesus gives his followers the task
of going out to all persons and teaching
them of this reconciling *agape* that
aims at bringing us all to love each other.
All nine points that make up *agape*
as Matthew spells them out aim at
this reconciliation of all of God's people.
As Matthew shows us Jesus explained
agape in terms of *hesed* and of *ahava*
and the notions of glory for the Jews
were connected with this and can be
fulfilled if all Christians become good Jews
in really loving God and all as our neighbor.

Part One

Experiencing Problems

Agape and *Hesed*

At Mt. Angel

I,1   Mt. Angel's Spiritual, Intellectual, Vital, Physical Values

I,1.1   Our alma mater's Spiritual Nourishing

On that Labor Day Weekend of 1952, at the time of mother's birthday
on September 6, Father Heeren came to our house for dinner.
After dinner he would begin the 500-mile drive to take me
to Mt. Angel, near Portland Oregon, where I would enter
the Minor Seminary with the Benedictine Monks where for
the next six years I would begin my studies to be a priest.
As we sat there for dinner in our humble little kitchen
daddy knew that mother and Father Heeren greatly loved each other
in an *agape* that sublimated affection, friendship, and *eros*.
And he knew that mother could think of nothing better for me
than that I become a priest like the priests she had come to know.
He could see how I had identified with my mother's values
and how I had received a vocation to become a priest and
to serve God and others by greatly admiring Father Heeren.
So we drove a third of the way, stayed at a motel, and
arrived at Mt. Angel in the middle of the day on Monday.
Fr. Heeren who had grown up in Ireland had gone to
the Minor Seminary there and then he came to Mt. Angel
when he decided to be a priest for the Diocese of Boise, Idaho.
He knew Mt. Angel and the monks very well and he and
Father Bernard, who was rector of the seminary, had been classmates.
As we drove, Father Heeren told me about the Benedictine Monks.
He said that their motto was "*Ora et Labora*" and with them
I would learn "to work and to pray" and most of all I noticed
the spiritual atmosphere of the monastery and the seminary,
which at one time had been sacred to the Indians as Topalamaho.
I was familiar with the world of the spirit since my father
lost his father to that world when he was five and my mother's
mother and father both learned of it when they lost a parent when young.

Part One: Experiencing Problems

I,1.2   Our alma mater's Intellectual Nourishing

As we drove up the hill a flood of feelings came over Father Heeren.
He pointed out to me the Stations of the Cross there among the trees.
Father Heeren was coming home to his nourishing mother whom
he loved so much and he was happy and proud to be bringing me.
We parked in front of the seminary, went in and found Father Bernard
who was so glad to see Father Heeren and so welcoming to me.
We were taken to the first- and second-year dormitory with my bags.
Father Heeren said goodbye to me, went with Father Bernard, and I
would not see him again until I went home for Christmas vacation.
From day one we got into the routine of seminary life arising
as 5:30 a.m. each morning and going to bed each night at 9:30 p.m.
We had the great silence from 7:10 each evening until
breakfast the next morning and we did not even look at each other.
There were many spiritual exercises beginning with daily Mass
each morning in the crypt where we would receive holy communion.
Then there was the sung Mass after breakfast with the monks.
During the day we recited Lauds, Sext, None, Vespers, and Compline.
We had spiritual reading each day before lunch and Father Bernard
gave us a spiritual talk five days a week in the evening.
But the intellectual life was just as important as the spiritual life
in terms of the time we spent in classes and in the study hall.
In our freshman year we had seven courses: Religion I, English I,
Latin I, General Science, World Civilization, Algebra I, and Chant I.
From Monday to Friday when we were not taking classes and during
the evening we had study hall and would work on our assignments.
Learning all the vocabulary and the grammar for our Latin class
was the most difficult task and it really trained our memory.
Father Louis was our first-year Latin teacher and learning grammar
helped us not only with English but with all the liberal arts
of reading, writing, speaking, and listening because we came
to reflect upon all the grammatical ways of our language.

Agape and *Hesed*

I,1.3   Our alma mater's Vital Nourishing

"I came to give you life and to give it to you more abundantly."
Those words of Jesus were the basis of our life at the Angel Mount.
Spiritual love, intellectual light, moral life, and physical logos
all fit together in such a way so as to contribute to each other.
Like tributaries of the same stream that contribute to living waters
theological, intellectual, moral, and physical virtues were forms
of excellence nourishing the fresh seeds in that seminary seedbed.
Those moral virtues of prudence, justice, fortitude, and temperance
were very important for future priests for they would have to be
excellent examples of those virtues that their people might imitate them.
The exercise that was most focused on growth in moral virtue
was our practice of weekly confession with our own confessor.
The virtue of temperance or *self-control* was central to confession.
Week after week I would tend to confess the same vices or sins,
of getting angry, swearing, or indulging in uncharitable thoughts,
words, or deeds and I just did not have consistent *self-control* .
We learned of a self-realization ethic that we could be happy
if we were virtuous for virtues are means to happiness.
This self-realization ethics for seminarians also aimed at
an other-realization ethics for priests loved as good shepherds
attempting to bring their flock to a healthy, happy, holy life.
We had to grow in vitality that we might help others do the same.
People tend to be so incompatible that they cannot be happy
and be at peace together and living closely with one another brought
many opportunities for disgust at each other's strange tastes.
We were often told about the battle between the flesh and the spirit
in St. Paul's letter to the Galatians in which he wrote:

> You cannot belong to Christ Jesus
> unless you crucify
> all self-indulgent passions and desires.

We had to become free from sin to be free for serving others.

I,1.4 Our alma mater's Physical Nourishing

At Mt. Angel we were nourished in the heart's love, the mind's wisdom, the soul's moral virtue, and the body's physical strength. Building up good habits of physical exercise was part of our seasonal and daily routine. In the fall we played football, in the winter basketball and we trained for boxing, and in spring we had track and field and we were each on a softball team. We often heard about a strong mind in a healthy body and to that was added a warm heart and a virtuous self-sacrificing soul. The monks imitated Jesus in all of that and their very lives of poverty, chastity, and obedience let each of us know their love. Even as freshmen we were told about cardiovascular exercise and at the football field we would run around the track until we were perspiring profusely and lift weights and stretch. We would practice passing and catching the football and blocking. In High school we had about eight football teams with members from each of the four classes and we would compete to see who won at the end of the season as we also did in basketball. For the first three years I did not really understand what was demanded to be really competitive in track and field even though I was very interested in running and jumping especially because I had delighted in my father's high school annuals, and he was a star athlete in all sports, but especially in the half mile. With him when I was six years old I had already started learning to box when he taught boxing at Carey High School. So already as a freshman I was eager not only to play basketball during the winter but also to train for boxing. Father Louie called it the manly art of self-defense and we had great fun sparring with each other and learning how to work the rapidfire punching bag and even skipping rope. That was the main thing about sports for me—they were lots of fun. Play is fun and we did play football, basketball, and baseball.

Agape and *Hesed*

I,1.5 Father Bernard and the Spiritual

Father Bernard Sander was the rector of the minor seminary
and as the person in charge of everything he primarily
concentrated on making sure each of us got deeply involved
in each of the spiritual exercises we could practice each day.
He was an excellent speaker and each day for about ten minutes
he would explain to us the deeper meanings of the mass,
of the divine office, of confession, and during May of the rosary.
During their fifteen-hundred-year history the Benedictines
have been forerunners in developing a beautiful liturgy.
Father Bernard would talk to us about the church's year of grace.
He explained to us how the daily sacrifice of the mass was
at the very center of our spiritual exercises and how it was
divided into the liturgy of the word and the liturgy of the Eucharist.
Each morning there would be a special reading from
the Hebrew Bible and from one of the New Testament Epistles
and from one of the Four Gospels. Father Bernard often
picked the connecting point between the three and spoke on that.
The Benedictine fathers would come together in the choir stalls
and chant back and forth the eight parts of the divine office.
Father Bernard explained to us how they sang the 150 psalms
of the Psalter each week and how many of the older fathers
had all the psalms memorized, which made them very dear.
As parish priests we too would eventually pray the Breviary
made up of Matins, Lauds, Prime, Terse, Vespers, and Compline.
Each day we would recite Lauds, Sext, None, Vespers, and Compline.
Thus already as freshmen we started learning the Old Testament
and began to see what Matthew meant when he claimed
that Jesus was the fulfillment of the Law and the Prophets.
Father Bernard began to help us see how love and justice were
so important throughout Hebrew history and how Jesus came
to take them further even with a love for all our enemies.

I,1.6 Father Ambrose and the Intellectual

Father Ambrose Zenner had gone to Rome to get his doctorate
in sacred theology and the word was that he was being groomed
to become the next abbot of the monastery and he did become
the rector of the major seminary when the new building
was built in 1956, and there were then two seminaries.
When I arrived in 1952, Father Ambrose was the vice rector
of the entire seminary under Father Bernard and every two months
he would talk with each of us as he gave us our report cards.
He was very encouraging and right away I liked him.
I would ask him why a priest had to study algebra and science
and he would tell me why a liberal arts education was important.
We students would talk with each other about such questions
and we would discuss with each other what he told each of us.
Already as freshmen we began to hear about the intellectual virtues
of science, art, practical wisdom, intuitive reason, and philosophical
wisdom and in the seminary there were those studying philosophy.
We called the students in the major seminary logicians,
philosophers, and theologians because that's what they studied.
Philosophy especially began to have a mysterious appeal
and it was good to believe that mathematics and science
could teach us special methods that would help us love wisdom.
My algebra teacher's name was Father Method and Father
Ambrose joked that Father Method was teaching us a method
of clear and correct reasoning that could help us in everything.
My grandmother Coates had a book on her shelf called
The Story of Philosophy by Will Durant and I loved
looking through it and certain quotations stayed in my mind
such as the saying of Dmitri from *The Brothers Karamazov*
"I don't want millions, but only an answer to life's questions."
I mentioned this quotation to Father Ambrose and he told me
that I already seemed to be a philosopher with all my questions.

Agape and *Hesed*

I,1.7 Father Anthony and the Vital

Father Anthony was both my confessor and my science teacher.
As freshmen he introduced us to chemistry, physics, and biology.
We put water in a container and after a few days looked at
a bit of it under the microscope and pretty soon bacteria began
to appear and after a couple of weeks it was loaded with many
kinds of little swimming critters visible only with the microscope.
We would remember forever how quickly germs could multiply
in water or any sort of unrefrigerated thing such as meat.
We were each growing rapidly and he kept a record of
each of our growth in weight, height, leg length, and even
the size of our muscles when we flexed our biceps, and we
each went individually to the laboratory for these measurements.
One day as he was measuring the inside of my leg his finger
touched my testicles and he asked me if I was missing one.
I asked him what he was talking about and he told me that
one of them felt diminished and I said to him: "I wonder why?"
He asked me if I ever played with myself and he said that
masturbation could momentarily cause the testicles to shrink.
I said that I had recently played with myself and he said
that I should confess that and break the sinful habit.
I told him how in the seventh grade some eighth-grade boys
had told me about it and I tried it and occasionally continued.
He explained to me how just thinking about a girl sexually
or how just touching myself for the pleasure of it was a venial
sin but ejaculation was a mortal sin and I should not
go to communion until I confessed it and amended not to repeat.
He did help me to become honest and to try to stop my self-abuse.
I did get the sin down to a few times a year and he told me
that there was a relation between my lust and my anger.
I never could understand what he meant but I tried to move
from self-abuse to self-realization and to increase my vitality.

I,1.8 *Father Louis and the Physical*

When I was a first-year student in grade nine and the minor
and major seminarians were still together in one building
the three administrators were Fathers Bernard, Ambrose, and Louis.
Father Bernard, the rector, primarily concentrated on the spiritual.
Father Ambrose, the vice rector, concentrated on the intellectual.
Father Louis, the prefect of discipline, concentrated on the physical.
He was very convinced that a strong mind in a healthy body
was essential if one were to live a long, happy, and productive life.
His conviction was convincing to us and each year our physical
exercises became more pleasant, significant, and deeply habitual.
Down by the football field there were two hardly used tennis courts.
Father Louis had some tennis rackets and said we could use them
whenever we wanted and he taught a few of us how to serve,
hit backhands, forehands, and to keep score and he said
that learning hand-eye coordination was valuable for any sport.
I believed him and saw a relation between the arts of fly-fishing,
wing-shooting, and tennis playing and I looked forward to more tennis.
However, as the prefect of discipline, Father Louis
not only got us into the physical exercises of sports
but we also did physical work especially on many Saturdays.
The monks had a very large farm with acres of hops below
the hill and various kinds of orchards and even a pig farm.
Brother Fidelis, a saintly little monk with a white beard,
took care of the pigs for years and we liked to help him.
The fathers all spoke of him with great praise for his life
of obviously sweet prayer and work and we were told how
he prayed all the time as he was taking care of his dear pigs.
In the seminary there was the activity of working on "The Chain
Gang." If someone broke a rule Father Louis would assign him
to a Saturday morning of digging a ditch, or shoveling snow,
or some fairly strenuous type of hard, physical labor.

Agape and *Hesed*

I,1.9 From Money—to Death—to Sex—to Religion

My father had always stressed that each of his five children
should get a college education so that we could get good jobs
and have happy lives without all the difficulties he suffered.
He made sure that we each did well in grade school and that
we worked and saved our money to pay for our college tuition.
But when I decided to become a priest the motive of money
was put into a new perspective and was no longer a priority.
Instead I began to move into the realm of the three great secret things.
Sex, death, and religion became more and more the center of my life.
Religion comes from the verb *ligare*, which means to bind
and *re-*, which means again, so religion is a binding of oneself
to God over and over again in the spiritual, intellectual,
emotional, and physical ways that made up our seminary life.
Prayer was the primary way in which we kept binding ourselves
to God again and again and prayer is rooted in a love that is
stronger than death, which my father learned when his father died.
With his mother and sisters he went through the mourning process
in a successful way by learning how to pray for his father
and his family by asking his father to pray for them.
He learned to converse with his guardian angel and Mary
the Mother of God and Jesus and the Father and the Holy Spirit.
When I was five he taught me to do the same and I prayed
especially with my mother as she too bound herself to God
over and over again in her prayer and by all that she did.
In the sacrifice of the mass twice a day we reenacted
the death of Jesus and we were bound together in communion.
You cannot take your money with you when you die and
religion with its crucifixion and resurrection can make sense
of death so that we can pray: "Oh death, where is thy sting?"
and as I tried to pray with purity sex began to take me
through various transformations in the religious life.

I,2 Growing Spiritually in that Seminary Seed Bed

I,2.1 *Nourishing Agape for All Persons with the Liturgy*

Already during our first year in the seminary we began
to practice the spiritual, intellectual, vital, and physical exercises.
We all knew that as future priests the spiritual were the most
important and that the others were for the sake of the spiritual.
At the center of our spiritual exercises was our praying of
the mass twice a day and all of our prayer was a practice
of *agapeic* love by which we would love God more and more
with our whole heart, mind, and soul and our neighbor as ourself.
The mass consisted of two parts: the liturgy of the Word and
the liturgy of the Eucharist, and Father Bernard in his teaching
focused most of all in relating Jesus and his love to both of these.
The church's year of grace was organized around the main events
in the life of Jesus so that the seasons of Advent, Christmas,
Lent, Holy Week, Easter, and Pentecost each had a buildup of lessons
in the readings from the Hebrew Bible, the Epistles, and the Gospels,
which let us pray in detail about each moment of Jesus' love.
This first half of the mass in its liturgy of the Word also
included the beautiful prayers, "I will go up to the altar of God,"
which, as an altar boy in the sixth, seventh, and eighth grades,
I had said in Latin with Father Heeren, and the Kyrie or *Lord
Have Mercy*, the *Gloria in Excelsis Deo*, and *The Creed*.
This liturgy of the Word prepared us for the liturgy of the Eucharist
with its three main parts of the offertory, consecration, and communion.
We brought all of our thoughts, words, and deeds, all of our praise
repentance, thanksgiving, and petition, and offered them up
with the bread and the wine the priest offered to God.
And then with the bread and the wine they became the body and
the blood of Jesus, which were separated in the consecration
so that the sacrifice of the mass is the center of the priest's life.
Then there is communion in which the resurrected Jesus lives on.

Agape and *Hesed*

I,2.2 *Nourishing Agapeic Affection with the Liturgy of the Word*

Love and personal growth in the seminary had to do most of all
with cultivating the three theological virtues of faith, hope, and charity.
Loving everybody is a very unnatural sort of thing for people are
so different that they irritate each other very frequently with
negative reactions that are habitual and that they often express.
Even our family members who are closest to us might be of
different body types and have tastes that tend to disgust us.
The whole seminary lifestyle with its lengthy silence and all
of its spiritual exercises aims at a self-overcoming so that we
could come to affirm all others constantly even with a loving affection.
Father Bernard helped us to see how the liturgy of the Word
operated on three planes at once: the historical, the plane of grace,
and the eschatological plane involving us in past, present, and future.
During the six seasons of the year the liturgy of the Word told us
the story of salvation as it was foretold by the prophets and lived out
by Jesus from his birth to his death and resurrection and his Spirit's coming.
But all of this historical reality offered us grace in our present life.
It was our task to appropriate it and love with the love that Jesus
loved as he came to teach love and to live it out in suffering joy.
And finally the liturgy of the Word was always preparing us for
the life to come when we would die but resurrect in glory with Jesus.
So the liturgy taught us faith in the past, hope for the future, and a life
of love for all in the present so that all the readings during mass
with new stories each day brought us to reflect upon and understand
the mass that as priests we would pray each day and teach to others.
We came to see how certain Saints like St. Francis especially
imitated Jesus in his affection as Francis would love brother moon
and sister sun and have affection for all persons and living beings.
The monks loved us with a certain affection that we could hear
in the tone of their voice and they began to teach us the history of
this special *agapeic* affection that would last forever as we lived it now.

Part One: Experiencing Problems

I,2.3 Nourishing Agapeic Friendship with the Word's History

Affection and friendship are two different kinds of love and the liturgy
of the word taught us of each throughout the history of the Hebrew Bible
and throughout the twenty-seven books of the New Testament
and on into history.

For besides the Sunday masses, which took us into a prayer life
of the development of the seasons of the year, there were also
the feast days of the saints who exemplified the kinds of love.
We knew of the affection of the family life of Jesus, Mary, and Joseph.
We also came to know of the friendship between David and Jonathan.
Affection seemed special because it was a felt sort of warm kindness
within a family and you would not feel that familial love for all.
Friendship also seemed to be a special kind of shared interest
between two or a few and it could be quite exclusive of others.
In fact, in the seminary we were warned about the dangers
of special friendships in which two seminarians would spend
much of their time together and even want to exclude others.
There is a self-love in the natural loves of affection, friendship,
and *eros* insofar as I have a special preference for my child,
my friend, or my beloved and universalizing these loves with
agape and letting them give a felt content to *agape* was the
lesson of Jesus and what the liturgy of the Word was teaching us.
St. Augustine was a great example of sublimated friendship and
St. Francis was a beautiful example of sublimated affection.
In the way they imitated Jesus we came to see how Jesus
had a special *agapeic* affection for everyone, a special
agapeic friendliness for all, and *agapeic eros* for each woman.
We came to see how Jesus loved each person as having
an equal worth, each person as unique and each person in
relation to all other persons so he would even love each woman
with a special sublimated *eros* that went out to her uniqueness.
The liturgy of the Word's history taught us of Jesus' friendliness.

Agape and *Hesed*

I,2.4 *Nourishing Agapeic Eros in the Word's Present*

The liturgy of the Word taught us the history of many examples
of love that we should practice in the present for the sake of
a blessed eternity in which every true love will conquer death.
Trying to be celibate and get my *eros* sublimated into *agape*
was the main trial of my life for I still a few times a year
fell into mortal sin, and sex for some of us was the great temptation.
In our first year there was a handsome, blond, curly-headed
youth from California who told me that sometimes
even when he was going up to communion he had impure thoughts.
He did not return in our second year and must have decided
with his spiritual advisor that the celibate life was not for him.
My confessor in my sophomore year was Father Justin who
had previously been a rector of the seminary and yet again
told me as he listened to my sins that my lust and anger
were related as are the concupiscible and irascible appetites.
I must have inherited from my father and his example
the habit of getting angry and swearing and no matter
how hard I tried I would still get angry on the spur of the
moment at something that hurt me and use God's name in vain.
The liturgy of the Word taught us a lot about *eros* for we could
wonder about the polygamy of Abraham and all the sexual sins
of David that are right at the center of the court history of David
and that brought him and his family the punishment of the rods of men.
And then there was Solomon and *The Song of Songs*, which began
with those words of a woman, "Let him kiss me with the kisses of his mouth."
When Father Bernard became a Benedictine he took the new name
of Bernard after St. Bernard of Clairvaux and Father Bernard
told us that he wrote over sixty sermons for nuns that were
based upon *The Song of Solomon* and that had to do with the kisses
of the feet, the hands, the mouth, and the breasts and somehow
the female within us was supposed to be the beloved of Jesus.

Part One: Experiencing Problems

I,2.5 Nourishing Agapeic Mourning in the Word's Future

The three great secret things that make their way into great art
are sex, death, and religion and the liturgy of the Word is filled
with meditation upon the death and resurrection of Christ Jesus.
The history of art since the beginning with the Egyptian pyramids
and with the early cave painting and with all early literature
like *The Tibetan Book of the Dead* has had to do with the mourning
process that lets us help our blessed dead with prayer and ask
the community of saints to pray for us so that the very core
of spirituality is also to live in the world beyond the material.
St. Paul's epistles which form a big part of the liturgy of the Word
focus most of all upon the death and resurrection of Christ's body
and upon how we should live now to be resurrected with him.
The Hail Mary, which we prayed many times a day, ended with
those words: "pray for us sinners now and at the hour of our death."
The eschatological theme of death, purgatory, heaven, or hell
was always there in the liturgy of the Word and we prayed often
for the poor souls in purgatory that they might go through
their reconciliation process and come to love all with no negativity.
As the liturgy of the Word taught us more and more of the lost
things we came to see how the theological virtue of hope was
being strengthened by all of our prayer, for the *Our Father*
brought us to pray: "Thy kingdom come, thy will be done
on earth as it is in heaven." And the *Glory Be* taught us to pray:
"As it was in the beginning, is now and ever shall be, world
without end. Amen." And that was the pattern of our spiritual life.
So we came to see that sex had to do with beginnings and death
with endings and that religion dealt with both and the eternity
that was there before sexual beginnings and our mortal endings.
Of course, as a second-year fifteen-year-old student I thought
a lot more about sex than about death and it was as if
I was coming to mourn a sex life and family I could never have.

Agape and *Hesed*

I,2.6 Nourishing Agapeic Affection in the Liturgy of the Eucharist

The second part of the mass that we prayed twice a day was
the liturgy of the Eucharist in its offertory, consecration, and communion.
As our teachers and especially Father Bernard taught us,
the Eucharist makes history become present and our hope
becomes so real that our *agapeic* love makes real for us
our faith in all that Jesus did 2000 years ago and it makes real
our hope in a future life with Jesus and all he came to save.
At the consecration of the mass when the bread and wine became
the body and blood, soul and divinity of Jesus my heart grew
in affectionate love as I prayed: "I praise, love, worship and adore you."
Adoration is a special kind of feeling that we might have for
the baby Jesus and for the suffering Jesus and for God once
Jesus makes God known as the love between the persons of God.
A lover might feel this love for his beloved and a parent might
feel it for a baby and adoration is a kind of affectionate
feeling that can grow as we say prayers of love for each other.
Twice a day in the liturgy of the Eucharist at the making
sacred of the bread and the wine we were reminded of Jesus'
incarnational love that went beyond atonement justice as
the Son of God became flesh that he might even suffer and die
for us to show us the love that loves all others even enemies
with a love that goes out to them as more important than ourself.
As we prayed with an adorational affection at the consecration
there was cultivated in our hearts an affection for everyone
even those who hurt us or disgusted us so that we could
see through any of their faults to the person for whom Jesus died.
The sacrifice of the mass at the consecration not only brought
forth the body and blood of Jesus into the bread and the wine
but also as they were separated there was a renewal of the
very sacrifice of Jesus as he died for us upon the cross.
From Jesus' *agapeic* affection for us we learned to have that for others.

I,2.7 Nourishing Agapeic Friendship with the Eucharist's History

The middle part of the liturgy of the Eucharist focused on Jesus
as present with us in the present moment there on the altar
when as the lamb of God he came to die for us again out of love.
As St. Paul puts it in 1 Corinthians 11:26,

> Until the Lord comes, therefore every time
> you eat this bread and drink this cup,
> you are proclaiming his death
> and so anyone who eats the bread
> or drinks the cup of the Lord unworthily
> will be behaving unworthily
> toward the body and blood of the Lord.

Receiving Jesus in communion in his body, blood, soul, and divinity
was the highlight of our day and St. Paul called it the *agape* meal.
We came to the seminary that we might become priests and offer
the sacrifice of the mass for God's people throughout our lives.
The whole purpose of the daily mass and communion was that we
might spend our lives growing in love for God with our whole
heart, mind, and soul and in loving all our neighbors as ourselves.
We learned from Jesus and the monks who taught us how to love
especially our enemies by praying for them even at communion.
In the seminary we were warned about the dangers of being
special friends with some to the exclusion of others and we learned
that as priests we had the common task of bringing the kingdom
of love to all humans that we might all live in communion.
In receiving communion together we became friends in the
common task of bringing communion to all the peoples of the earth.
God is the love or *agape* between the Father, Son, and Holy Spirit.
Human persons have an equal dignity like the persons of the Trinity
and deserve our *agapeic* affection and all persons belong to
the mystical body of Christ in a communal personhood and thus
we should have an *agapeic* friendship for every person.

Agape and *Hesed*

I,2.8 Nourishing Agapeic Eros in the Eucharist's Present

The liturgy of the Eucharist makes Jesus present in the past,
present, and future dimensions of his presence and nourishes
our love with a special kind of felt affection that is universal.
The third part of that liturgy, the communion, especially nourishes
an *agapeic*, affectionate friendship uniting all in bringing about
the kingdom of God's *agape* so that all might be reconciled.
My special problem was *eros* or sexuality so that sometimes
in my sinfulness like a black sheep I could not receive communion.
Thus the offertory come to have a special meaning for me
as I offered myself up in all my sinfulness with the bread and
the wine praying that I might be transformed in the consecration
and become a sacred priest set apart to serve God and his people.
Whereas each part of the liturgy of the Eucharist had past,
present, and future dimensions the offertory made Jesus present
to me in a heartfelt way as I tried to imitate him in his celibacy.
As time went on I came to see that many women loved him and
he loved many women for there was the Samaritan woman who
had five husbands and Mary and Martha and Mary Magdalene.
I was especially struck by how after the resurrection Magdalene
recognized him by the way he said her name with a love
that let her know right away that it had to be her Lord.
Jesus had a sublimated *eros* that let him love each unique
woman in a very special way even in all of her female uniqueness.
Many women came to love him with that sublimated *eros*
that would give a special content to their *agape* and a universality
to their *eros* even as Father Heeren had that toward my mother
and she toward him and she named her youngest son, Tommy
Joe, after Father Thomas Heeren and her husband Joseph.
Could such a transubstantiation ever happen to me in which
my sinful habitual substance would become a sacred substance.
I prayed each morning to become a sacred, *sacerdos* priest.

I,2.9 *Nourishing Agapeic Mourning in the Eucharist's Future*

The liturgy of the Eucharist is all about a love stronger than death.
It is about death and dying and a mourning process that can be
totally successful if one can live out the sorrowful mysteries
in light of the glorious mysteries to bring about the joyful mysteries.
In the sacrament of the sacrifice of the mass the sacred heart
of Jesus who is the high priest is slaughtered as the lamb of God.
He was born for us in his incarnation that he might be killed
for us in his crucifixion but then in the reliving of this in the mass
he lives on in us in communion in his glorious resurrection.
The glorious mysteries that began with the resurrection bring
out the futural dimensions of the liturgy of the Eucharist,
which we can begin to understand by thinking about the prayer,
Glory Be:

> Glory be to the Father and the Son and the Holy Spirit
> as it was in the beginning, is now
> and ever shall be world without end. Amen.

Levinas explains in *Otherwise Than Being* (pp. 144ff.) how "Glory is
that which manifests the unmanifest even in its unmanifestness."
So each day in communion we would give glory to God and
experience the glory of God by knowing God's love more dearly.
Each day in communion it would become manifest to us
that Jesus who had died for us was now living within us.
So in communion we went through a mourning process
in which the lost, dead Jesus would be found alive within us.
As we were nourished day by day in communion the Love
that is God became more and more manifest to us even
though it remained beyond us in its mysterious unmanifestness.
The manifest is that which we can hold fast in our hand
or even in our mouth as we held Jesus in holy communion.
No matter which of our loved ones dies our mourning
for them through prayer and communion lets them be present.

Agape and *Hesed*

I,3   Growing Intellectually in That Seminary Seed-Bed

I,3.1   *Nourishing Agape with the Trivium*

In the seminary our alma mater constantly cultivated within us
the theological virtues of faith, hope, and charity and we came to see
how the intellectual virtues of science, art, practical wisdom,
intuitive reason, and philosophic wisdom aided the theological virtues.
Growing in the love of wisdom and the wisdom of love contributed
greatly to understanding *agape* and its various sublimations.
Right from the beginning in the minor seminary our teachers
began to train us in the trivium of grammar, rhetoric, and logic.
In our first year Father Louis taught us Latin and in our
second year Father Ambrose started us with German while
we continued with Latin and we studied English in both years.
So we began to get a very good training in the basics of grammar.
During our third year we were also being trained in the rhetorical arts
of expressing ourselves in both writing and in public speaking.
In English we learned to write an essay with an introduction, a body
with three parts, and a conclusion and we talked about defending
a thesis with demonstration, definitions, distinctions, and dialectics.
We were also introduced to public speaking and down in the Little
Gym we began to see fourth-year students address an audience
in a speech contest and we knew that next year we would do the same.
We would not study logic in depth until our sixth year
but we knew and were friends with the logicians and looked
forward to learning both the traditional and the new mathematical logic.
We came to understand how our study of algebra, of geometry,
and of trigonometry was already introducing us to logical thinking.
When we got our report cards in November of my second year
I received 89 in Latin II, 84 in German I, 81 in Geometry
and 84 in Chant II, plus 95 in Religion II, 95 in English II,
and 98 in World History and when Father Ambrose gave me my
report card he said I could do better and I believed him.

Part One: Experiencing Problems

I,3.2 Nourishing Agapeic Affection with Grammar

That conversation with Father Ambrose about my report card
started a mysterious new phase of my life in the seminary.
In January I got basically the same grades and I even fell
from 84 to 81 in German, which he was teaching me.
But he must have inspired me to a New Year's resolution
because by June all my grades were much higher and
I went from 81 in German to 92 and he was pleased.
From then on I got good grades and I continued to talk with
Father Ambrose and I told him about my troubles with celibacy.
In my third year we decided together that he would be my confessor.
And so once a week I went to his office, knelt before him,
and confessed my sins and somehow as long as he was my
confessor and spiritual advisor I never committed another sexual sin.
He was as affectionate to me as was my own father who,
when I was in the third grade, worked hard with me to keep
my grades up and it was as if they were parallel events.
It seems that Father Ambrose with his celibate life had sublimated
his erotic passion in such a way that it even gave him the power
of a sublimated *agapeic* affection and a sublimated friendship.
Because Father Ambrose was celibate with no wife or children
of his own he could be affectionate and friendly toward each of us.
Somehow the power of his celibate *agape* even let me be
celibate and to become a much better student with that new
concentrated and passionate energy channeled over from
the black horse to the white horse and the charioteer.
Father Ambrose was my German teacher and all the intricacies
of grammar were becoming clear to me as I declined nouns
and conjugated verbs in both Latin and German and started
learning the tenses and voices of the verbs and the nominative,
genitive, dative, accusative, and ablative roles of the noun.
Growth in attention to grammatical structures increased loving attention.

Agape and *Hesed*

I,3.3 Nourishing Agapeic Eros with Rhetoric

Perhaps Father Ambrose's sex drive was quite strong and thus
the sublimation of his *eros* into *agape* could be so powerful
that I could identify with it and be graced with celibacy myself.
Up at Sun Valley where I worked during the summer and Christmas
vacation there was a beautiful waitress by the name of Myrna.
I remember wishing that she and Father Ambrose could meet and marry.
She was a very devout lady who would go to daily Mass each
Tuesday and Friday and I felt a reverent love for her myself.
My continued study of grammar helped me with reading and
listening so that if I heard any incorrect grammar I would
silently notice it unless it were from my brothers whom I corrected.
In certain classes such as English we would be called upon
to read out loud and being able at once to spot sentence structure
with its phrases and clauses helped me to be a good reader.
Constantly working with grammar gave me a familiarity with
language and that familiarity became an affection for speaking,
which encouraged me to always speak with affection to all,
as Father Ambrose and the other monks would always speak to us.
Before Father Ambrose became a monk his name was Joseph Zenner.
Perhaps he chose the name Ambrose partially because of the way
Ambrose helped Augustine not only by teaching him about the
four senses of Scripture—the literal, moral, mystical, and typological—
but also advised Monica that a child of so many prayers and tears
would never perish and thus helped Augustine become celibate.
Father Ambrose was a great rhetorician and as a public
speaker he had a sense of presence plus a well-argued
message that enabled him to be a truly inspiring teacher.
If we think back to Plato's Phaedrus at 245c and following
and that first great example of erotic sublimation it seems that
the power of Father Ambrose's creative speaking and writing
fits right in with that creative enthusiasm and divine madness.

I,3.4 Nourishing Agapeic Friendship with Logic

Father Gerard Marx went out to Notre Dame and studied
symbolic logic with Bochenski and in our sixth year
we had a great time learning traditional logic and mathematical
logic in the notation of Whitehead and Russell and the Polish logicians.
But, of course, from year one on we were always learning the logic
of practical consequences for if I did not confess my sexual sins
then my conscience would harden and not grow in sensitivity.
In our third year a happy-go-lucky Irishman Father Brendan
was teaching us religion and Pat Carney from Boise, Idaho knew him.
As a joke we hid a pillow under each of our desks and as he
was lecturing we pulled them out and put our heads on them as if
we were going to sleep and Father Brendan sent us to Father Ambrose.
Father Ambrose got a laugh out of it but said that we were being
insulting to Father Brendan by suggesting that he was boring.
Father Ambrose told us that for our penance we should each write
a thousand-word paper and Father Brendan would correct them.
The title of mine was "My Last Night with a Renegade" and
when Father Ambrose read the title he got a great belly laugh but
really it was only about fishing with my dad and using renegade flies.
So by our third year we clearly saw that any unkindness and
lack of friendliness would have its consequences and we
were learning from the Benedictine community that any act
of friendly *agape* would have its logical consequences for now
and for the future and that acts of love built the kingdom of love.
As we grew in experience we learned more and more about the logic
of opposites for there could be exclusive, inclusive, dialectical,
and mixed opposites and we were always told about loving enemies.
We were told that even a terrible criminal would have much good
within him and that we should reach out in loving prayer to enemies.
In the seminary we came to see the transcendental logic that any being
is beautiful, good, true, and therefore worthy of affirmative love.

Agape and *Hesed*

I,3.5 Nourishing Agape with the Quadrivium

In the seminary the spiritual life and the intellectual life fit together and promoted each other in natural Benedictine harmony. We learned about the Dark Ages after the fall of the Roman Empire and we came to see how the only light burning was in the monasteries. The Benedictines always taught the Trivium with its grammar, rhetoric, and logic, and the Quadrivium with its mathematics, music, science, and history, and we were constantly trained in both. After algebra in my third year all my grades were in the 90s, except for trigonometry in which I received a final grade of 83. I do not understand why but I always had a difficult time in math. One time in our first year Father Method had me up at the board working on an algebra problem in front of the rest of the class. He kept asking me this and asking me that and I just wasn't getting it. Finally, I slammed the chalk into the board and started working out the answer and he said, "Good, Goicoechea, get mad, maybe you will wake up and see that this isn't so difficult after all."
I did get angry quite easily but did it really wake me up and did sexuality also awaken me from some lack of passionate energy? Father David was the Gregorian Chant Master for the Monastery and the teacher of chant to the seminarians and I did learn to sing but I never made the choir, for others sang far better. Science was also greatly appreciated by the monks and after general science in year one with Father Anthony we then had chemistry and a wonderful full year biology course with Father Mark. We learned about the scientific method and did many experiments. But most of all I really liked history and we learned Roman History when we studied Latin and the history of music and also of science as we learned of Mendel, Copernicus, and Galileo. All of this learning was a way of more deeply loving all of being with an *agape* that appreciated more and more all of nature.

I,3.6 Nourishing Agapeic Affection with Mathematics

No matter what the monks taught us they did it with that
universalized affection for which their celibate lives prepared
them so that they truly were fathers to us their adopted sons.
My father as a professional gambler was a kind of mathematician.
As he would count the cards and remember with laws of addition
and subtraction what had been played and what had not he
greatly appreciated a good memory well trained by mathematics.
He made sure that we each learned rapid-fire addition,
subtraction, multiplication, and division but I just never
seemed to have the talent for building on that with higher math.
However, when you think that all things can be understood in
terms of mathematics then you come to a new appreciation
for the complexity and the simplicity of each thing, that is, one
being with two parts of this and five parts of that, and so on.
If you are a monk with a sublimated *eros* and thus a new
agapeic affection for all persons, places, and things then you
can see how training in the various kinds of math
could bring about a greater affection for all the orderly detail.
The world is charged with the grandeur of God and it does
flame out like shining from shook foil, and a mathematician
can better love all the wondrous complexity of that simplicity.
Our math teachers Father Method and Father Hilary had a vision
that they imparted to whomever could share in their delight.
And even though I seemed to be limited in my capacity to
follow all the nuances with them, their affection for me, which
I tested, still taught me. And the math I could learn definitely
helped me to better love the world of Euclid and the geometricians.
That those earth measures and those who knew trigonometry
were privileged to see certain laws of the universe impressed
me and though I could not easily get it I at least learned
enough to trust in the order of all, even with a kind of faith.

Agape and *Hesed*

I,3.7 Nourishing Agapeic Eros with Music

As we practiced singing our scales and learned about the history
of the growth from plainchant in its various kinds to polyphony
we came to see that music is all based on mathematical measuring
just as is science and we learned about whole, half, and quarter notes.
Could you say that music is math transformed into lovely sound?
Some of the eighteen masses that we sang on different feast days
were especially sweet and sorrowful songs, like *Stabat Mater*, and
still had a beautiful sweetness about them so that as mathematics
could build up affection so music could build up a lovely *eros*.
We not only studied music in class every year but it was
a big part of our prayer life since each day we sang high mass.
The Benedictines not only sang high mass each day but they sang
the eight parts of the divine office, for music was a major part
of their life of "Ora et Labora" and its beauty let them grow in love.
For Christmas in my second year my mother gave me the three-volume
set of *The Works of St. John of the Cross* and during my third
year at meditation at the end of each morning I studied intently
The Dark Night of the Soul and I took many pages of detailed notes.
I condensed them down and talked about that beautiful poetry
with Father Ambrose and I came to see a metrical music in poetry.
That poetry together with the Gregorian chant formed me further
in the *agape* of a sublimated *eros* for it sang:

> On a Dark Night enkindled in love with yearning
> oh happy chance, I went forth
> my house being now at rest.

Once the internal and external senses of our interior castle
are at rest Jesus can recline his face upon our flowery
breasts, kept wholly for himself alone. I came to see
how celibacy can develop a loving femininity even in the male.
From then on deep in the anima of my animus I would never
think of having sex but always of making love even in celibacy.

I,3.8 Nourishing Agapeic Friendship with Science

In our science classes we learned how physics and biology were
still parts of philosophy before modern times and how Aristotle not only
wrote the first book on physics but was also the father of biology.
In defining genus, species, difference, property, and accident he worked
out a classification for the various species of plants and animals.
In his psychology he distinguished scientifically plant, animal, and
human souls and went on to give proof for the immortal human soul.
We learned how Gregor Mendel, a monk himself, worked out the laws
of genetics and how Copernicus, a Catholic priest, came up with
the Copernican revolution that encouraged Galileo and his experiments.
Father Mark had us make a biology book and Bill Wiegand,
a brilliant student from Idaho who was a year ahead of me,
let me use his notebook that he made the year before and I can
remember even tracing some of his drawings and copying much.
Learning the scientific method was a big part of seminary schooling
and we learned how to put forth an hypothesis and to try to
prove it mathematically, logically, and with experimentation.
The five intellectual virtues according to Aristotle are science,
art, intuitive reason, practical wisdom, and theoretical wisdom.
Our schooling was meant to teach us many kinds of knowledge
so that our intuitions could guide in science and help us
to find a fruitful hypothesis as Mendel and Copernicus did.
Intuitive reason and the scientific search that could grow out of it
aided us even in getting a kind of certitude in our faith, hope, and love.
Aristotle defined science as a certain knowledge of things through
causes and our liberal education helped us to intuit probabilities
so that with a practical wisdom we could integrate our lives
as a universal whole within the big picture seen by wisdom.
For Aristotle friendship was a unity of one soul in two bodies
based upon common values but once we saw Jesus' *agapeic* love
for all, even enemies, we knew that we should be friendly to all.

Agape and *Hesed*

I,3.9 Nourishing Agapeic Mourning with History

The monks nourished their *agape* artistically with music, scientifically with the sciences, mathematically with intuitive reason, and came to a practical wisdom that revealed their celibacy as a sublimated *eros* that facilitated a new affection and friendship. They nourished us in all of that historically, for we had art and music appreciation courses in which we came to know the history of art and music and we learned the history of ideas. We studied the Hebrew Bible in the nine stages of its history. All the fathers had majored in philosophy before they studied four years of theology and then studied their specialties. Just at the time that I went to the seminary around 1950 Scripture study went through a revolutionary change in the Catholic world, for the higher biblical criticism was making an impact. Father Mathias was back from Rome and teaching us after getting his Doctorate of Sacred Scripture and William Foxwell Albright's "From Stone Age to Christianity" was being read by Catholics. We saw how the Law and the prophets with their loves of *Ahava* and *hesed* prepared the way for the new *agape* of Jesus. We were beginning to understand the history of the various spiritualities, from the Benedictine to the Franciscan and Dominican to the Jesuit and the Carmelite; we started to understand the history of modernity, from Luther and Descartes to Calvin and Hobbes to Henry VIII and Locke to Spinoza and Leibniz to Berkeley, Adam Smith, Hume, Kant, Hegel, and Marx; and all of this at bottom was a history of *agape*, which gave us confidence even as high school students that all things work together unto the good. The monks, who knew this history so well because much of it was their own Benedictine history, gave us such a positive attitude that we could successfully mourn any loss that came our way.

II. With Levinas and Derrida

II,1   Levinas's Ethics as First Philosophy

II,1.1 Levinas Grew up with the Jewish Religious Ethics

Emmanuel Levinas tells us that the Hebrew Bible directed his
thinking from the time of his earliest childhood in Lithuania.
He was born in 1905, and entered the University of Strasbourg in 1923.
Besides studying philosophy and learning its history in the West and
besides learning the contemporary philosophy of Heidegger and Husserl,
he made a study of Talmudic sources under the guidance of a teacher
who communicated the traditional Jewish mode of exegesis.
Just as Maimonides came forth with a Jewish version of Aristotelian
philosophy in the thirteenth century and just as Spinoza gave us his
Jewish version of ethics in modern times, so Derrida and Levinas
give us their Jewish version of the postmodern approach to ethics.
From his perspective of Jewish responsibility Levinas reworked
the whole history of Western philosophy and *Totality and Infinity,*
which he published in 1961, gives the full view of the early Levinas.
My world is a totality and I try to control every aspect of it.
I might even explain it to myself and others with a philosophical theory
that gives an account of its beginning, its process, and its purpose.
Each person's religious worldview could let him or her order
everything in a totality that again makes sense of all the parts.
But, according to Levinas, the face of the other can call me out of
my totality into an infinity of responsibility of care for others.
Levinas entitles the first section of *Totality and Infinity* with
a parallel when he calls it "The Same and the Other" and it is the face
of the other than can breach my totality and open me to transcendence.
Levinas sees ethics in the West as a self-realization ethics in which
I will be virtuous in order than I might be happy but he sees Judaism
as having an ethics that looks out for the good of the other and especially
for the needs of widows, orphans, and aliens who look to me for help.
The Hellenic philosopher loves wisdom to understand the totality
and the Hebraic sage is given wisdom's love when he welcomes infinity.

Agape and Hesed

II,1.2 Philosophy's Love of Wisdom and the Wisdom of Love

In his book *Levinas and the Wisdom of Love* Corey Beals quotes Levinas's *Otherwise than Being* (p. 161):

> Philosophy is the wisdom of love
> at the service of love.

This formula of the wisdom of love as distinct from the love of wisdom may distinguish Hebraic ethics from Hellenic philosophy and get to the main point of Levinas's philosophy of ethics in which he wants to show how ethics is beyond philosophy. On page 13 Beals quotes Derrida who, after reading *Totality and Infinity*, said that it "proceeds with the infinite insistence of waves on a beach." Beals says that this means that Derrida sees Levinas as just insistently repeating the same point and Richard Bernstein takes up the metaphor and agrees that Levinas is always repetitious. However in trying to be clear about Jewish postmodernism we will here explore the ideas that once Derrida criticized *Totality and Infinity* Levinas took it to heart and moved on to the new position of *Otherwise than Being*, which stresses the wisdom of love. As we examine the repetitious points of *Totality and Infinity* we will prepare ourselves to see why and how Derrida criticized the very relation of totality as logically exclusive of infinity. In *Totality and Infinity* Levinas's main point is that Jewish ethics is based upon a belief in a bond of responsibility between all members of the family of man and I should be responsible to the face of others especially widows, orphans, and aliens. The look of need on their face calls me to an infinite responsibility. However, Derrida shows how Levinas is working with a logic of exclusive opposites characteristic of modern logic.
Totality and infinity might better be conceived as mixed with each other, and with that in mind Levinas moves from the image of widows, orphans, and aliens to that of the suffering servant who reveals the glory of God by suffering for others with love.

II,1.3 By Letting my Totality Welcome your Infinity

In Section One of *Totality and Infinity* Levinas discusses
the same and the other and the totality of the same has to do
with everything in my world making it up in the same way.
I can enjoy each thing within my world and the peace
of this enjoyment is the first form of my egoism, which is
a movement by which my self-centered life is a being for-itself.
But then the face of the other can look at me and make
a demand upon me and I can become responsible to the other.
If I in my totality welcome the other I discover that they can
make infinite demands upon me and thus infinity invades
my world by making more claims than I can imagine.
In my world I can enjoy others but if I respond to the call
of the other and become responsible to him or her my responsibility
is not a pleasure but a pain and an affliction in which I
welcome my neighbor so that he is more important than myself.
Welcoming the other's infinite demands becomes
more important to me than the totality of my own world.
On page 75 of *Totality and Infinity* Levinas gives a good description
of what it is like for my totality to welcome your infinity.

> The nakedness of the face is destituteness.
> To recognize the Other is to give.
> But it is to give to the master, to the lord,
> to him whom one approaches as "you"
> in a dimension of height.

In a footnote he says that the "you" is the "you" of majesty
in contrast to the "thou" of intimacy so that widows, orphans,
aliens, and any one whose face pleads with need is my lord
and master and thus they have a special height and majesty.
The welcoming of Levinas sees the great worth and dignity
that is equal in every person and takes responsibility for that person.

Agape and *Hesed*

II,1.4 With a "me voici" beyond Buber's "I and Thou"

Martin Buber's *I and Thou* beautifully expresses how the Jewish religious ethic works as it poetically shows how love is the responsibility of an I for a thou, which is an attitude that is given me by grace and which I then will. This attitude that I can have toward nature, humans, and spiritual beings is contrasted with the I-it attitude in that the I-thou is exclusive, direct, present, and mutual while the I-it does not relate to the other as unique and mediates the relation with knowledge and relates to it in the past and the it does not relate mutually to me. Buber shows how it is the exalted melancholy of our fate that every thou in our world must become an it, but with grace and will they can once again become our thou. Also, in every I-thou relation we do meet the eternal thou. On pages 68 and 69 of *Totality and Infinity* Levinas says that he does not have the ridiculous pretension of "correcting" Buber, but he is critical of the mutuality of the I-Thou relation and thereby thinks of our responsibility called forth by the face of the other as a *"me voici"* relation rather than an "I-Thou" relation in order to give the other that height of being more important than myself. For Levinas the I is the subject of my totality that is nourished by enjoyment and will kill for a crust of bread in preferring self. The me of the *"me voici,"* the "here is me" at your service, is the me of the accusative, genitive, dative, ablative, vocative, responsible self who will give the bread out of my mouth to the other so that it is given to me to give by the call of the other who is to be served by me with a duty that is mine before the other I. Levinas builds upon the notion of love as responsibility of an I for a thou by seeing love as coming from the lowly humble me who can serve the noble other as the I who makes demands on me.

Part One: Experiencing Problems

II,1.5 *And a Transcendence beyond Plato's Divine Madness*

Plato's philosophy explains this world of Heraclitean physical becoming in terms of the Parmenidean metaphysical realm of Being. This realm of Being is central to Heidegger's ontology and is not all that helpful when it comes to formulating a sensitive ethics. But Levinas sees in Plato's metaphysics a Good beyond Being that the Platonic philosophy of love in both *The Symposium* and in *The Phaedrus* gets in touch with as the Beautiful Good. On page 43 of *Totality and Infinity*, Levinas writes:

> Western philosophy has most often been an ontology:
> a reduction of the other to the same
> by interposition of a middle and neutral term
> that ensures the comprehension of being.

Just above that on the same page he writes:

> A calling into question of the same
> which cannot occur within the egoist
> spontaneity of the same
> is brought about by the other.
> We name this calling into question
> of my spontaneity
> by the presence of the Other ethics.

On page 48 Levinas begins to discuss "Transcendence as the Idea of Infinity" and he shows how the metaphysics of Plato and Descartes discovers a divine infinity that is transcendent. To think the infinite, the transcendent, is not to think an object. On page 49 he writes:

> The "intentionality" of transcendence
> is unique in its kind;
> the difference between objectivity and transcendence
> will serve as a general guideline
> for all the analyses of this work.

He then discusses the divine madness of Plato's sublimated *eros*.

Agape and *Hesed*

II,1.6 And an Infinity beyond Descartes' Infinite

Levinas treats Plato and Descartes together as he shows how
they each in different ways had a transcendent infinity
in their metaphysics and this was felt in Plato's *Phaedrus*.
On page 49 Levinas writes:

> Against a thought that proceeds from him
> who "has his own head to himself,"
> he affirms the value of the delirium
> that comes from God, "winged thought."

This enthusiasm and divine madness is thought in its highest
sense and is a kind of ecstatic possession by the divine Other.
Plato discovered something akin to Levinas's infinity that calls
me and teaches me of the other when I behold the face of the other.
Levinas shows how Plato and Descartes are not thinking of
an object but are in touch with the transcendent, the other.
However, the transcendence that is the point of Levinas's book
does not empower the I by sublimating the power of vulgar passion
to become the energy of noble passion and its new creativity.
Rather, the face of the other, as Levinas writes on page 50,

> lets the desire proper to the gaze
> turn into a gen*eros*ity incapable
> of approaching the other with empty hands.

This has to do with the Jewish loves of *hesed* and *ahava*
which are called to care for widows, orphans, and aliens and
which will even let the Jewish people become a suffering servant.
As Descartes considered what it was that let him be certain
when he was able to say, "I think, therefore, I am," he saw
that his criterion had to be an idea of perfection within his mind
that only a perfect being could cause.
That standard that let him know when an idea was certain
or not was the idea of the infinite or the perfect beyond limits.
But again this is not the infinite transcendence of the needy other.

Part One: Experiencing Problems

II,1.7 And a Face beyond Heidegger's Ontology

Levinas sees his ethics as totally opposed by Heidegger's ontology. On page 46 Levinas writes:

> A philosophy of power, ontology is,
> as first philosophy which does not
> Call into question the same,
> a philosophy of injustice.

Aristotle really emphasized an ethics of self-realization and did not emphasize my self-sacrifice to love and serve the needy other. Heidegger is like that with his ontological ethics of authenticity. I can be authentic if my life is a connected whole throughout my time. If I see that every decision makes me guilty because in choosing for something I must choose against something else then I can go back to my first decision and live it in my guilt, just as I can see that anxiety is being threatened by the indefinite so that if I anticipate my death in anxiety my ecstatic time can be authentic. With anticipatory resoluteness as a being-unto-guilt and a being-unto-death I can realize myself as an authentic *Dasein*. Levinas sees this ontology as a first ethic as being a philosophy of power in which I empower myself by integrating my life. But this only builds up the ego and does not call it into question as does the look of the other for Levinas. And consequently Levinas sees the whole project of *Being and Time* as a philosophy of injustice. Heidegger's philosophy is still part of modernity in standing alone before Being as the powerful, authentic individual looking down on the inauthentic.
In an article by William Richardson in Adriaan Peperzak's book *Ethics as First Philosophy* (p. 123) we get a good picture of how Levinas thought of Heidegger as even working with the Nazis. Richardson quotes Levinas:

> In 1943, my parents were in one concentration camp
> and I was in another.

He implied that Heidegger had something to do with that injustice.

II,1.8 And a Responsibility Beyond Kierkegaard's Subjectivity

Levinas mentions Kierkegaard only twice in *Totality and Infinity*. On page 40 he writes:

> It is not I who resist the system
> as Kierkegaard thought; it is the other.

On page 305 he writes:

> The I is conserved then in goodness
> without its resistance to system
> manifesting itself as the egoist cry
> of the subjectivity still concerned for
> happiness or salvation, as in Kierkegaard.

In *Proper Names* Levinas explains this more fully with two articles on Kierkegaard and on page 76 he writes:

> [W]hat disturbs me in Kierkegaard
> may be reduced to two points: . . .
> he bequeathed to the history of philosophy
> an exhibitionist, immodest subjectivity . . .
> The second point. It is Kierkegaard's violence
> that shocks me . . . That harshness
> of Kierkegaard emerges at the exact moment
> when he "transcends ethics."

When Kierkegaard leaps from the ethical stage on life's way to the religious stage of absolutely relating to the absolute Levinas points out the violence that is done by paying attention totally to God and not being concerned with other human beings in our world here. As Kierkegaard leaps into the religious he leaves behind the ethical, but then for Kierkegaard there is the second movement of the leap by which the knight of faith in *Fear and Trembling* gets Isaac back a second time and returns to the ethical and loves the neighbor. Levinas seems to take literally with nothing further in it that "unless you hate your father, mother, wife, child and even yourself, you cannot be my disciple." So Kierkegaard is violent.

Part One: Experiencing Problems

II,1.9 And beyond Nietzsche's Philosophizing with a Hammer

Levinas also mentions Nietzsche only twice in *Totality and Infinity*.
On page 28 Levinas writes:

> The relation between the same and the other
> is not always reducible to knowledge
> of the other by the same, not even to
> the *revelation* of the other to the same,
> which is, already fundamentally different
> from disclosure.

In a footnote to this he discusses Nietzsche's notion of "drama."
There can be a dramatic unfolding of Apollo or Dionysus
through their actions in maybe five acts of a tragic drama.
On page 203 Levinas continues this contrast between the ethical
of me and the other and Nietzsche's character as a work of art.
In *Proper Names* Levinas links Kierkegaard and Nietzsche together
in going beyond the ethical to a religious level that is more mystical
than ethical and concerned with my fulfillment rather than the other's.
He sees them both as contributing to a Heideggerian view of a self-
centered, egoistic authenticity that can support National Socialism.
So Levinas does not look into the face of Nietzsche any more than
he looks into the face of Kierkegaard: he treats neither
The Works of Love, which belong to Kierkegaard and not his pseudonyms,
nor the amor fati and love of all existence that in *The Antichrist*
Nietzsche connects with the all-loving Jesus.
Nietzsche's Jesus has an *agape* that really loves the enemy
for Nietzsche loves most of all the Jesus of the Sermon on the Mount.
Derrida is a much more complete reader of both Kierkegaard
and Nietzsche than is the Levinas of *Totality and Infinity* and
so when Derrida deconstructs the early Levinas and helps
him move to the later Levinas of *Otherwise Than Being* Derrida
will have the complete Kierkegaard and the complete Nietzsche
in mind and not settle for a misreading of the faces of those two.

Agape and *Hesed*

II,2 Derrida's Deconstruction of *Totality and Infinity*

II,2.1 With a Jewish Aporetic Ethics That Deconstructs

Derrida greatly appreciates Levinas's ethical philosophy and in his seventy-five-page essay on Levinas's early thought, which he called *Violence and Metaphysics: An Essay on the Thought of Emmanuel Levinas*, Derrida refers to "[t]he great book *Totality and Infinity*" and approaches it with an Introduction and five parts:

	Introduction	79
I.	The Violence of Light	84
II.	Phenomenology, Ontology, Metaphysics	92
III.	Difference and Eschatology	109
IV.	Of Transcendental Violence	118
V.	Of Ontological Violence	134

Right away, at the beginning of his preface to *Totality and Infinity* Levinas discusses the violence of war and reminds us that we are constantly involved in war and winning at any price, which means that we are most concerned about conquering our enemies. Ethics, insofar as it has to do with loving other persons, even our enemies who do not love us, is forgotten and self-defeating. Most ethical ways of thinking have to do with self-realization and to even preserve ourselves in a state of nature that is "nasty, mean and brutish" we have to be constantly unethical. From his Jewish tradition Levinas knew about caring for widows, orphans, and aliens and, as he says right away in his preface, he does think of an eschatology and a place that living ethically can help bring about if we really take responsibility for responsibility and try to bring about shalom. Derrida, also a Jewish philosopher, wants to lessen violence as much as possible and to do that he wants to become more and more aware of the limits of making ethical decisions and even to decide to have an infinity that excludes any totality for already that distinction is violent.

Part One: Experiencing Problems

II,2.2 Levinas' Logic of Exclusive Opposites

At the beginning of his essay on Levinas in *Writing and Difference* Derrida (p. 79) quotes Matthew Arnold's *Culture and Anarchy*:

> Hebraism and Hellenism—between these two points
> of influence moves our world.
> At one time it feels more powerfully
> the attraction of one of them
> at another time of the other;
> and it ought to be, though never is
> evenly and happily balanced between them.

As Derrida thinks back to the ethics of the Greeks he goes especially to Socrates, who first moved from Greek physics to ethics. Socrates was concerned for the care of the soul and in taking this responsibility he decided that the best approach was skepticism. He claimed that he was the wisest man in Athens because he alone knew that he knew nothing and he trusted in that humble way. In Greek a road or pathway and even the pathway of thinking is called a *poros* and "a" negates that so that aporetic means that there is no certain way of knowing just how to decide things. As Derrida claims, following Socrates, we can only make decisions over the abyss of indecidability because things are so complex that we never know the total big picture with certainty. Because we live in a world about which we are always learning more we should have the best of intentions but given that the future might reveal all sorts of things of which we were ignorant. When Derrida thinks about Levinas's ethics he appreciates the infinity of things so much that he is skeptical about totality. We may think we know a totality but we never really can. In following the Socratic aporetic ethics Derrida begins to deconstruct Levinas's non-skeptical logic of exclusive opposites. As Derrida develops his aporetic ethics in which deconstruction is justice he opts for a metaphysics of excess and a logic of mixed opposites.

II,2.3 And Levinas's Deconstruction of Buber's I and Thou

Buber's theory of the I-thou relation is strongly criticized by Levinas for four reasons: (1) it is reciprocal (2) it is a private relation between two (3) it is a reality that can change into its opposite and (4) it makes ethics depend upon theory so it is not first philosophy. The four characteristics that make the I-thou relation different from the I-it relation are each critically destructed by Levinas. Buber's mutual, exclusive, direct and present I-thou relation is not at all like the ethical responsibility of Levinas for the face of the other who teaches me his paradoxical destitute-height demands of me to give to him and others the bread out of my mouth. Derrida mentions Buber on page 105 of his essay and shows how Levinas is opposed to Buber because Buber has his intimate reciprocity and does not start with any ethical relation. Derrida is doing a very careful reading of Levinas looking at him from many angels and helping his readers read Levinas. Derrida takes up Levinas' thinking about the face of the other which calls me before I think and by page 108 he is thinking the face of God or the face of Yahweh who is never named in *Totality and Infinity* and Derrida discusses the face of Yahweh that is hidden from Moses and quoting Jabes on page 109 Derrida wonders what Levinas would think:

> "All faces are His; this is why He has no face."

Buber's I-thou always reveals the eternal Thou but Levinas' infinite face of the other does not reveal the Face of God. So are there some insights of Buber that might help us in questioning Levinas as Derrida seems to be questioning him? Levinas with his destruction of metaphysics which is like Heidegger's leads Derrida's to a deconstructive reading instead which comes out of Derrida's aporetic first ethics which does not simply treat Buber as right or wrong but lets Buber by way of Jabes help us with a better reading of Levinas.

Part One: Experiencing Problems

II,2.4 And Levinas' Deconstruction of Husserl's Phenomenology

As Derrida treats Levinas' use of Husserl's phenomenology he primarily concentrates on three main points: (1) It is a theory of consciousness which sees all consciousness as being intentional. (2) It is an attitude of respect for the concrete. (3) It is a method of description. Husserl's first philosophy was to go to the things themselves and to describe them in their great variety of relationships with the sciences and philosophy. Husserl saw all consciousness as consciousness of something. As Levinas used phenomenology to develop his ethics as first philosophy he saw consciousness not as intending an object but rather as being intended by a subject whose face is calling out to me and teaching me of the one who needs my care. In the Preface to *Totality and Infinity* Levinas writes on page 27:

> This book will present subjectivity
> as welcoming the Other, as hospitality;
> in it the idea of infinity is consummated.
> Hence intentionality, where thought remains
> an adequation with the object, does not
> define consciousness at is fundamental level.
> All knowing qua intentionality
> already presupposes the idea of infinity,
> which is preeminently non-adequation.

Derrida discusses Levinas' critique of Husserl and on page 87 of *Violence and Metaphysics* writes:

> In his critique of Husserl,
> Levinas retains two Heideggerian themes . . .
> Husserl perhaps was wrong to see
> in this concrete world,
> a world of perceived objects, after all.

As we will now see in looking at Derrida's treatment of Levinas on Husserl and Heidegger Derrida will try to be non-violent.

Agape and *Hesed*

II,2,5 And Levinas' Deconstruction of the Heidegger's Ontology

Derrida develops his practice of deconstruction out of
Heidegger's practice of the destruction of metaphysics that enabled
him to move from Husserl's phenomenology to his hermeneutical way.
In *Being and Time* Heidegger did a hermeneutical phenomenology
of the existential in order to develop his ontological way of thinking.
Heidegger made a fresh start as he identified the metaphysical
preconceptions that underlay Husserl's theory of consciousness.
Heidegger thought that words such as "consciousness", "subject"
or "substance" are the results of metaphysical theories which
keep us from really getting to the phenomena of human being.
Thus Heidegger had to destroy the history of metaphysics
in order to get a view of human being or *Dasein* and thus
on page 41 of *Being and Time* he writes:

> The thing-in-being whose analysis
> is our task is we ourselves.
> The being of this thing-in-being
> is each one's "mine" (*je mines*)

This *jemeinigkeit* or *Ipseity* helps Levinas move toward
the me who is responsible to the face of the other and Heidegger
also moves towards ethics as he analyses *Dasein* in his or her
mood-discourse-understanding for we can be in the world
inauthentically in ambiguity, idle talk or curiosity or we
can become authentic and have a proper care for being itself.
Heidegger did develop a philosophy of responsibility and saw
man as the shepherd of Being and thought of thinking as thanking
with a sort of Nietzschean affirmation Heidegger thought that
we should be grateful for all that is and that is responsibility.
So Derrida points out how Heidegger moved beyond Husserl
toward and ethical viewpoint, but Levinas must still move
beyond Heidegger to develop a philosophy of love for
others who call me from desire to possess to desire to serve.

Part One: Experiencing Problems

II,2.6 And Levinas Destruction of Plato's Metaphysics

The title of Derrida's essay on Levinas is *Violence and Metaphysics* and already at the beginning on pages 85 and 86 Derrida says a great deal about how Levinas gets beyond Heidegger with Platonic *eros* and then Levinas must still get beyond the violence of that metaphysics. Levinas' philosophy of love and his loving ethics has to do with two kinds of desire: that which desires to possess and for the infinite which does not satisfy desire but which opens it to transcendence. Plato's metaphysics has to do with the Good beyond Being or the *epekeina tes ousias* and as Derrida says on page 85:

> In *Totality and Infinity* the "Phenomenology of *Eros*"
> describes the movement of the *epekeina tes ousias*
> in the very experience of the caress.

Levinas entitles the last section of *Totality and Infinity* *Beyond the Face* and section a of that is *The Ambiguity of Love* and then B is *The Phenomenology of Eros* which Derrida considers. As Derrida explains on page 93 the affectivity of need and desire as love are very different for need is self-centered but

> Desire, on the contrary, permits itself
> to be appealed to by the absolutely irreducible
> exteriority of the other to which
> it must remain infinitely inadequate.

Platonic *eros* in its Divine Madness in *The Phaedrus* is open to this kind of infinite for it is not an intentionality of disclosure but of search: a movement into the invisible. In a certain sense it expresses love, but suffers from an inability to tell it as Levinas explains on page 258 of *Totality and Infinity*. However, while Greek love can go this far and prepare the way for Jewish ethics it does not reach the alterity of the other in the face of the poor, the stranger, the widow, and the orphan and thus Levinas must with Heidegger destroy the history of Platonic metaphysics, which Derrida prefers to less violently deconstruct.

Agape and *Hesed*

II,2.7 And Levinas' Destruction of Aristotle's Metaphysics

Having learned philosophy as a Catholic Heidegger knew Aristotle very well as he was developed in different ways by Aquinas and Scotus. When Heidegger destroyed the history of metaphysics by showing all of its ideas that should not be used by the phenomenologist he dealt with the notion of substance which is a thing in itself that forms the core of the Aristotelian tradition; but Levinas does not even bother with Aristotle because his ethics is so different. Levinas sees the ethical relation as totally asymmetrical so that there is no mutuality or reciprocity between humans and thus Aristotelians would think that Levinas' ethics is impossible. Aristotle does not get rid of the I and develops a self realization ethics in which by being virtuous I can be happy. Love for him is friendship and the friend is the other half of my soul. Derrida stands in between Aristotle and Levinas and sees the subject as decentered and never at home so I am not a Levinasian accused me and I am not an Aristotelian substantial thing in itself. So Derrida deconstructs what would be both the Aristotelian destruction of Levinas and the Levinasian destruction of Aristotle's metaphysics. Levinas can identify with Platonic *eros* and take it in the direction of his infinitizing desire but Aristotelian friendship has nothing to offer him and though his philosophy of an ethical asymmetry would be critical of Aristotle and Aristotelians argue to a first cause which is pure act and the Supreme Being but Levinas is interested in the Infinity beyond any such Being. As Derrida think of the Jewish reciprocal ethics of Buber and the asymmetrical ethics of Levinas he chooses the ethics of asymmetry and what he comes to call the ethics of pure giving. Already in *Violence and Metaphysics* Derrida is thinking of the notion of the pure and on pages 146–47 he begins to think of pure violence and pure non-violence together.

Part One: Experiencing Problems

II,2.8 And Levinas' Destruction of Descartes' Infinite

At the beginning of his essay on page 82 Derrida writes:

> The consciousness of crisis is for Husserl
> but the provisional, almost necessary covering up
> of a transcendental motif which in
> Descartes and in Kant was already beginning
> to accomplish the Greek end;
> philosophy as science.

Aristotle defined science as a certain knowledge of things through causes and Descartes begins with the quest for that certainty. His tree of philosophy has the three metaphysical roots the second of which is the God of Infinite perfection or infinity which idea enables him to doubt any idea that is imperfect. Then growing out of the roots is the trunk of physics and then there are the branches of medicine, mechanics and morals. Levinas shows how this Cartesian idea of the infinite does not have the transcending value of Platonic metaphysics but belongs to the Aristotelian criticism of Platonism and thus on page 83 Derrida writes:

> Levinas seeks to raise up metaphysics
> and to restore its metaphysics of the Infinite
> in opposition to the entire tradition
> derived from Aristotle.

The Platonic Infinity, which has to do with the Good beyond Being, is central in *Totality and Infinity* as Levinas uses it in going beyond the Being of Heidegger to his ethics of the Infinity of the other. The desire for that Infinity that is an ever increasing desire is central to the love in *Totality and Infinity* and remains so in *Otherwise than Being* for it makes up the very core of the wisdom of Love. Descartes as the father of modern philosophy has none of this and puts all his emphasis on the ego that is not essentially related to others. The scientific method seeking certainty fits with this individualism.

Agape and *Hesed*

II,2.9 And Levinas' Destruction of Kierkegaard and Nietzsche

Of course, Kierkegaard and Nietzsche together with Dostoyevsky and
Hopkins are the founders of the postmodern ethics as first philosophy.
But Levinas never does come to appreciate Kierkegaard or Nietzsche
even though Heidegger was so positive in many ways to both of them.
Levinas did not seem to know of Kierkegaard's *Works of Love*
and his philosophy of loving others as more important than self.
Levinas always seemed to think of Nietzsche as violently
philosophizing with a hammer and only announcing the death of God.
On pages 110 and 111 of his essay on Levinas Derrida defends
Kierkegaard against Levinas and shows that Kierkegaard is not an
egoist thinking only about his own salvation and on page 93 he writes:

> Despite his anti-Kierkegaardian protests,
> Levinas here returns to the themes of *Fear and Trembling*,
> the movement of desire can be what it is
> only paradoxically, as the renunciation of desire.

These two kinds of desire are central to *Totality and Infinity* and
as Derrida is deconstructing what Levinas says about Kierkegaard
he shows that Levinas is contradictory in critiquing Kierkegaard.
Derrida is very favorable toward both Kierkegaard and Nietzsche
and does speak positively of Nietzsche in *Writing and Difference*.
Jack Caputo pictures Derrida as a Dionysian Rabbi or a
Nietzschean Levinasian and Derrida is very much a Nietzschean.
As Derrida helped Levinas move from *Totality and Infinity*
to *Otherwise Than Being* perhaps Derrida's Nietzsche had more
of a role to ply than Derrida's Kierkegaard because already
on page 8 of *Otherwise Than Being* Levinas refers to Nietzsche's
poetic writing and the reversal of time in a laughter refusing language.
We must now examine the love ethic of *Otherwise Than Being*
and see if Levinas is being more true to Jewish *Ahava* and
Hesed here than he was in *Totality and Infinity* and again
we can continue to think of this Levinas in comparison with Buber.

II,3 The Wisdom of Love in *Otherwise Than Being*

II,3.1 *How the Notion of the Third Opens Levinas*

Levinas took Derrida's deconstruction of *Totality and Infinity* to heart and wrote *Otherwise Than Being* to more consistently state his Jewish ethics. Corey Beals's book *Levinas and the Wisdom of Love* is wonderful in clearly explaining all that is new in the Later Levinas and he concentrates on the notion of the third in order to answer many of Levinas' critics by showing how justice and philosophy are grounded in it. However, Beals discusses the ambiguity of Levinasian love in terms of *agape* and *eros* and does not make a distinction between the *Ahava* and *hesed* of the Hebrew Bible and Christian *agape*. On page 254 of *Totality and Infinity* on "The Ambiguity of Love" Levinas does distinguish between a desire that can be the most egoistic and cruelest of needs and a desire which is ever open to the infinity of the other in a responsible love for the other. Throughout his book Beals develops this distinction, which he calls the two types of love, on page 2:

> desire (as a satiable desire, or neighbor love)
> and need (as satiable desire, or self-love).

The commandment in the Hebrew Bible is "Love your neighbor as yourself" and this love of neighbor did become part of Christian *agape*. But Levinas does not write about loving oneself; rather, I am to be responsible to widows, orphans, and aliens even at my own expense and this is the difference between Buber and Levinas. In Levinas with the widows, orphans and aliens of *Totality and Infinity* and the suffering servant of *Otherwise Than Being* there is only an asymmetrical relation that invited much criticism as we shall see but with *The Third* Levinas got symmetry. Beals's explanation of how *The Third* opens the way for justice and philosophy is excellent and he does answer the critics. But does he not equate wrongly this symmetry with *agape*?

Agape and *Hesed*

II,3.2 To the Double Responsibility of Love and Justice

Beals refers often to the book *Entre Nous: On Thinking of the Other* in which Levinas in interviewed by a Christian interlocutor. Especially in chapter 9, "Philosophy, Justice and love," Levinas is asked about his views on love:
"So, love is originary?" and on page 108 Levinas answers:

> Love is originary. I'm not speaking theologically at all;
> I myself don't use it much, the word love,
> it is a worn-out and ambiguous word.
> And then, too, there is something severe
> in this love; this love is commanded.

Then on page 113 the interviewer asks:

> In this perspective, what, according to you
> would be the difference between *eros* and *agape*?

Levinas responds:

> I am definitely not a Freudian; consequently
> I don't think that *agape* comes from *eros* . . .
> I can say no more about it now; I think
> in any case that *eros* is definitely not *Agape*
> that *agape* is neither a derivative
> nor the extinction of love-*eros*.

To be faithful to Levinas we have to be clear that *agape* is not part of his technical vocabulary and that is why he resists getting serious with the interviewer about both love and *agape*. Beals like the interviewer calls the two loves of Levinas *agape* or responsible love of neighbor and then a selfish need love. But in spite of that his book on *Levinas and the Wisdom of Love* is excellent in showing how Levinas develops the idea of the third. When the face of the other looks at me with a request ethics as first philosophy is born but for there to be philosophy proper following upon that first ethical responsibility the look of a third at us is necessary for us to start thinking philosophically.

Part One: Experiencing Problems

II,3.3 With a Wisdom of Love at the Service of Love

On page 157 of *Otherwise Than Being* Levinas writes;

> The responsibility for the other
> is an immediacy antecedent to questions.
> It is troubled and becomes a problem
> when a third party enters.

When the third party looks at the other and me we become
self-conscious and questions begin to arise about justice and
thus philosophy is born so that even responsibility is questioned.
On page 161 Levinas writes:

> Philosophy is this measure brought to
> the infinity of being-for-the-other
> and is like the wisdom of love.

And then on page 162 he writes:

> Philosophy is the wisdom of love
> at the service of love.

This is the central thesis of Beal's book and by explaining
this wisdom of love and its serving of love he wants to
explain the central core of all of Levinas' writing.
Chapter 3 of Beal's book on *Levinasian Love* pages 43-64
deals with the relation between altruistic love and self-love.
He gives the criticism of many against Levinas for his exclusion
of self-love and some like Paul Ricoeur see Levinas'
description of altruism as excessive and Ricoeur argues
that especially being a hostage for the other is excessive.
It is Beal's task against Derrida, Caputo, Kearney,
Ricoeur, Irigaray, and others to show that according to Levinas
altruism and self-love are compatible and it is with the
appearance of the third that the extreme asymmetry is
overcome by the wisdom of altruism than can serve even self.
As a result of Derrida's deconstruction of *Totality and Infinity*
Levinas works out this new theory of love in *Otherwise than Being*.

Agape and *Hesed*

II,3.4 Which Goes from Loving Widows, Orphans and Aliens

Derrida would see Levinas as an advocate of pure giving which is impossible because there is always a return for any gift I give. The asymmetrical relation between me and widows, orphans and aliens is such that for Levinas I expect nothing in return but Derrida argues that there will be all kinds of unexpected returns. As a Jew I might feel happy and proud that I take care of the poor and do not participate in a caste system helping the rich. Levinas took such criticism to heart and in *Otherwise Than Being* he made the asymmetry even greater with his suffering servant. When I offer my cheek to the smitter I suffer so much in my giving it is hard to say that I receive some gift in return.
Levinas gets around Derrida's problem of pure giving with his notion of the third that lets responsibility become first philosophy. The third who can always be there looking at us when I take responsibility for others brings about an interpersonal personhood. Max Scheler already developed a philosophy of persons in relation and Buber and Marcel were influenced by him so Levinas' notion of the third had precedents and this is why he is postmodern. With the third he is explicitly going beyond rugged individualism and the modern approach that makes of every man an island. The notion of a trinity prevents an egoism for two even though with the best intentions one may seek to be a most pure giver. It is at this point on page 162 of *Otherwise Than Being* that we get to "Philosophy is the wisdom of Love at the service of Love." Once the third opens us to philosophical questions about justice we can begin to work out the relation between altruism and self-love which is the main issue between Derrida and Levinas. Kierkegaard had to work out the relation between self-love and the love of God and neighbor so how does Levinas do it? Is he able to make altruism and self-love compatible? Does he deal with loving God as well as self and neighbor?

Part One: Experiencing Problems

II,3.5 To being the Suffering Servant

In Second Isaiah there are four Suffering Servant poetic pieces
that Mark in the first Synoptic Gospel applies to Jesus.
Levinas' philosophy has the same structure as Mark's Gospel.
First in Galilee Jesus goes about caring for widows, orphans, and aliens.
Then he goes up to Jerusalem and Mark shows him as the Suffering
Servant of Isaiah who offers himself even for those killing him.
The early Levinas takes responsibility for widows, orphans, and aliens.
The later Levinas portrays the hostage being persecuted for others.
As Derrida and others point out there can be a self-love even
in the two kinds of altruistic love so as Levinas seeks to be
consistent he develops his notion of the third and a philosophy
of justice that takes him beyond the collision of altruism and egoism.
As Beals (p. 57) points out, Peperzak thinks that compatibilism is
only an option after the arrival of the third and he explains
this further on page 55 when he quotes Peperzak:

> the asymmetry of this relation does not seem
> to exclude a double asymmetry in which
> I am as "high" for the Other as the Other is for me.

Beals (p. 55) invokes Peperzak's quotation of Levinas:

> I myself can feel myself
> to be the other for the other.

Also on page 55 Beals goes on to write about Merald Westphal:

> As both Levinas and Kierkegaard emphasize,
> neighbor love runs counter to our natural self-love.
> and as such, taken seriously,
> "the command to practice it is truly traumatic.
> How at all, is it possible, even imperfectly?"

For Kierkegaard the natural loves of affection, friendship, and *eros*
have a built in self-love and he does explain how to overcome this.
So it can help if we see how Levinas and Kierkegaard compare.

Agape and *Hesed*

II,3.6 Who Loves the Enemy in a Proximity

As Beals writes on page 83, Levinas says quite clearly:

> Consciousness is born as the presence
> of 'the third' party in the proximity
> of the one to the other.

On the same page Beals explains:

> This view is in contrast to theories of
> original hostility, such as Hobbe's,
> which describe humans as naturally at war.
> Levinas, on the other hand, describes an ego
> naturally obligated to the other.

This obligation, which is one of Jewish justice, has to do with
my being a host and a hostage for every other even if his face
is not calling me because there is a nearness to every human
that obligates us to become our brother's keeper and lover.
This is what the wisdom of love can teach me as it serves love.
This wisdom of love originates in the responsibility of one for the other.
This is what makes Levinas postmodern in that he goes beyond
the social contract theories that originate in a war of all against all.
The ethical relation is the beginning of political states and institutions.
As Levinas puts it on page 82 of *Otherwise Than Being*:

> Proximity is not a state of repose
> but, a restlessness outside the place of rest.

He explains that further on page 88.

> In a sense nothing is more burdensome
> than a neighbor. Is not this desired one
> the undesirable itself.

When the face of the other calls me I should respond with caring love.
But when the third then appears looking at us I see that I am
responsible for him and all others as well and being a host for
any other makes me a hostage to all near me in proximity.
In my passivity I am persecuted as proximity becomes obsession.

II,3.7 *That Lets Me Lovingly Substitute for Him*

Throughout *Otherwise Than Being* Levinas has many sayings
that relate to substitution and on page 113 he begins a six-
page section on substitution in which he shows that
we are all responsible for everyone else and that the
material needs of my neighbor are my spiritual needs.
His idea of substitution clearly shows how ethics for him
is not a self-realization ethics such as Aristotle taught.
We do not practice virtue in order to be happy.
Rather, we should live in the best way possible in order to
help others to be happy; the face of the other
calls me to work hard to let that other be happy.
Whereas I used to work for my good I should now
substitute the other for myself and work for them.
Once we are looked at by the third and realize the brotherhood
of all men in newly felt proximity we see that we are the
suffering servant for all and a substitute taking on their needs.
The self as a suffering servant is an hostage and because of
our being the hostage there can be, as he says on page 117,

> pity, compassion, pardon and proximity—
> even the simple "After you, sir."

All of this presupposes substitution (page 117):

> the possibility of putting oneself
> in place of the other.

so that his guilt and pain can become mine and not only his.
The wisdom of love shows us all of this so that we can come to
serve others in love as did the Suffering Servant of Second Isaiah.
Before that image was applied to Jesus the Jews saw themselves
as being persecuted by many people and they came to the wisdom
of love which let them offer their suffering even for their enemies.
That is a great wisdom that is at the heart of Levinas' philosophy.
He explains it even further in terms of the glory of the sufferer.

Agape and *Hesed*

II,3.8 With a Glory that Manifests the Unmanifest

On the next to last page of *Otherwise Than Being* as Levinas is giving a summary of his book he writes, p. 184:

> Signification, the-one-for-the-other, the relationship
> with alterity, has been analyzed in the present work
> as proximity, proximity as responsibility for the other,
> and responsibility for the other as substitution: The subject
> was shown to be an expiation for another, the condition
> or unconditionality of being hostage.

When by my responsible action I say "here I am for others" as Abraham, Jacob, Moses, Samuel and Isaiah said "Here I am" I bear witness to their infinity and to the weight of their worth. That weight or *kabod* in Hebrew is the glory of infinite worth. Whereas the five mentioned here gave glory to God by their saying of "here I am" to Him Levinas has us bear witness to the infinite worth of every other by welcoming them even by being their hostage. So the last big theme of *Otherwise Than Being* is that of glory. Levinas' definition of glory is that which manifests the unmanifest even in its unmanifestness so we must now understand this. As Levinas begins to treat glory on page 140 in a section called *The Glory of the Infinite* he writes about inspiration and witness. I bear witness to the glory of the other when I respond *"me voici"*. That puts it better than even "Here I am" because the me is in the accusative case and in my lowliness I witness to the height of the other. Levinas thinks that this is the deepest truth of Judaism that it can bear witness to the glory of all other faces calling out to me. Levinas starting on page 142 contrasts his view with Descartes and Kant and he even speaks off modernity for by keeping philosophy and religion within the limits of reason alone there is no glory. On page 146 he writes about the glory of the infinite that orders me to the other so when I respond I am making this glory manifest. Others can begin to see this glory when I bear witness to it.

II,3.9 Even in its Unmanifestness

To make manifest means to show somebody something by
holding it in your hand for them so they can hold it in theirs.
According to Levinas the glory of the other calls us to our duty
so that by responding to the other and the third can see that glory.
On page 149 Levinas writes:

> witness is humility and admission;
> it is made before all theology;
> it is Kerygma and prayer,
> glorification and recognition.

All of this helps us better understand the manifestation of glory.
As a witness the face of the other will bring me to humility with its
infinity that is so high and weighted with such a holy worth.
As a witness I do admit even before any theology that the other
is so wonderfully glorious that I can spend my life as a
suffering servant trying to aid others as they call for my aid.
Once the third comes and sees me doing this and begins to respond
to my witness the justice of all this can be called into question and then
philosophy can begin and so will theology but maybe not for Levinas.
If I read him correctly he is trying to stay this side of theology.
His point is that we can witness to the infinite glory of the other
before we get to any theology that explains what glory is and why
we should always be giving glory to God as our life's purpose.
Witnessing to the infinite glory of any face of the other is Kerygma.
Kerygma refers to the basic core of a religion and for Christianity
it is the incarnation, crucifixion, resurrection, ascension and Pentecost.
So Levinas is saying that bearing witness to the face of the other is
the very core of the Jewish religion and it includes prayer for the other.
When one bears witness to the glory of the other he does recognize
that glory and make that glory more recognizable to others.
Of course, this glory even as it becomes manifest becomes even
more unmanifest in the infinity of its rich loveliness.

In *Hesed* and *Ahava*

III,1 Glueck's Treatment of *Hesed* as Mutual Love

III,1.1 *Hesed as Secular, Religious and Divine Conduct*

Nelson Glueck's foundational book on *Hesed in the Bible* which was published in 1927, stresses that *hesed* is a mutual relation. As he reflects on the occurrences of *hesed* in the Bible he divides them into three types: the secular, the religious and the Divine. In the section headings for each of these parts he stresses mutuality and thus in chapter one on page 38 he writes:

> *Hesed* as conduct corresponding to a
> mutual relationship of rights and duties.

In chapter II, *Hesed as Human Conduct—Its Religious Meaning* he writes on page 63:

> *Hesed* in the Prophetic and cognate Literature
> as the Reciprocal conduct of men toward
> one another and explicitly toward God.

In chapter III, *Hesed as Divine Conduct*, he writes on page 70:

> *Hesed* as the Reciprocal Relationship
> of God to the Patriarchs.

In each chapter he seems to make a point of mentioning the mutual or the reciprocal in all the many sub-headings. So Glueck together with subsequent scholars of *hesed* treat three different kinds of *hesed* and he and they begin with the secular. Without any religious overtones there can be a covenant bond between: A. Relatives by blood or marriage, related clans and related tribes; B. Host and guest; C. Allies and their relatives; D. Friends; E. Ruler and subject; and F. Those who have gained merit by rendering aid and the parties thereby put under obligation. Religious *hesed* as he sums it up on page 69, is religiosity, piety, kindness, and love of humankind. Divine *hesed*, which is initiated by God, is the reciprocal relationship of God with the Patriarchs, David, and his house, and his faithful people in which the demands of loyalty, justice, righteousness, and honesty are mutually kept.

III,1.2 A Secular Covenant Bond with Lasting Loyalty

As Glueck treats the three kinds of *hesed* he brings out
fourteen traits that belong to the fullness of Divine *hesed*.
As he thinks his way through the passages that have to do
with *hesed* with no religious dimensions he finds three traits.
The three Hebrew words are *hesed*, *b'rith* and *emeth* which
mean a bond of agreement in a covenant with lasting loyalty.
Hesed is a bond, *b'rith* is a covenant and *emeth* is lasting loyalty.
Glueck writes on page 35:

> In Gen. 47:29 (J1) Jacob about to die,
> asks his son Joseph, to swear to him
> that he will show a loyal *hesed*.

The swearing indicates that they make a covenant between
themselves and the word loyal always accompanies any *hesed*.
From pages 38 to 54 Glueck gives several Biblical examples
of each of the six kinds of human relations and their *hesed*.
On pages 54 and 55 he gives a summary of his conclusions.

   A. It is conduct corresponding to a mutual relation of rights and duties.
   B. Only those participating in this bond can receive or show *hesed*.
   C. *Hesed* confirmed by an oath constitutes the essence of a covenant.
   D. In includes mutual assistance, sincerity, duty and loyalty.
   E. In the older sources, the common usage of *hesed* never means

an arbitrary demonstration of grace, kindness, favor or love.
So *hesed* is a reciprocal covenant bond in which persons who
who have made an agreement work to support each other.
So in the Jewish world there is a widening series of persons
who are loyal to this covenant bond between themselves.
It begins with father and son, and husband and wife and goes
out to relatives and to members of the same tribe and then
to related tribes and then it goes out host and guest and then
to allies and then to new friends and then to rulers and subjects.
Hesed is something you do because of its special bond of love.

Agape and *Hesed*

III,1.3 A Religious Bond with Justice and Law

Glueck begins chapter 2 by discussing *hesed* in the prophetic literature as the reciprocal conduct of men toward one another and explicitly toward God and he at once brings out how *hesed* becomes the conduct of all men toward one another. This is so because we are all children of God our Father. Glueck begins with a treatment of *hesed* in the Prophet Hosea. The two new traits of *hesed* that arise with the religious are Zdakah or the justice of right conduct and mispat or the law. Right away in Hosea the notion of a right conduct that is just and of an *order* laid out in the *law* further explain *hesed*. Once Glueck introduces us to the notions of justice and law as related to God and as constitutive of *hesed* he writes on page 58,

> It is difficult to translate the word *hesed*.
> "Love" would be correct if one understands
> under this rubric what has just been said.
> However, for "love" Hosea uses *ahava*.
> Perhaps one could best render *hesed*
> as "religiosity" or "pietas."

So how does *hesed* become a religious piety with the addition of the notions of justice and law as they make demands on us? Mishpat should be understood as doing good and hating evil. It is a divinely ordained conduct in terms of justice and righteousness. In his summary on page 69 in point G, Glueck writes:

> Subjectively understood, *hesed* can appear
> as favor, mercy, compassion.
> Objectively, *hesed* remains obligatory,
> determined by the divinely based ethical
> commandments which are the laws of society.

God has given the Jews the 10 commandments which all humans should obey for that would bring justice to the family of man. On page 63 he especially explains *hesed* toward the sick, poor, and helpless.

III,1.4 Hesed as Divine Conduct with Nine New Traits

Once Glueck studies the passages that have to do with God promising his *hesed* to his favored ones he explains nine new traits of *hesed* that further clarify the first five essential traits. After examining (1) *hesed* as (2) a covenant (*b'rith*) to which we should have (3) the lasting loyalty of (*emeth*) and after seeing how it demands (4) a just conduct (*zdakah*) (5) in accord with the law of God's commandments (*mishpat*), Glueck relates (6) *hesed* to God's promise, which we should trust (*emunah*). (7) And if we break the covenant God will show mercy (*rahamim*). (8) If we have fear of the Lord (*yirah*) and repent and thus (9) believing in God's promised *hesed* can give us peace (*Shalom*). (10) Also trusting in God's *hesed* can let us *know* God (*da'at*). (11) Those who practice *hesed* with devotion are the (*Hasadim*). (12) Even though some might despair over death the Hasadim have *confidence* in an everlasting love stronger than death. (13) God for our good will use his punishing powers (*az*), (14) but he does offer salvation and redemption (*t shuah*). The main point about *hesed* as divine conduct is the promise of Yahweh to his people that he will care for them with his *hesed*. God's people should always have *emunah* or faith and trust in his promise which was made most clearly to David at 2 Sam 7:14–18 which Glueck begins to treat on page 75:

> I will be his father, and he shall be my son.
> When he commits iniquity, I will chasten
> him with the rod of men, with the stripes
> of the sons of men; but I will not take away
> my *hesed* from him, as I took it from Saul,
> whom I put away from before you. And
> your house and your Kingdom, shall be made
> sure forever before me; your throne shall
> be established forever.

Agape and *Hesed*

III,1.5 The Hesed of the David Promise

One could argue that the most important passage of the Hebrew Bible when it comes to preparing for the Good News of *Agape* is this passage of 2 Sam 7:14–15, which promises *hesed* to David and his house for ever for Jesus is of David's house. Jesus' *agape* can be seen as a development of this Davidic *hesed*. Glueck is familiar with Wellhausen and his theory of how the Penteteuch was a writing of the oral tradition in four voices. The Book of J which refers to God as Yahweh or Jahweh was written in about 930 BC from the viewpoint of the Davidic Promise. After the Kingdom divided and Samaria became the capital of the Northern Kingdom they were no longer true to David and the E version of the oral tradition which referred to God as Elohim was written from the viewpoint of the Mosaic Covenant. There is no allusion to the *hesed* of Elohim in the Book of E. So all the references to the Promise of *hesed* in the Book of J could be influenced by the Promise to David in 2 Sam 7:14–15. The Promise of land, nation and name made to Abraham is probably best understood in terms of the *hesedic* promise to David. This promise tells Abraham that his family will have a land flowing with milk and honey and that children will be more numerous than the sand of the sea and the stars of the sky and that his name will be a blessing to all the peoples of the earth. Through Jesus this promise made to David and read back into Abraham has been being fulfilled during the past 2000 years. So to best understand the *hesed* that Yahweh promised to David we need to go back nearly a thousand years after him to Jesus. I think that it is just possible that all three types of *hesed*: the secular, the religious and the Divine *hesed* promised to David could have gotten their start with this promise made to David. As we go along we will continue to think about this possibility.

III,1.6 The Trusting Faith and Mercy of Davidic Hesed

When the Prophet Nathan told David of Yahweh's promise of *hesed*
Yahweh's faithfulness or *emunah* began to become evident.
Yahweh would be faithful to David and his Kingdom forever and
he would not take away his *hesed* from David as he did from Saul.
God's promise of being faithful to his people let them have a faith
and trust in him that would have to undergo all kinds of temptations.
David became king of the twelve tribes of Israel in about 1000 BC.
He and his people would have thought that they would all have
been faithful to God and his promise of faithfully caring for them.
But during the reign of his grandson Reheboam the Northern
tribes under Jereboam split away without concern for *hesed*.
The Northern Kingdom was punished with the stripes of men.
They were destroyed by the Assyrians in about 725 BC
but the Kingdom of David at Jerusalem was divinely spared.
Then at about 625 BC the Babylonians were threatening Judah
and the Deuteronomist warned them that they should perform
the Mosaic Covenant renewal ceremonies which, being followers
of the Davidic promise theology, they had not attended to.
But the Kingdom of David seemed to come to an end when the
Babylonians destroyed Jerusalem and the temple bringing
an end to the Davidic line of kings and maybe to God's promise.
Under God's inspiration they became a Kingdom of of priests
and thereby let the Kingdom of Yahweh's *hesed* continue.
They were able to return from captivity and under the priests
Ezra and Nehemiah they did rebuild the temple and see the *hesed*
of the Davidic line as continuing under Yahweh's promise to them.
God punished them with the rods of men but he did have mercy
for his *hesed* was filled with *rahamim* which could shine
forth because a remnant did have faith in God's faithfulness.
The remnant of David's Judean people were faithful in the
most impossible of times and God did show them his mercy.

Agape and *Hesed*

III,1.7 And Its Peace for those who Fear the Lord

The peace that God promises with his everlasting merciful love
for all of those who trust in his trust in them is a great gift.
When Paul thought of Jesus' *agape* which is the fulfillment
of this peace giving Davidic *hesed* he talked about love, joy
and peace as being so connected that love always implies peace.
On page 79 Glueck quotes Psalm 85:11:

> *Hesed* and *emeth* will unite;
> Zedek and *shalom* will kiss each other.

The Jewish people could believe in the everlasting merciful love
promised to David and his people because it was most glorious.
This love of God for them and their love for God was surely
humankind's highest affirmation for they could not think of a better.
This twofold emphasis on love first and justice second did bring
them to fear the Lord because there is a natural punishment connected
with any morality and any suffering could be seen as a punishment.
The Jewish people underwent many trials after the promise of *hesed*
was given to David but they could see all that as God loving them more.
And no matter what the suffering and even the loss of the Davidic
line they could have peace in their faith, hope and love that
God would keep his promise and reveal something even better.
As Glueck brings out on page 91, Psalm 31:17 says:

> Let your face shine on your servant;
> save me by your loyal covenantal love.

As Glueck says in his summary on page 102:

> In His *hesed* God manifests
> strength and power on behalf of His faithful
> and brings them aid and salvation.

So those who love this God of love can have a great peace for they do
come to know his glory and see his face shining upon them.
They know him as the God of almighty power and might and
they can feel safe and peaceful believing that they are his.

III,1.8 God's Hesed gives the Hasadim Knowledge and **Confidence**

As Glueck points out on pages 90–91, Psalm 143:12 has been much discussed because it asks God to destroy the enemies of God's servants, the hasadim, and thereby to be cruel to all enemies. This goes against Glueck's idea that *hesed*ic love goes out to everyone. Glueck writes that:

> God is entreated to destroy His enemies,
> not because of His mercy, but in His *Hesed*,
> in accordance with the demands of loyalty
> and justice-the attitude based on the relation
> between Him and His servant. The *hesed*
> might be appropriately translated as
> "loyalty" or as "loyally given help."

So as the hasadim or God's servants try to be loyal to God's law they believe that God will be loyal to them and destroy their enemies. So to respond to God's gift of *hesed* given to David is a life-long process of coming to know God and oneself and *hesed* better and better. Thus the notion of *da'at* which lets us know Yahweh by serving God through acknowledging and recognizing his as God is part of *hesed*. The very attempt to meet one's side of the bargain is always making one wonder how to understand such mysteries as to how to relate to our enemies for many can be an enemy in some way. *Hesed* is not yet the *agape* which will love enemies as did Jesus. But the questions are being raised and even life after death is being questioned for if there was an everlasting for each of us maybe through reconciliation enemies could become *hasadim*. As Glueck shows on pages 92– 93, Psalm 88 asks in verses 12–13: "Is your *hesed* declared in the Grave?" for right in the *hesed* given to David there is the word "everlasting." The servants of God who are loyal to his law have confidence that he will protect them even though they may deserve punishment. That seems to be the point of the Davidic Promise maybe even for all?

Agape and *Hesed*

III,1,9 For Even though He Punishes there is Salvation

This *hesed* passage in 2 Sam 7:14–15 can be seen to contain
all fourteen traits of *hesed* that Glueck brings out in his book.
As we think of an everlasting merciful love for David's house
the notion of *tshuah*, which is root for the name of Jesus,
on page 100 Glueck quotes Psalm 40:10 and writes about it:

> Even if verse 10 is not completely in order
> it is still significant that *Zdakah, emunah*
> and *tshuah*, occur before *hesed* and *emeth*.

The verse begins with the words:

> Your righteousness I have sealed in my heart.
> I have spoken of your faithfulness and salvation.

So salvation, the fourteenth trait of *hesed*, is implied by the notion
of God's love for us insofar as we can trust that he will save us.
David and his holy people who served God came to see that *hesed*
is the very nature of God and was promised to us because of who
God is and not because of what we need, desire or deserve.
Hesed includes grace and mercy and compassion but much more
for in some way it includes salvation which may be everlasting.
Thus while *hesed* is a love like *ahava* its connotations are
much broader than those of loving as such for it can save us.
This notion of salvation *tshuach*, prayed for and witnessed to
in Psalm forty is a preparation for the *agape* of Jesus.
Jesus will be the *tshuah* who will be the son of God who
will become flesh that all flesh might see the salvation of the Lord.
So *hesed* as it is understood better and better by God's servants
after it was promised to David shows us what God's love is
and what our love can be and it is more than any other known love.
Glueck started his pioneering work by revealing these
fourteen essential attributes of *hesed* but other scholars
have tried to declare the meaning of *hesed* even more clearly
so we can now go to their work and look more deeply into *hesed*.

III,2 Correcting Glueck's Understanding of *Hesed*

III,2.1 *Masing Rejects the Pattern of Mutual Reciprocity*

In the 1967 edition of Glueck's book a person by the name
of Gerald A. Larue writes a thirty-two-page article on *Recent Studies*
in *Hesed* in which he reports on eighteen different authors.
Quite a few disagree with Glueck's notion of a *hesed* that
is mutual or reciprocal and Uku Masing is especially clear.
From pages 21 to 26 Masing develops three important theses
about the non-mutuality of *hesed*, about its non-universality
and about the Davidic Promise not really being a covenant.
On page 22 Larue writes:

> Nor did Masing accept the idea that involved
> in *hesed* was a pattern of mutual reciprocity,
> for he argued that the aid or favor given
> by any inferior to a superior was not *hesed*.

As we are trying to understand how the notion of *hesed* is a
preparation for the Good News of *agape* this question of mutuality
is of key importance as we have already seen with Levinas and Derrida.
Hesed as a duty love to care for others could be a pure giving
that gives without expecting anything in return as Levinas
argues concerning care for widows, orphans and our aliens.
Lerue writes on the same page:

> Masing rejected Nelson Glueck's analysis
> as "a talmudizing theory" failing to achieve
> clear distinctions between *hesed* and *Zadikah*.

So it seems that Buber and Glueck would not distinguish
clearly enough between everlasting merciful love and justice.
Yahweh had an everlasting merciful love for David and his
house and that was a gift that could not be reciprocated by humans.
David as the inferior could keep God's law and try to be one of
the faithful Hasidim but the reciprocation of David's house
could never equal God's gift for he loved them in spite of anything.

Agape and *Hesed*

III.2,2 *Masing Rejects Glueck's Universal Hesed*

On page 57 Glueck writes:

> In Hosea *hesed* is a lofty concept
> highly refined in the heart of the prophet.
> It is no longer conduct corresponding to
> a reciprocal relationship within a narrow circle,
> but the proper conduct of all men toward one another.
> On the one hand mankind is regarded
> as one large family, and on the other,
> as children of one heavenly father.

Masing also rejects a concept of a universal *hesed* that extends to all of humankind and on page 24 Larue writes that Masing writes:

> It is necessary to remember that the prophet
> did not speak to all of mankind but
> to a special group, and only later was it
> assumed that prophetic writings were
> directed toward all men.

Did the idea that it was a duty to practice love for all first come with Jesus and his *agape* as he fulfilled the prophets? Masing goes on to write that

> Such an assumption tends to move *hesed*
> from its earlier meaning of concrete action
> to a way of thinking . . .
> *Hesed* in Hosea is an attitude rather than
> a concrete act and perhaps
> "loyalty to divine law which protects the weak"
> would suitably translate the sense of *hesed*.

So Masing suggests that Hosea does see *hesed* as an attitude that all people should have just as the promise given to Abraham had to do with there being a blessing for all humans. But as action and concrete behavior Jewish *hesed* meant being loyal to each other against any threat of any enemy.

Part One: Experiencing Problems

III,2.3 Masing Questions the Idea of a Davidic Covenant

On page 25 of the Glueck book Larue refers to Masing as saying:

> The concept of a Davidic Covenant
> appears only in a few places.
> And there appears to have been a difficulty
> in making the idea that God made a covenant
> with David generally acceptable.

The Mosaic Covenant was a two way treaty in which God proposed that he would take care of his chosen people if they would keep the Ten Commandments and all the details of his laws. The Davidic Promise is not quite like this because Yahweh promises his everlasting merciful *hesed* even if David is a sinner. Masing goes on to say on page 25:

> The covenant of Yahweh with his people
> is not stressed as much as Yahweh's
> goodness, and Yahweh forgives the sin of the people.

So there are many interpretations of *hesed* in the Hebrew Bible and Glueck has proof texts in mind for this overall interpretation. But if we focus on that *hesed* that God promised to David there is no "do ut des" as Derrida would say, no "I give that you might give." The *hesed* that prepares the way for *agape* is this love that Yahweh promised to David and it is not a covenant and is not mutual. It primarily emphasizes the goodness of God and his love for David. Insofar as it is promised to David and his house it is not universal. Later scholars of *hesed* took these three points of Masing seriously. Doob Sakenfeld's *The Meaning of Hesed in the Hebrew Bible* tends to agree with Masing and she goes further in disagreeing with Glueck in her book which was published and copyrighted in 1978. She again writes of many authors who have worked on *hesed* and she is especially appreciative of Sidney Hills who in 1951 presented an unpublished paper on *hesed* that she used very much. Before coming to her work we can reflect on her treatment of Hills.

Agape and *Hesed*

III,2.4 Hills Shows How Hesed Is Done by the Superior Party

On pages 10–11 of her book Sakenfeld lists seven points
about the *hesed* of the human subject and seven points about
the *hesed* of God in each case Hills stressed that *hesed* is an action
and not a psychological state which will help distinguish it from *ahava*.
In both of his lists Hills writes:

> *Hesed* denotes unilateral assistance for the helpless,
> granted without compensation or condition
> not a mutual exchange: (there may be)
> two successive unilateral acts in opposite directions.

Concerning this point Sakenfeld writes on page 12:

> Hills performed a great service for the study
> of *hesed* in his recognition that *hesed* is done
> by the situationally superior party
> for one who is completely lacking
> in present resources or future prospects.

This essential structure of *hesed* as a unilateral assistance for
the helpless fits right in with the *hesed* promised to David and
it shows how *hesed* is not strictly mutual nor covenantal.
What Hills brings out here seems to fit all the cases that Glueck
brought out in terms of secular, religious and Divine *hesed* so you
really wonder how Glueck could so completely stress mutuality.
Hills brings *hesed* ever closer to the non-reciprocal pure giving
of Levinas and Derrida and there stress upon caring for widows,
orphans and aliens and upon the Suffering Servant's love.
So we are completely reshaping the eleven point definition of *hesed*
by Glueck by showing that it is not mutual and covenantal.
The *hesed* promised to David comes from a loving and merciful God
and does not need a strict reciprocity from David and the Hasidim
and once we see this unilateral loving activity it lets us see all
the cases of *hesed* in a new light and this is what Sakenfeld
will bring out in her book as she redefines Biblical *hesed*ic love.

III,2.5 And is Distinct from Judicial or Legal Action

Glueck's fourth and fifth points in defining *hesed* brought out
the notions of a just and right conduct in accord with law and order.
Together with the notion of *b' rith* or covenant he brought in the
notions of *Zdakah* or just conduct and *mishpat* or law and order.
Thus he defined *hesed* on page 69 as

> a reciprocal ethical and religious conduct
> that fulfills the demands of loyalty, justice,
> righteousness and honesty.

On the other hand Hills writes on page 11 of Sakenfeld's book:

> *Hesed* denotes action determined not by law
> or custom but by personal decision:
> it is non-legal, fundamentally unlike law or custom.

Hills writes this concerning *hesed* between human subjects and
and concerning Divine *hesed* he writes:

> God grants *hesed* not as a divine judge
> but as a personal friend and benefactor
> who fulfills his responsibility to the helpless
> whoever they may be, without regard
> to their merit and often in direct
> contradiction to his own law.

So the God of the Mosaic Covenant would be a strict judge
and take an eye for an eye and a tooth for a tooth but this God
contradicts himself when he comes to David and loves him and
blesses him even though he is a great sinner and law breaker.
Hesed in all three realms: the secular, the religious and the Divine,
according to Hills, does without the further traits of Glueck
so that is it is not a covenant that demand justice according to the law.
Hills says that God does fulfill his responsibility with *hesed*
so it is a moral but not a legal phenomenon even among men.
It is an activity that arises spontaneously from within
rather than an activity that is required externally by the law.

Agape and *Hesed*

III,2.6 *Hesed* is Action with Special Moral Qualities

Sakenfeld on page 11 quotes Hill's unpublished paper:

> *Hesed* denotes action that is not optional
> but rather obligatory on moral grounds.
> *Hesed* denotes action which requires special
> moral qualities: viz., initiative, courage,
> constancy, and trustworthiness.

It seems that Hill is arguing that *hesed* brings with it
a new kind of morality unlike both Mosaic and Greek morality.
Plato would show how ethics is based upon prudence, justice
fortitude and temperance but it seems that *hesed* is not based
on prudence or justice while it does retain fortitude and temperance.
Plato and the Greeks did develop a self-realization ethics but
the ethics of *hesed* is another realization ethics and may be
contrary to Greek or Mosaic moralities that make justice explicit.
So Hills seems to be making a distinction between the legal and
the moral and arguing that God acts contrary to his own law
in performing the moral act of *hesed* as, for example, with David.
Hills goes on to write in point 7 concerning divine *hesed*:

> The *hesed* of God is worthy of highest praise,
> and is to be rewarded not by reciprocal
> *hesed* but by love and obedience.

So there is a progressive revelation in scripture and when we
think of the God of the Mosaic Covenant we think of a just God
who will punish serious sin with an everlasting punishment.
But when we come to the God of the Davidic Promise we see a God
with higher moral standards who will have an everlasting merciful
love for David and his house and will care for David in spite of sin.
David and his should pray with highest praise to this wonderful
God and obey and love him presumably with heart felt *ahava*.
God reveals himself in his promise to have special moral
qualities and these should bring out special moral virtues in David.

III,2.7 Hills Shows how Hesed Responds to an Essential Need
In point 3 under both human *hesed* and divine *hesed* Hills says:

> *Hesed* denotes essential and often
> indispensable assistance, not extra privilege.

As Glueck tried to define *hesed* he worked out his fourteen points
and then other scholars cast doubt on covenant, law and justice,
and now we will have to explore what Sakenfeld will do with Hill's
notion of essential assistance and not extra privilege as we wonder
about the shalom or peace that *hesed* gives us according to Glueck.
It seems that peace, at least in some of its aspects, would be a kind
of extra privilege and would not be given with God's never failing constancy.
In the case of the dynasty of David there is little peace with the
constant threats against the Kingdom and then the dividing of the
Kingdom and then finally the termination of the dynasty by the Babylonians.
The Hasidim could have an inner peace in spite of external turmoil.
But, is Hills here showing that another of Glueck's traits is not essential?
The Davidic Promise is the beginning of the Messianic promise and that
there will be a Messiah who carries on the Davidic Dynasty seems essential.
Glueck does not bring out any link between *hesed* and the Messiah.
But we already know what Derrida does with this notion and how
he distinguishes himself from Christianity by being without a Messiah.
So now as we think of the view of Hills and how Sakenfeld will
build on his points in defining *hesed* again we will have to see how
she will treat the prophecy of the Messiah in relation to *hesed*.
This is a key point concerning *agape* as the fulfillment of *hesed*.
As Matthew looks upon Christ's kingdom of love will he go to
certain prophecies throughout the Hebrew Bible pertaining to the
Messiah and will he show how the Messiah's *agape* fulfills those?
How will Jesus Christ, the Davidic Messiah, treat peace and will it
be essential when he says, "I come not to give you peace, but the sword"?
Widows, orphans and aliens have essential needs and Levinas
following Hills' notion of *hesed* wants to satisfy their basic needs.

Agape and *Hesed*

III,2.8 Hill's *Hesed* has its Source in God

Hills concludes his nine points on human *hesed* on page 11:

> *Hesed* denotes action which has its source in God.
> He desires and commands it, recognizes and
> rewards it, and punishes its omission.

This seems to suggest that all *hesedic* relations, even the so called secular, have their source in God who got the idea started. Of course, the entire J text is a Davidic Promise rendition of the oral tradition so anything from that text that mentions *hesed* could well have its source in God who first revealed it to David. Also the promise given to Abraham of land, nation and name could have to do with *hesed* even though it is not mentioned and is anachronistically read back into the story of Abraham and his family. The idea of land, nation and name also reveals to us what Hills calls essential needs or indispensable assistance, not extra privilege. Abraham's family and offspring will need a land even if it is not flowing with milk and honey and they will have to become a great nation if all peoples are to be blessed by Abraham's name. There is a connection about essential needs between the promise of *hesed* given to David and the promise given to Abraham for at 2 Sam 7:16 we read:

> Your dynasty and your sovereignty
> will ever stand firm before me
> and your throne be ever secure.

Again, the continuance of the family is essential and the Messianic Kingdom is also essential even if their land is overcome by the Babylonians and even if the Davidic Dynasty is terminated. When we come to Matthew's Gospel we will see the fulfillment of the promises in Jesus, the Davidic Messiah, who will carry on the Dynasty and let the Name of Abraham be a blessing for all. Hills says that with *hesed* extra privilege is not promised, but a special privilege even though it is not extra is promised.

III,2.9 Stoebe Claims that Hesed was Introduced by J

In 1952, Hans Joachim Stoebe published his thesis on "The Meaning of the Word *Hesed* in the Old Testament" and Sakenfeld refers to him on pages 8, 9, and 10 of her book:

> Stoebe suggested that the theological use
> of *hesed* was a special development
> introduced by the J writer . . .
> This attribution seems consonant
> with the high degree of creativity
> assigned by J von Rad and others.

So Glueck and Sakenfeld and many others agree that *hesed* is found in the three contexts as the secular, religious and divine. Stoebe is here arguing that the theological or divine use of *hesed* begins with the Davidic Promise and is used by the J writer. Because her text was probably written at about 930 BC and because it covers the whole sweep of history from Adam and Eve down through Abraham and right through to the time of the Judges her theological working out of the meaning of *hesed* could have been very influential also on the secular and the religious usages. The main point of the Davidic Promise and the theological use of *hesed* is that it was an unconditional love with mercy so that even if David and his offspring sinned God would still bless them with his everlasting merciful *hesedic* love. This Davidic Promise is very different from the Mosaic Covenant in that the covenant was a mutual relation based on justice. But with the *hesed* of the Davidic Promise atonement justice is made secondary to merciful love, for David will receive a natural punishment for any immorality but in the long run he and his house will endure forever because Yahweh loves him as a father loves a son and he will love him always that way. The unconditional love of *hesed* is not stressed throughout the Hebrew Bible and for the most part Mosaic Justice is primary.

Agape and *Hesed*

III,3   Doob Sakenfeld's Treatment of *Hesed*

III,3.1 *Also Studies "Secular," "Theological," and "Religious"* **Usages**

Sakenfeld's book, like Glueck's, works with three different kinds of *hesed*, but what he calls Divine *hesed* she treats as theological *hesed*, and whereas he treats the religious before the Divine she treats the theological or the Divine before she treats the different religious usages. As we go along we will make clear the significance of these two changes which arise from her new way of understanding *hesed*. The Hebrew Bible is understood as the revelation of God to his people. What Catharine is beginning to suggest is that *hesed* is revealed by God and it gets its secular and religious meaning from revelation. She does not make this explicit but we can explore its possibility. To do this we can study with her first what she calls Theological *Hesed* and see the texts in which it appears and make clear its nature. Then we can consider the secular usage and finally the religious. On page 148 she makes what is perhaps the key distinction when it comes to understanding the nature and history of *hesed*. After writing that "[t]he conditional (Mosaic or Sinaitic) tradition emphasizes the importance of obedience," she goes on to write:

> The unconditional (Davidic, Abrahamic) tradition,
> by contrast, handles the problem of sin by
> describing God's relationship to the people
> as one based on the divine promise alone,
> not subject to collapse because of human failure.
> Here *hesed* as the basis for the preservation
> of the covenant is understood as promised
> rather than unexpected.

In linking together the Davidic and Abrahamic promise she is working with the idea that the J writing when treating Abraham is doing it from the viewpoint of the unconditional Davidic promise. She writes of the puzzle of how God can be present in the midst of a sinful people and how the theological language of *hesed* solves it.

Part One: Experiencing Problems

III,3.2 The Primacy of the Theological Davidic Hesed

In explaining what she means by the theological approach to *hesed* Sakenfeld writes on page 147:

> The theological meaning of the word *hesed*
> developed within the framework of various polarities:
> the individual-communal, the deserved-undeserved,
> the surprising-promised, and the varying
> covenant traditions of the Patriarchs, Moses and David.

She points out that there were two central polarities, for *hesed* was used to express God's free care for individual suppliants and for his people as a whole and it expressed the central character of God's action both in conditional and unconditional types of covenant theologies, that is in the Mosaic and the Davidic types. On page 149 she writes:

> Psalm 89 gives classic expression to the fully developed
> theology of God's *hesed* as promised faithfulness
> to the Davidic line, epitomized in vs. 28:
> "My *hesed* I will keep for him forever,
> and my covenant will stand for him."

God is related to his people indirectly, through his anointed. As she begins chapter 3 on the *hesed* of God in Pre-exilic prose she writes that she will use four types of text: (1) those treating the relationship of Yahweh to various individuals in a context of aiding the person (2) those texts consisting of blessing / benediction formulae directed to specific individuals, (3) Liturgical phrases or formulae from the context of the Sinai covenant and (4) those texts of the Dueteronomic historians' application of *hesed* concerning David. So as Glueck has already made clear there are many kinds of texts treating the *hesed* of God and as Sakenfeld shows all these texts work with a theological tension in which *hesed* is connected with covenant and is not connected with covenant, is connected with justice primarily and is not by being more love oriented.

Agape and *Hesed*

III,3.3 Does God's Revelation of Hesed Prepare for the Secular?

When the J writer wrote her (I say her following Harold Bloom in his *The Book of J*) epic account of the oral tradition that forms the skeletal structure of the Book of Genesis her theology is that of the Davidic Promise, which puts Yahweh's unconditional *hesed* up-front. The several secular usages of *hesed* in Genesis could well be given direction by the understanding of *hesed* in terms of the promise. On page 24 Sakenfeld summarizes secular *hesed* under four points all of which have the structure of Davidic *hesed*:

(1) The human actor always has some recognizable responsibility for the person who is to receive *hesed*, either because of an obvious personal relationship or because of some previous action; yet

(2) Situationally the actor is always quite free not to perform the act of *hesed* — no pressure can be brought on him and no reprisal is available within the legal system.

(3) Two additional factors are that the act of *hesed* usually fulfills an important need for the recipient

(4) and that it is something which he cannot possibly do for himself and often is something which no one but the actor can do for him.

If we consider the examples of secular *hesed* in Genesis such as Gen 47:29 when Jacob, about to die, asks his son Joseph, to swear to him that he will show him loyal *hesed* or when Abraham asks his wife Sarah, to render *hesed* to him we can see the four points that Sakenfeld summarizes here. So you wonder how secular this *hesed* is that appears throughout the Hebrew Bible in that it is in the context of the religious Bible and its structure seems to be influenced by God's *hesed* for David. It is a freely given grace or gift to a situationally inferior who cannot help himself just as David whose dynasty would collapse.

Part One: Experiencing Problems

III,3.4 Does Theological Hesed Support Religious Hesed?

On page 169, Sakenfeld introduces her treatment of religious *hesed*. She begins by saying:

> The occurrences of *hesed* in prophecy are evenly divided between *hesed* done by man (IIX) and that done by God (IIX).

This seems to be the point of the distinction between the religious done by man and the Divine or theological as the *hesed* done by God. In comparing the three kinds of usage she goes on to write on page 169:

> We are dealing with a new category of usage for pre-exilic texts, that which has been called "religious," as opposed to "secular" or "theological." As is to be expected, there are certain tensions which result in a "stretching" of the word as it is transferred from the secular to the religious realm, just as we have already seen "stretching" in the theological adaptation.

So she calls the move from the secular usage to the "religious" usage a "stretching" and says that also happened to the "theological." She presents three key "religious" texts in order to set the stage for a discussion of the question of "stretching" or of influence. The first example she used is from Hosea 4:1

> Hear the word of Yahweh, O Israelites,
> For Yahweh has controversy with the inhabitants of the land:
> For there is no *emet* and there is no *hesed*
> And there is no knowledge of God in the land.

She says it is not clear whether it is *hesed* toward men or toward God that is missing but is could be toward both and even if it were only toward men that might keep them from knowing God. God as superior promised and showed *hesed* to David and it seems that the Jews thought they should imitate God in showing *hesed*.

Agape and Hesed

III,3.5 The Modification of Hesed in Religious Usage

On page 173 Sakenfeld writes:

> With these three examples before us we can examine the modification of the word *hesed* which takes places in "religious" usage.

She gives another example from Hosea and one from Jeremiah which are similar to Hosea 4:1 and she points out that in Hosea 4:2 the sins against *hesed* are listed: "false swearing, lying, stealing, murder, adultery" which review the ethics of the commandment. Still on page 173 she writes:

> The examples make clear that religious *hesed* is directed both to God and also to fellow men ... with respect to God, it is clear that Israel has a responsibility, but it is to him, not for him.

Concerning the religious meaning of *hesed* to our fellowmen she writes on page 174 that

> [t]he basis for responsibility, religiously speaking, is the membership of all Israelites in the covenant community.

So the responsibility of *hesed* was that of the stronger person for the weaker and theologically that was the case when Yahweh made his promise of everlasting merciful love to David and his dynasty. This was also the case in all secular *hesed* in which the stronger would be loyal in protecting and doing things for the weaker. But now it is as if Mosaic Covenant theology and David Promise theology are being joined together in this new religious *hesed* with its double duty of keeping the Ten Commandments toward neighbor and of obeying God thereby and of coming to a knowledge of him. Sakenfeld speaks of the stretching of the word *hesed* and maybe this is how it was stretched in a logical and understanding way. God revealed his unconditional love to David and then humans could bind themselves to another that way and finally to the whole people.

III,3.6 Hesed is Primarily not Covenantal

Hesed is a love of duty rather than an emotional feeling like *ahava*. It is primarily a promise to be loyal in benefiting another who is weaker and the benefit can be of: assistance, blessing, Davidic Dynasty, Deliverance, Forgiveness, Preservation and worship. Most of the time it is God, the giver, who benefits man, the receiver. Nelson Glueck thought of *hesed* as a covenant or *b'rith*, but later scholars such as Aubrey Johnson disagree. According to Larue (in Glueck, *Hesed in the Bible*, 27) Johnson maintains:

> The particular expression that Yahweh will keep *b'rith* and *hesed* is of Deuteronomic origin.

On page 25 Larue writes as we have already pointed out, that

> [t]he concept of a Davidic covenant appears only in a few places and there appears to have been a difficulty in making the idea that God made a covenant with David generally acceptable.

Deuteronomy was written around 625 BC as the Babylonian threat began to loom large and the Kingdom of Judah began to think that they should take the Mosaic Covenant much more seriously. It means "The Second Law" and as we will see it will stress *ahava* or a love of God with our whole heart, mind and soul so that while the David Promise is *hesed* oriented the covenant relates more to *ahava*. In his book, *Understanding the Old Testament*, Bernhard Anderson on page 308 of the fourth edition gives a definition of *hesed* and he begins by writing that:

> The word is exceedingly difficult to render into English, as evident in various translations of the term in Hosea 6:6 "mercy" (King James Version), "steadfast love" (Revised Standard Version), "goodness (American Jewish Translation) "loyalty" (New English Bible).

With Sakenfeld he stresses that *hesed* is faithfulness in action.

Agape and *Hesed*

III,3.7 *Hesed is Primarily not Reciprocal*

We have seen how strongly throughout his book Glueck stresses that *hesed* is a reciprocal relation and that may have to do with his stressing that *hesed* is always a covenant between two. However as Anderson again says on page 308

> *Hesed*, then, is loyalty manifested by a stronger party
> toward someone who is in a weaker position . . .
> It is an act of inner faithfulness and therefore of grace.
> One is free to be loyal or not to be loyal,
> although the weaker party in the relationship,
> in a time of distress, may have no other source of help.

So if we take as our paradigm case the Promise of *hesed* that Yahweh made to David we can see that it is a non-reciprocal relation. So as we go along in trying to understand the two forms of Jewish love and to see how they interact and then prepare the way for the *agape* of the New Testament we will be asking if the *ahava* first belongs to a covenant relation and if the *hesed* in a promised duty of the stronger to the weaker which is not mutual nor covenantal. Once again we might recall that Larue (in Glueck, *Hesed in the Bible*) writes on page 22:

> Masing rejected Nelson Glueck's analysis
> as "a Talmudizing theory" . . . Nor did
> Masing accept the idea that involved in *hesed*
> was a pattern of mutual reciprocity, for he
> argues that the aid or favor given by an
> inferior to a superior was not designated as *hesed*.

The Talmudizing theory must tend to stress the Mosaic Covenant between Yahweh and his chosen people and really stress the Ten Commandments and justice rather than unconditional *hesed*. It is very important to understand *hesed* correctly so that we can better understand Levinas and Derrida and better understand just what *agape* will get from *ahava* and from *hesed*.

Part One: Experiencing Problems

III,3.8 Hesed is Primarily not Related to Justice

Nelson Glueck stressed that *hesed* was a mutual, covenantal
bond which involved just and loyal assistance in accord with love.
But those who came after him and focused on *hesed* as such
before it became mixed with the Mosaic covenant theology
argue that mutuality, the covenant and justice and loyalty
are not primarily related to the unconditional love of the Promise.
Of course, already in that passage of 2 Samuel 7 when Nathan
reported Yahweh's promise to David there was a mention of justice.
He and his would be punished with the rods of men for an injustice
that they might bring about by omission or commission and justice
in all its forms of distributive justice and social justice as well as
justice to individuals is right at the heart of any Jewish thinking.
But with his merciful *hesed* Yahweh will look after the Davidic
Dynasty because God loves David as a father loves his dearest son.
So the Talmudizing influence started way back perhaps with
the Deuteronomic historians and Glueck emphasizes this trend.
It seems that the Jewish Prophets, Priests, Kings and Sages all
tended to mix Mosaic covenant and Davidic Promise theology
together and lose sight of the pure meaning of *hesed* as the
scholars after Glueck began to make it clear step by step.
The Talmudizing influence has its roots deep in biblical history
and in our day seems to be followed by scholars like Glueck and
Buber but seems to be argued against by the like of Levinas and Derrida.
This tension seems to be there in the Gospels also so that John's
Gospel, for example, seems to be more judgmental than the Gospel
of Q1 as it is found in Matthew and Luke as we will see when we
come to the Gospel of Matthew and see how revelation unfolds for him.
Revelation in the Hebrew Bible and in the New Testament is not
piped in directly from God as it was from Allah to Muḥammad.
Rather, it takes place through a conflict of interpretations and
as Derrida would say with the complexity of Aporetic voices.

Agape and *Hesed*

III,3.9 Hesed is like a Mother's Love for her Child

The Book of Isaiah with its three different historical parts is especially concerned with the House of David and does not take away the primacy of an everlasting merciful love from *hesed*. At the beginning of chapter 11 Isaiah writes about David who will spring from the stock of Jesse:

> A new shoot will grow from his roots.
> On him will rest the spirit of Yahweh,
> the spirit of wisdom and insight,
> the spirit of counsel and power,
> the spirit of knowledge
> and fear of Yahweh;
> his inspiration will lie in fearing Yahweh.

Even though there be this fear of Yahweh there can still be a greater trust for justice and punishment are not primary given the Promise of everlasting merciful love of *hesed* which brings comfort to Israel. In chapter 49:15–16 Isaiah says

> feel no pity for the child she has borne?
> Even if these were to forget,
> I shall not forget you.
> Look, I have engraved you
> on the palm of my hand.

The word *hesed* appears fifteen times in *The Book of Isaiah* and even though it does not appear here the pity that Yahweh will have for his child is a beautiful image of God's *hesed* for David and for his house which will come to include all peoples with Jesus. Through Jesus we will all become part of the Davidic Dynasty and will all spring from the root of Jesse and the gifts of the Holy Spirit of the Risen Lord Jesus can belong to each of us and we will all be like a child of our mothering God Yahweh and even have our name carved into the palm of his *hesedic*, Godly, loving hand.

The Idaho Seminarians with Father Bernard

The Major Seminary Community in Kenmore Washington

Agape and *Hesed*

IV With Matthew

IV, 1   The *Agape* of Matthew's Infancy Narrative

IV, 1.1 Can be seen in terms of The Sermon on the Mount

The most clear statement in Matthew about the meaning of the new *agape* and how it fulfills *ahava* appears in the middle of Jesus' Sermon on the Mount at Matt 5:43–47:

> You have learned how it was said: you must
> love your neighbor and hate your enemy.
> But I say to you: love your enemies
> and pray for those who persecute you.
> In this way you will be sons of your Father
> in Heaven, for he causes his sun to rise
> on bad men as well as good, and his rain
> to fall on honest and dishonest men alike.
> For if you love those who love you,
> what right have you to claim any credit?

This is the key to unlocking any hidden meaning of *agape*.
Even today with their *ahava* the Jews are not going to pray
for Hitler; but it is their *ahava* for their fellow Jews that Jesus
begins with as he expands the idea of *ahava* with his new *agape*.
This *agape* also takes us beyond the modern Lutheran position
that we cannot merit any new grace for ourselves or others
with our works of love for if we love enemies we can claim credit.
This passage even lets us understand better the whole of
The Sermon on the Mount for it not only presents a new *agape*
for enemies but implies that there is a new *ahava-agape* for God.
In the Hebrew Bible the Jews were commanded to love God with *ahava*
and their neighbor with *ahava* but now this new love of enemy
reveals a new dimension of our heart, mind and soul with
which we must love God for now we see him ordering love of enemy.
We will be sons and daughters of God in a new way if we love
our enemies and pray for those who persecute us for he is
also the father of our enemies and even of all of his enemies.

IV, 1.2 For its New Ahava-Agape for the Enemy

Jesus preaches his Sermon on the Mount to those who are
beginning to love him and his *agape* must be totally new
because as the God-man he is totally new and so to love him
is to love him with an *ahava-agape* for God and for neighbor.
Jesus makes God and his love for us known to us since he is God.
He makes love for neighbor known to us in a new way because
he is our neighbor and a brother of all of us even our enemies.
By loving our enemies we are not only obeying his new
commandment but we are loving his brothers and sisters for
now all humans are children of the father even sinful children.
The disciples of Jesus who hear these words of *hesed* will
come to love him more if they begin to obey these words and in
loving him more they will love God and neighbor also even more.
The main point of the Sermon on the Mount is "resist not evil."
If we really love our enemies we will be able to see things
from their point of view and with purity of heart we will be able
to see the good in all beings even though there may be evil too.
This new commandment to resist not evil and to love our enemies
is a new *ahava-agape* but *hesed* is primarily God's love for us
and now we begin to see how out of love for us God becomes man.
This interplay between the *ahava* in *agape* and the *hesed* in
agape will be the main point of our meditation on Matthew.
Already even though it is not explicit God's *hesed-agape*
for us is at work here in this Sermon on the Mount for Jesus
as God is teaching us with his merciful love a new way of love.
As we go now to the beginning of the Gospel and its Infancy
Narrative we will see that a key point is that Jesus is born
into the family of David and as Messiah-Christ he will bring
God's everlasting merciful love of *hesed* to all of mankind.
The main gift of God's *hesed* for us is to give us a new
ahava that will be the revolutionary turning point in our history.

IV, 1.3 Lets us see the Infancy Story's New Hesed-Agape

Matthew's Gospel begins with a great emphasis on the house of David's and Matt 1:17 sums up the genealogy by saying:

> The sum of generations is therefore;
> fourteen from Abraham to David;
> fourteen from David to the Babylonian deportation
> and fourteen from the Babylonian deportation to Christ.

Christ Jesus is the anointed offspring of King David and he is bringing the Kingdom of David to all that they might be saved. So right from the beginning we see that *hesed* is being expanded to become a new *hesed-agape* through which God loves all persons. We begin by seeing how Jesus Christ came to be born for his Mother Mary who was betrothed to Joseph was found to be with child by the Holy Spirit and an angel appeared in a dream to Joseph telling him at Matt 1:20–21:

> Joseph, son of David, do not be afraid
> to take Mary home as your wife
> because she has conceived what
> is in her by the Holy Spirit.

Joseph is son of David and Jesus his son will therefore belong to the house of David and Joseph knows that Mary could be stoned according to Jewish law for being an adulteress. But Joseph now loves her with a new *ahava-agape* because in a way she could be seen as his enemy by betraying him with her pregnancy. Already here right from the beginning we get a new picture of God as the Father, the Son and The Holy Spirit and this God is becoming incarnate out of *hesed agape* for all of humankind. This son of Mary will be named Jesus, because he is the one who is to save his people from their sin because "Jesus" means "savior" and he will save all by teaching them of a new *ahava-agape*.

Part One: Experiencing Problems

IV, 1.4 Especially in Four of Mary's Predecessors

In 1:3-6 Matthew writes in his genealogy:

> Judah was the father of Perez and Zerah,
> Amar being their mother . . .
> Salmon was the father of Boaz.
> Rahab being his mother,
> Boaz was the father of Obed,
> Ruth being his mother . . .
> David was the father of Solomon,
> whose mother had been Uriah's wife.

The story of Judah and Tamar in Genesis 38, is one of prostitution,
adultery and all sorts of crazy, mixed-up, wicked, sexuality.
Judah thinks Tamar is a prostitute and with him she conceives of
the twins, Perez and Zerah, who get the tribe of Judah going and who
will be ancestors of King David and as we see here of Jesus himself.
Also Rahab is a harlot who lived in Jericho and helped Joshua
to take that city and she too became an ancestress of the Christ child.
The Book of Ruth right after the Book of Judges tells the story of
a lovely young lady who came from Moab to Bethlehem
with her mother-in-law, Naomi, and then marries a Jewish man
by the name of Boaz with whom she has a child named Obed.
Obed is the father of Jesse who was David's father and thus Ruth
who was not Jewish became the great grandmother of King David.
Finally King David had relations with Bathsheba, the wife of Uriah
the Hittite and with her King Solomon was brought into being.
David was not only an adulterer but he had Uriah killed in battle.
So we do see God loving sinners and non-Jews in that these
four women are connected with Mary and her miraculous conception.
Once we see God's *hesed-agape* as a love even for the enemy
we see that he had this kind of merciful love for sinners all along.
The everlasting, merciful love of *hesed* that was promised to
David goes out to sinners and is made clear by Jesus' *agape*.

Agape and *Hesed*

IV, 1.5 And in God's Love in the five Dreams

In just two pages of *The Infancy Narrative* we read of five dreams with which the loving Father God takes care of his Son who is born of Mary and is already being threatened by the King of the Jewish people. The Magi are warned in a dream not to go back to King Herod because the king feels threatened by Jesus and wants to get rid of him. Also Joseph is warned in four different dreams by an angel of the Lord what he should do in order to protect God's Son and his foster child. First, when Mary is found to be with child Joseph is told in a dream that the child was conceived by the Holy Spirit and that he should take Mary as his wife and become the foster father of her child Jesus. Second, he is warned by an angel of the Lord in a dream to take Mary and her child into Egypt in order to protect them from King Herod. Third, he is told by an angel of the Lord in a dream that it is now safe to bring the child and his mother back to their own land. Fourth, he is told by an angel of the Lord that it is still dangerous and they should go to Bethlehem for safe living. God the Father's love for his Son, the baby Jesus, is being revealed here right at the beginning of the New Testament. Throughout the history of revelation in the Hebrew Bible God revealed his will to young men and old men in dreams and visions. Now he is directing the three foreign kings to follow the Star of Bethlehem and to celebrate the first Epiphany of the Lord Jesus. With a dream to protect his and Mary's infant Son God warns \the kings not to let King Herod know where he is because he will kill him rather than pay him homage as he says he wants to do. With this dream God the Father is revealing his love and thus teaching the magi how to love the baby all the more and thus right from the beginning of the New Testament universal *agape* is revealed. So it is with Joseph for in his four dreams he is learning of God the Father's lover in a new way which he himself must now practice for his foster child who is also God's only Son.

IV, 1.6 And in Fulfilling the five Prophecies

Right away in the Infancy Narrative Matthew begins to show how Jesus is the fulfillment of the Law and the Prophets and how *agape* is the fulfillment of the two Jewish loves of *hesed* and *ahava*. Matthew tells us that Joseph's first dream about Mary's conceiving of a child by the Holy Spirit was to fulfill the prophecy of Isaia7:14.

> The virgin will conceive and give birth to a son
> and they will call him Immanuel.

The chief priests and scribes told Herod that the child would be born in Bethlehem because of the prophecy in Micah 5:1:

> And you Bethlehem in the land of Judah
> are by no means least among the leaders of Judah,
> for out of you will come a leader
> who will shepherd my people Israel.

The *agape* of this shepherd will fulfill the *hesed* promised to that first shepherd King for Jesus will fulfill the Davidic dynasty. Joseph's dream to take Jesus and Mary to Egypt and bring them back at the right time fulfilled Hosea 11:1:

> I called my Son out of Egypt.

In trying to kill Jesus Herod had baby boys under the age of two in Bethlehem put to death in fulfillment of Jeremiah 31:15:

> A voice was heard in Ramah
> sobbing and loudly lamenting
> it was Rachel weeping for her children,
> refusing to be comforted
> because they were no more.

Finally, Joseph's dream to take his family to Nazareth fulfilled the prophecy in Matthew 2:22:

> He will be called a Nazarene or to Nazareth.

Matthew's plan to show how Jesus and his new love of *agape* came right out of the revelation of *hesed* and *ahava* makes itself clear right here in the beginning with these dreams and prophecies.

Agape and *Hesed*

IV, 1.7 And God's Hesed let the Magi Adore with Ahava

The story of the visit of the magi (Matt 2:1–12) which only
Matthew tells shows how non-Jewish foreigners are the first
to love Jesus and how from the beginning Jews want to kill him.
We are introduced here to a strange paradox in Matthew in that
he focuses on the Jewish revelation that leads up to the Christian
and yet he emphasizes how so many Jews do not accept the Christ.
On the other hand he shows how God so loved these foreign Kings
that he enabled them to be the first to manifest the God-man's glory.
King Herod learned from these foreign kings of the new born King.
And so they were the first apostles to bring the Good News of Jesus.
With the Magi the Davidic promise of an everlasting merciful *hesed*
is now being universalized and given even to all non-Jewish people.
When J told the story of Abraham he was given the promise of
land, nation and name and he was told that all the peoples of
world would be blessed by his name and now that is happening.
God with his *hesed* leads the Magi to come and give homage
to the child Jesus and thus they begin to love God with *ahava*.
So right here in the beginning of Matthew's Gospel *agape* as
the fulfillment of *hesed* and *ahava* is practiced by the Magi.
This love is miraculously revealed and would never be known
except Yahweh and his Holy Spirit give it as a gift to the Magi.
Already here in the story of the Magi we see faith, hope and *agape*
working together for they have faith in the star that leads them and
they have faith that the baby is God himself whom they adore.
As they offer their gifts of gold, frankincense and myrrh they
hope to praise and thank God who has given them his three gifts.
With their three gifts they hope to thank God for his three gifts.
They do have faith in God's love and faith and hope in their love.
God's *agape* for them and theirs for God is worth more than gold.
They have been given the gift of faith that this baby is God.
Thus they have trust that God will be pleased with their gifts.

IV, 1.8 As these Aliens Manifest the New Universal Love

When the three Kings meet the three members of the Holy Family
Joseph knows this is the moment of the first public epiphany.
Joseph had already had his epiphany and he began to wonder about this.
When he learned that Mary was pregnant he was shocked into
a trauma of fear and trembling, of anxiety and of a near despair.
But then the Angel of the Lord came to him and said, "Be not afraid."
And all was made manifest which is the meaning of epiphany for
he was told of the Holy Spirit and of the Son of God and he believed
in the three persons of the Trinity even though it was new and obscure.
Whereas Luke's *Infancy Narrative* is told from the viewpoint of Mary
Matthew's is told from the viewpoint of Joseph and hence the new
Christian view of *agape* and personhood and of *agape* and the
four loves was first revealed to Joseph but not in a public epiphany.
That public epiphany happens first with the Magi for they
begin to make the God-child manifest to the Jews and King Herod.
But they are gentiles and so God's love of *agape* is first made
manifest in a public way to the Gentiles and now we see
that all persons are the chosen people of God for at the moment
of the Magi's visit all persons can now be seen as God's people.
This is the great meaning of this Epiphany for it reveals that
hesed and *ahava* now become *agape* for the family of man.
Herod does not accept this because he feels threatened by this
new upstart King and many Jews down through the ages do
not accept this Messiah any more than will Levinas and Derrida.
Paul becomes very impressed with the new *agape* and becomes
the apostle to the gentiles realizing that people like the Magi
do not have to become Jews first in order to be Christians.
Like the Magi, gentiles can have faith and hope in Christ
and love him but when it comes to the essentials there
are faith, hope and *agape* and the greatest of these is *agape*.
And this *agape* is the fulfills of *hesed*, *ahava* and the four loves.

Agape and *Hesed*

IV, 1.9 Of Agape that Governs the Infancy Narrative

Joseph is constantly by a messenger of God given the gift of
an *agape* with which he loves the God-child with his whole heart,
mind and soul and Mary as himself throughout *The Infancy Narrative*.
Joseph is told to name the child, Jesus, because he is the one
who is to save his people from their sins and with the coming
of the Magi Joseph knows that all persons are to be saved by Jesus.
When the Angel addresses Joseph he calls him the son of David.
And the promise given here to Joseph that Jesus will save his people
expands the promise given to David because through Joseph and
Jesus all people will belong to the house of David and receive *hesed*.
Joseph must have been absolutely astounded to receive in his
dreams all these wondrous truths and as the foster father of
Jesus he must have felt that he was caring for all of humankind.
To protect the baby Jesus he had to brave his way to Egypt
and then back again and he had to hide out in Nazareth.
From the beginning he believed in all of this with firm faith
and had trust in God and the Angel of the Lord that it was
the will of God for him to cooperate in all of this unbelievable story.
The whole point of Matthew's Gospel is to show how the Kingdom
of God has come to the earth with the love of Jesus and how it
is our task to help bring it about on earth as it is in heaven.
Joseph is the first of all humans to work on this task of *agape*
and he did it so well that he is the patron saint of good fathers.
No wonder of it that my grandparents named my father Joseph
and gave him the second name of Manuel for God is with us.
In Matthew's Gospel we hear no more of how Joseph cared for
Jesus but we can be sure that with his faith, hope and love
he was united with Jesus most intimately as his constant caregiver.
Joseph found *agape* gave to fathering affection a new meaning.
It gave to his eros with Mary a new meaning as she remained
a virgin and he was now a friend of the Angel of his Lord and God.

IV, 2 *Agape* in Matthew's three Q Texts

IV, 2.1 *The Agape of the Historical Jesus of Q1*

After his *Infancy Narrative* Introduction the first of the five parts of Matthew's Gospel treats *The Kingdom of Heaven Proclaimed*. Chapters 3 and 4 make up its *Narrative Section* and chapters 5, 6, and 7 comprise this part's teaching section of *The Sermon on the Mount*. This Sermon contains many of the sayings of the historical Jesus of Q1 and Jesus' new understanding of love is first revealed here. We have seen at the beginning of this part at IV, 1.1 how Jesus brought about his great *agape*ic revolution in the words of Matt 5:43-44:

> You have learned how it was said: you must
> love your neighbor and hate your enemy.
> But I say unto you: love your enemies
> and pray for those who persecute you.

Just before this at 5:43 Matthew records the Q1 saying:

> You have learned how it was aid:
> Eye for eye and tooth for tooth. But I say this
> to you: offer the wicked man no resistance.

The *agape* of the historical Jesus of Q1 as the Jesus people recorded it was a fulfillment of both Jewish *hesed* and *ahava*. Jesus is primarily teaching a new *agape-ahava* because with *ahava* we should love our neighbor as we love ourself and now we get a new commandment to love our enemy as we love ourself. Jesus as the child of wisdom is loving us with a new *hesed* by teaching us to love our enemies with an everlasting mercy. Jesus tells us to be perfect even as our heavenly father is perfect. We should love widows, orphans, aliens and our own enemies. Jesus himself did this as he prayed for those who were killing him: "Father forgive them for they know not what they do." This love of enemy and non-resistance is very difficult and may at times look like suicide but it could bring reconciliation.

Agape and *Hesed*

IV, 2.2 Fits in with Matthew's Doctrine of Reconciliation

In his *Sermon on the Mount* as Matthew's Jesus is explaining how he does not come to abolish the Law or the prophets, he says that our ancestors said *You must not kill* but he says at 5:23 that

> if a man calls his brother "fool"
> he will answer for it.

And then at Matt 5:24–25 Jesus says:

> So then, if you are bringing your offering
> to the alter and there remember that
> your brother has something against you,
> leave your offering there before the altar,
> go and be reconciled with your brother first,
> then come back and present your offering.

Jesus wants us to be reconciled especially with our enemies. We are children of the Father and brothers and sisters of each other. Loving our enemies and turning the other cheek aims at reconciliation for the whole point is that we should not be enemies. I should be my brothers' and sisters' keeper and do all I can to remove any obstacle between us especially my own sin. I have made many enemies by offending many other persons. If I do not blame them for being an enemy to me but look into myself for the fault then I will promote possible reconciliation. We are being told here that we cannot have *ahava-agape* for God unless we successfully have it with even our enemies. I need to so love my enemy that he or she no longer has anything against me and only then should I praise God. This gift and task of *agape* that Jesus is here giving us is a harder commandment to live out than any other commandment. And yet interspersed with these very passages are the Q2 sayings which present a very judgmental Jesus who does not love enemies. All throughout these first chapters of Matthew there seems to be a contradiction between the loving Jesus and the punishing Jesus.

IV, 2.3 But the Jesus of Q2 is a Punisher

In Chapter 5 Jesus teaches us to love our enemies and he is the all loving peacemaker, but as this section begins with the preaching of John the Baptist at the beginning of Chapter 3 there is no love of enemy by John or the Jesus he portrays. Some Pharisees and Sadducees come to John seeking baptism but he warned them that they had to fully repent or they would be punished and at Matt 3:10–12 he says:

> Any tree which fails to produce good fruit
> will be cut down and thrown into the fire.

And he says that Jesus will

> gather his wheat into the barn;
> but the chaff he will burn
> in a fire that will never go out.

There are several passages like this throughout Matthew so that his Jesus seems to have a contradictory message about love. The Q scholars, as we see in Burton Mack's book *The Lost Gospel*, explain the sixty-two sayings that Matthew and Luke share as being divided into three attitudes toward love, justice and the enemy. The Q1 sayings belong to the historical Jesus and the Q2 sayings were attributed to him by the Jesus community in Galilee after Jesus was killed and the Jews were threatening the Christians. They did kill Stephen and some Christians became traitors and left the Jesus community out of fear and a lack of strong belief. With the Jewish enemy and the traitors in mind the community of Jesus' Galilean followers attributed these sayings to Jesus. They had him say that he would judge the enemy and the traitor. Between the time of Jesus' death and the Jewish-Roman conflict that brought about the fall of Jerusalem to the Romans is 70 AD Jesus was seen as a rewarder-punisher who tolerated no enemies. Once the Jews are no longer such a threat Q3 is not so contradictory to Q1 and attributes a third attitude to Jesus.

IV, 2.4 With whom Matthew Himself Agrees

Matthew does all he can to bring about reconciliation with the Jews.
In chapters 3 and 4 he quotes scripture six times showing
how he totally agrees with the Law and the Prophets and how he
sees Jesus as their fulfillment which the Jews will not consider.
He goes out to then with his entire gospel but they will not listen.
He finds over and over again that the scribes and the Pharisees
are hypocrites for they make a show of following the Law but
do not keep the golden rule as Jesus clarifies it in Matthew 7:12.

> So always treat others as you would like them
> to treat you; this is the meaning of the Law and the Prophets.

The eighth and last of the Beatitudes is:

> Happy those who are persecuted
> in the cause of right:
> theirs is the Kingdom of heaven.

Matthew's Gospel is primarily about attaining the Kingdom of heaven
and it is addressed to the Jews who are his dear brothers and sisters.
They have been persecuted by the Romans and as Matthew is
writing his Gospel during the 80's he hopes they can be blessed.
The Christians in the time of Q2 were persecuted by the Jews
and they thought that their persecutors would suffer in hell.
Matthew now sees the Jews being persecuted in the cause of right
and if they can accept that and pray for their persecutors
they might become blessed even by turning to Jesus and his love.
They might find the Kingdom of heaven here on earth
especially if they could but begin to pray the Lord's prayer and
as Jesus says at the end of it in Matt 6:14–15

> If you forgive others their failings,
> your heavenly Father will forgive you yours.

But Matthew knows that if we do not forgive we will not be forgiven.
Just as Q2 was convinced of hell fire so is Matthew a believer.

IV, 2.5 *For while He is Sympathetic to Judaism*

If we ponder Jesus' revolutionary love of *The Sermon on the Mount* we can see that it is God's will that we love all persons everywhere especially our enemies and that we should aim at reconciliation. But any wrong doer does receive a natural punishment and any kind of persecutor needs to be warned that he will suffer for any wrong that he inflicts on another and Q2 and Matthew make this very clear for no one, including the Jews, can get away with sin. Matthew writes his gospel for Jewish Christians and he is concerned that Jews become Christians for it is obvious to him that Jesus makes it clear that Jews can be fulfilled as Christians. The preaching of John the Baptist is central to Matthew's vision for he believes what John says at Matthew 3:2

> Repent, for the Kingdom of heaven
> is close at hand.

The Jews should repent and believe that all are God's chosen. Matthew always sees this as a fulfillment of prophecy and thus he says that this was the intent of Isaiah when he said in Isa 40:3

> A voice cries in the wilderness
> prepare a way for the Lord
> make his paths straight.

Matthew shows how Jesus and John preached the same message for once John was arrested Matthew says at chapter 4:17

> From that moment Jesus began his preaching
> with the message, "Repent, for the Kingdom
> of heaven is close at hand.

So Matthew thinks that Jesus is truly Jewish and that the Jews should become truly Christian but there was much resistance. That is why John was already put to death before Jesus and Matthew knew that it was quite Jewish to persecute their own prophets but it would be wise for them to repent and change.

Agape and *Hesed*

IV, 2.6 He is Highly Critical of the Jewish Leaders

Immediately after Jesus preaches The Eight Beatitudes he says at Matt 5:11–12:

> Happy are you when people abuse you
> and persecute you and speak all kinds
> of calumny against you on my account.
> Rejoice and be glad, for your reward will
> be great in heaven; this is how they
> persecuted the prophets before you.

This is almost a ninth beatitude and it encourages Christians to imitate Christ for the blood of martyrs is a great teacher. Matthew is opposed to the Jewish leaders because they persecute the prophet Jesus and his followers and are therefore hypocrites. That is, they are a living contradiction, proclaiming righteousness and yet not be righteous in persecuting Jewish Christians. Righteousness is a major theme for Matthew and Jesus teaches it from the beginning of Matt 3:15:

> Jesus came from Galilee to the Jordan to be
> baptized by John. John tried to dissuade him.
> "It is I who needs baptism from you," he said.
> "And yet you come to me." But Jesus replied,
> "Leave it like this for the time being;
> it is fitting that we should in this way,
> do all that righteousness demands."
> At this John gave in to him.

Q and Luke do not have this passage about righteousness and at Matt 6:33 it is mentioned again:

> Set your hearts on his Kingdom first,
> and on his righteousness, and all these
> other things will be given you as well.

Jesus' people were to be righteous and they were persecuted because of it by Jewish leaders who did not know righteousness.

IV, 2.7 And He is Closer to Q2 than to Q3

As Matthew toils for years in writing his Gospel he has before
him Mark's Gospel and the Gospel of Q and in the narrative
part of the first of his Gospel's five parts he uses Q3 as
well as Q2 and Q1 and he interweaves them with bits of Mark.
The narrative park of Matthew's first section has three stories about
the baptism, the temptation and the call of the disciples and the story
of the temptation comes from Q3 and according to Mack has three
new themes as he suggests on page 173:

> They are (1) the mythology of Jesus as
> the son of God, (2) the relationship of Jesus
> as the son of God to the temple at Jerusalem,
> and (3) the authority of the scriptures.

After Jesus fasted in the desert for forty days and forty nights
the tempter came to him and said at Matthew 4:3:

> If you are the Son of God,
> tell these stones to turn into loaves.

In the Q1 sayings Jesus is called the child of wisdom and the son
of man a bit and in the Q2 sayings he is the apocalyptic son
of man who is judge, but now in the Q3 sayings he is called
the son of God and this is all important for Matthews Good News.
The Jewish leaders will not see Jesus as the Son of God and Matthew
writes his entire gospel to try to prove to all this one key point.
So Matthew focuses on Jesus as the Son of God in accord with Q3.
And yet in attitude he is closer to the Jesus of Q2 who is
intent upon judging persecutors who are threatening Christians.
Of course he has the Q1 sayings of the all loving Jesus and
he continues to use all the Q3 sayings as we will see, but
his overall tone is not like Luke's who stresses the Q1 Jesus
nor does he fully side with Q3 which is easier on Jewish leaders.
In all three parts of the temptation Story Jesus reveals how
God responds to temptation that we might all imitate our Lord.

IV, 2.8 Does Matthew Alter many Prophecies?

In the temptation story Matthew changes the original to suit his own purposes and he does that with many of the Hebrew Bible prophecies. A key point in Matthew's argument is at Matthew 5:17

> Do not imagine that I have come
> to abolish the Law or the Prophets.
> I have come not to abolish
> but to complete them.

In the original Q3 text Jesus responds to the tempter by saying as Luke puts it:

> No one lives by bread alone.

However, Matthew has the Son of God say:

> Man does not live on bread alone
> but on every word that comes
> from the mouth of God.

And Matthew's version gives the full version of Deut 8:3:

> He humbled you, he made you feel hunger,
> he fed you with manna which neither you
> nor your fathers had known, to make you
> understand that man does not live on bread alone
> but that man lives on everything
> that comes from the mouth of Yahweh.

So Matthew is a tremendous Bible scholar and can complete the Q text when it is appealing to the Bible even in a way that fits well with Matthew's own purposes in presenting the word of God to Jews. The sayings of Matthew's Jesus often alter original prophecy in order to explain God's word from his own new perspective. Howard Clark Kee in his book *Understanding the New Testament* on page 134 shows how Matthew often uses prophecies by giving them a new meaning that you would not see as a sincere Jew. Matthew knows that Jewish leaders will not agree with his interpretation so he is in a battle as were the people of Q2.

IV, 2.9 And know Jewish Leaders will Object?

On page 134 Howard Kee writes:

> A distinctive feature of Matthew's quotations
> is an introductory formula he uses eleven times:
> 1:22; 2:5; 2:15; 2:17; 2:23; 4:14;
> 8:17; 12:17; 13:35; 21:4; 27:9-10.
> With variations, the formula runs:
> "This was done to fulfill what was spoken
> by the Lord through the prophet ... "
> It must be acknowledged that, by current
> standards of biblical interpretation, none
> of these prophecies means in its original
> context, what Matthew has made it
> mean in his setting.

Matthew knows full well that given Jesus' *agape* all
the old prophecies will be fulfilled by being altered to fit
their new context and he knows the Jewish leaders will object.
This is why in his basic attitude he is like the judgmental
Jesus of Q2 because he must warn the Jews of the difficulties
that will come their way if they continue to hate Christians.
In this first of his five parts Matthew gives us so many of
the wonderful Q1 sayings of the *agape*ic Jesus from the
Eight Beatitudes to the Our Father and all the great sayings
about loving everyone even your enemy as your brother and sister.
Matthew gives us the sayings of Jesus about the revolutionary
agape that commands an unconditional, universal love for all.
In these few pages he also gives an excellent account of how
that *agape* still implies punishment for any sin or injustice.
And thus he begins to explain his battle with the Jewish leaders.
Finally, he introduces us to the Q3 sayings and attitude in
which the tension lessens between the Son of God and the Jews.
Besides this *agape*ic struggle of Q he introduces us to Mark's *agape*.

IV, 3 *Agape* in Matthew's use of Mark

IV, 3.1 *Mark's Agape appears in Matthew's First Part*

Already at Jesus' baptism Matthew brings in Mark's saying about the *agapetos*, when at Matt 3:16–17 he writes:

> As soon as Jesus was baptized he came
> up from the water, and suddenly the heavens
> opened and he saw the spirit of God descending
> like a dove and coming down on him.
> And a voice spoke from heaven, "This is
> my Son, the Beloved; my favor rests on him."

Already in this scene we see the three persons of the Trinity loving each other and the word *agapetos* describes for us Jesus. Mark uses this term for Jesus at the beginning of his Gospel and in the middle with the Transfiguration of Jesus where Matthew quoting Mark says at Matt 17:5,

> He was still speaking when suddenly
> a bright cloud covered them with shadow,
> and from the cloud there came a voice which said,
> "This is my Son, the Beloved; he enjoys
> my favor. Listen to him."

Mark's Gospel with its synoptic or bird's eye view of Jesus' life has a beginning, part one, a middle, part two and an ending. Part one treats the Galilean ministry in which Jesus lovingly taught and cared for widows, orphans, aliens and any in need. In the middle there is the Transfiguration and then in part two he goes up to Jerusalem and as the suffering servant undergoes the Agony in the Garden, the Scourging at the Pillar, the Crowning with Thorns, the Carrying of the Cross and the Crucifixion. Finally, there is the Resurrection which is the Good News. Matthew and Luke follow Mark in this synoptic outline and so for both at the beginning and in the middle we have the Father telling us to listen to his Son, the *Agapetos*.

Part One: Experiencing Problems

IV, 3.2 Markan Agape introduces Matthew's Second Part

Matthew begins his second part, *The Kingdom of Heaven is Preached*, with the story of the cure of a leper at Matthew 8:1–4 which he takes from Mark,

> After he came down from the mountain
> large crowds followed him. A leper
> came up and bowed low in front of him.
> "Sir," he said, "if you want to, you can
> cure me." Jesus stretched out his hand
> and said, "Of course I want to! Be cured!"
> and his leprosy was cured at once.

Mark begins this story at Mark 1:40 by saying,

> A leper came to him and pleaded on his knees:
> "If you want to," he said "you can cure me."
> Feeling sorry for him, Jesus stretched out his hand
> and touched him. "Of course
> I want to!" He said: "Be cured!"

This expression that Mark uses and that Matthew here drops about feeling sorry for him and then touching him is one of love. Mark often has Jesus speak this way, and, sometimes Matthew does too as for example at Matthew 14:13 and Matthew 15:32 following Mark at the first and second miracles of the loaves. "He took pity on them and healed their sick" and he has Jesus say:

> I feel sorry for all these people;
> they have been with me for three days
> and have nothing to eat.

This feeling of mercy for the suffering that Matthew finds in Mark is a new kind of *hesedic-agape* which Jesus practices all the time when he cares for the poor of the earth. *Hesed* meant God's mercy for David's house and the privileged were expected to practice *hesed* for the poor as Jesus here does. So Matthew sees in Mark's Jesus a new *agapeic hesed*.

Agape and *Hesed*

IV, 3.3 *The Kingdom of Heaven is Preached*

The Narrative Section of Matthew's second part on *The Kingdom of Heaven* is Preached tells the stories of ten miracles many of which come from Mark and continue to show Jesus' mercy. The very last paragraph before the very last section gives a kind of summary when it says at Matt 9:36–38,

> When he saw the crowds he felt sorry for them
> because they were harassed and dejected,
> like sheep without a shepherd. Then he said
> to his disciples, "The harvest is rich
> but the laborers are few, so ask the Lord
> of the harvest to send laborers to the harvest."

This *hesedic-agape* of the Good Shepherd again Matthew gets from Mark 6:34:

> So as he stepped ashore he saw a large crowd:
> and he took pity on them because they were
> like sheep without a shepherd, and he
> set himself to teach them at some length.

Jesus' miracles are an outpouring of the *hesedic-agape* and his feeling of mercy and he wants his followers to love this way. Many are called but few will choose to imitate Jesus in being a good shepherd but his first disciples do just that. So the love in Mark seems to have a strong *hesedic* nature while the love in Q1 seems to be more like *ahava* in which we are to love everyone including our enemy as we love ourself. So the followers of Jesus will have a double *agape* including merciful *hesed* and an *ahava* that is universal. *Hesed* and *ahava* are not distinguished by Jesus and we can begin to see how for Jesus they are two aspects of the same love. The *ahava-agape* Jesus requires means we love all others as we love ourselves unconditionally, universally and eternally. We must love others with merciful *hesed* as we would want that.

IV, 3.4 Matthew Builds on Mark's Agape for God's Kingdom

What Jesus wants his people to love most of all is the Kingdom of God.
As he begins his Galilean ministry his words as we
see at Mark 1:14-15 are:

> After John had been arrested, Jesus went
> into Galilee. There he proclaimed
> the Good News from God. "The time has come,
> and the Kingdom of God is close at hand.
> Repent, and believe the Good News."

Matthew follows Mark with the same words at Matt 4:17:

> From that moment Jesus began his preaching
> with the message, "Repent, for the Kingdom
> of Heaven is close at hand."

What Mark always calls the Kingdom of God
and Matthew the Kingdom of Heaven is also
called the Kingdom of God throughout the Q text.
So to bring about the kingdom of David is the reason why the
Son of God became man and thus his *agape* includes *hesed*.
The Kingdom since the time of David had to do with merciful *hesed*.
God has merciful *hesed* for us and wants us to enter his Kingdom.
While Mark remains in the context of the Davidic Kingdom and
its *hesed* Matthew sees Jesus as the new Moses and structures
his Gospel in five parts like the Pentateuch and in following
the Mosaic shema emphasizes *ahava* just as much as *hesed*.
The Lord's Prayer which Matthew takes from Q1 brings out this
main point of Mark's Jesus with its seven petitions:

(1) Our Father who art in heaven, hallowed be thy name.
(2) Thy Kingdom come—there it is, the main petition.
(3) Thy will be done on earth as it is in heaven.
(4) Give us this day our daily bread—including the Eucharist
(5) And forgive us our trespasses,
    as we forgive those who trespass against us.
(6) And lead us not into temptation,
(7) But deliver us from evil. Amen

Agape and *Hesed*

IV, 3.5 And on Mark's Preaching of the Good News

As we have seen Mark shows how Jesus begins his public career by preaching the Good News from God and he continues to show this at Mark 1:21–22:

> They went as far as Capernaum, and as soon as
> the Sabbath came he went to the synagogue
> and began to teach. And his teaching made
> a deep impression on them because unlike
> the scribes, he taught with authority.

And at Mark 1:38–39 Jesus says:

> "Let us go elsewhere to the neighboring country towns
> so that I can preach there too, because
> that is why I came" and he went all through
> Galilee preaching in their synagogues
> and casting out devils.

Matthew repeats this and after the first four disciples are called it is written at Matt 4:23,

> He went around the whole of Galilee
> teaching in their synagogues, proclaiming
> the Good News of the Kingdom and curing
> all kinds of diseases and sickness
> among the people.

So Matthew's Jesus following Mark's Jesus is a preacher and a teacher who speaks with authority about *agape* because he is a lover who shows the Kingdom is here with his casting out of devils, his healing the sick and his forgiving sinners. The fivefold structure of Matthew's Gospel is based on this:

(1) The Kingdom of Heaven Proclaimed
(2) The Kingdom of Heaven is Preached
(3) The Mystery of the Kingdom of Heaven
(4) The Church, First Fruits of the Kingdom of Heaven
(5) The Approaching Advent of the Kingdom of Heaven

IV, 3.6 And of Mark's Casting out of Devils

We have already seen Jesus' confrontation with the Devil
in the temptation in the Wilderness and this is very significant.
In the eyes of Jesus the world did belong to the Kingdom of
Satan and the devil had a point when he said at Matt 4:8-9,

> Next, taking him to a very high mountain,
> the devil showed him all the kingdoms
> of the world and their splendor.
> "I will give you all these," he said
> "if you fall at my feet and worship me."

Mark introduces the theme of exorcism very early when Jesus
begins teaching at Capernaum and cures a demoniac for
at Mark 1:23-26 we read:

> In their synagogue just then there was a man
> possessed by an unclean spirit, and it
> shouted, "What do you want with us,
> Jesus of Nazareth? Have you come to
> destroy us? I know who you are:
> the Holy one of God." But Jesus said
> sharply, "Be quiet! Come out of him!"
> and the unclean spirit threw the man
> into convulsions and with a loud cry
> went out of him. The people were so
> astonished that they started asking
> each other what it all meant.

At Matt 8:28-34 we have the a story of the two demoniacs
who were so fierce that no one could come near them and
Jesus cast out their devils and sent them into a herd of pigs.
So as Jesus begins to introduce the new Kingdom of Heaven
even on earth he is not only a preaching teacher but he
is also an exorcist who begins to take over the kingdom
of the demons and in doing this the angels are always with him.

Agape and *Hesed*

IV, 3.7 And on Mark's Healing of the Sick

We have already noted how in Mark and then in Matthew
Jesus felt sorry for the poor and the sick and how he healed
them with the loving touch of his merciful *hesed-agape*.
The Kingdom of Heaven which Jesus is preaching will be
a place with no sickness and Jesus wants to show how
life on earth can be more and more like the Kingdom of Heaven.
Mark's Gospel and Matthew's following him is divided into
the two parts of the Galilean ministry then the Jerusalem ministry.
First, he goes about healing the suffering and then he himself suffers.
Jesus is a paradigm of the compassion for the suffering and he will
identify with them to show them the worth of their sorrowful mystery.
In the Narrative Section of the second part of the Kingdom
ten miracles are described and we see much healing of the sick
for there is the cure of the leper, the cure of the centurion's servant,
the cure of Peter's mother-in-law, the cure of the paralytic,
the cure of the woman with a hemorrhage who "but touched
the hem of his garment," the cure of the two blind men and others.
The Kingdom of Heaven will be without sickness and suffering.
But life here is ruled by the powers of darkness and the point
of Matthew's Gospel following Mark is that Jesus' love is so great
that he is here to start revealing the Kingdom of Heaven to us.
In the second part of this section on *Preaching the Kingdom of Heaven*
Jesus explains to his disciples how they too must be compassionate.
At Matt 10:37–39 he tells them about renouncing self to follow him:

> Anyone who prefers father or mother to me
> is not worthy of me. Anyone who prefers
> son or daughter to me is not worthy of me.
> Anyone who does not take his cross and follow
> in my footsteps is not worthy of me . . .
> Anyone who loses his life for my sake
> will find it.

IV, 3.8 And on Mark's Forgiveness of Sin

Again following Mark Matthew tells the story of Jesus eating
with sinners for at Matthew's house Jesus eats with a number
of tax collectors and sinners and at Matt. 9:10 we read:

> When the Pharisees saw this, they said
> to his disciples, "Why does your master
> eat with tax collectors and sinners?"
> When he heard this he replied, "It is
> not the healthy who need the doctor,
> but the sick. Go and learn the meaning
> of the words: *What I want is mercy, not
> sacrifice.* And indeed I did not come
> to call the virtuous, but sinners."

So Jesus came for the sake of sinners and he practices and
teaches mercy for them and in the Our Father he prayed:

> And forgive us our debts
> as we forgive those
> who are in debt to us.

Jesus teaches us to forgive that we ourselves might be forgiven.
If we love our enemy as we love ourself then we are
forgiving for an enemy is an enemy because he sins against us.
It is not just an accident that people are widows, orphans
and aliens and that people are sick and are mad and possessed.
Adam and Eve sinned and as a result we have to suffer and die.
We ourselves continue to sin and many suffer because of that.
Jesus aims to set things right and announce the Kingdom of Heaven.
The main thing we have to do in following him is to forgive
sinners and love our enemy and we will begin to love the enemy
who is within ourself so that we can get reconciliation within.
Once we become Jesus' disciples he will help us with reconciliation.
In a way we are lucky we are sinners because Jesus came
to call the sinners and as virtuous we might not hear his call.

Agape and *Hesed*

IV, 3.9 Especially by the Suffering Servant

Jesus did not only heal and have compassion for the suffering
but he suffered greatly himself and so did his disciples.
We know of Peter's mother-in-law and so he must have had
a wife but once he was called he left his own and took up
his cross and followed in Jesus' footsteps also to be martyred.
In Second Isaiah there are the four Suffering Servant Songs
at Isaiah42, Isaiah 49, Isaiah 50:4-9 and Isaiah 52:13–53
and the Jewish people were the Suffering Servant.
But the Christians came to see Jesus as the Suffering Servant.
Isaiah 53:6 begins:

> We had all gone astray like sheep,
> each taking his own way,
> and Yahweh burdened him
> with the sins of all of us.
> Harshly dealt with, he bore it humbly,
> he never opened his mouth,
> like a lamb that is led to the slaughter house
> like a sheep that is dumb before its shearers
> never opening its mouth.

Jesus, the lamb of God, is the Good Shepherd who dies for sinners,
that they might be redeemed, that the Kingdom of Heaven might
come and that it might begin to come even here on earth.
Matthew following Mark shows how Jesus goes up
to Jerusalem and there undergoes his passion that as savior
he might save us all by his cross and then by his resurrection.
Matthew following Mark tells us the greatest story ever told
that invites us to follow Jesus and his followers in loving'
others even to the point that we will suffer like the lamb of God.
This is the story of *agape* that invites each of us to offer our
sufferings with Jesus that they might be consecrated and that
we might all live in communion with him and his Father forever.

When we were Freshmen with the Sophomores

JUNIOR CLASS from left to right bottom row: Jerry Smith, Steve Goodfriend, Peter Roerig, Bill Taylor, and Pat Carney. Top row: Tom Waddill, David Goicoechea, Jerry Eastman, Michael Jones, Ken Wyffels, and Ray Heuberger.

Our Junior Class

Running the Hurdles

The Tennis Court and Willamette Valley

Mount Angel Hill Top

The Grotto at Mount Angel

The Monastery Church

At Mount Angel in the play Christ in the Concrete City

Part Two

Seeking Their Causes

I. With Benedictine Spirituality

I,4 Growing Vitally in that Seminary Seedbed

I,4.1 Nourishing Agape with Poverty, Chastity, and Obedience

The Monks of Mt. Angel as our Nourishing Mother were focused upon cultivating within themselves and within us the spiritual, intellectual, moral and physical virtues that we might grow in vitality. Mortality, of course, would claim us all but we believed in a vitality and its love that would conquer death because of Jesus' resurrection. According to Kierkegaard the four stages on life's way have to do with the aesthetic, the ethical, religiousness A and religiousness B. Aesthetic beauty, ethical goodness, experiential truth and faith's holiness were the aim and goal of our life in that seed-bed. The Monks took their vows of poverty, chastity and obedience. Obedience was seen as the humility that listens to God's will. Just as pride was seen as the root of all evil so humility was seen as the root of all virtue so that with it one could practise self-control, courage, prudence, justice and the ten commandments. The whole experience of the Jewish people could be seen as a growth in a higher and higher morality that was progressively revealed. If they would live according to the Ten Commandments they would develop a great vitality for all based on the justice of the common good. The Monks taught us to examine our conscience by asking if we had broken any of the ten commandments and we would think about each and get to know them and ourselves better. Humility's obedience taught us to obey the Ten Commandments. If we did we would have a just self-control, courage and wisdom. We learned how the gifts of faith, hope and charity with their grace could help us to follow the commandments and practise virtue. As we were taught the intellectual virtues they helped us understand the moral virtues and the added vitality they could give us and others. The *agape* of Jesus which revealed personhood in the dignity, uniqueness and interrelatedness of each and which could sublimate each love let us grow in the vitality of a loving sociality.

I,4.2 Nourishing Agapeic Affection with Poverty

At Mt. Angel our Alma Mater taught us in many ways that
one can easily become possessed by one's possessions and my
father always taught us that we must get a college education
so that we could get great jobs and have healthy, wealthy lives.
Thus from the Monk's we learned of a non-worldly ideal
that gave a different meaning to education than my father had.
They emphasized gospel sayings from Matthew and Luke
that revealed a Jesus who in his special love said to them
to leave behind all they had that they might come and follow him.
It was as if the Monks saved themselves from the world,
the flesh and the devil through their poverty, chastity and obedience.
First, in their poverty the Monks focused on loving God
for they knew how easy it is to serve the false god of mammon
and it is true that where your heart is there your god is.
Secondly, they were able to completely love and care for us
because their vow of poverty enabled them to work for the good
of others rather than for any goods they might accumulate.
This vow of poverty with which they developed their *agape*ic
affection for all contributed to their vitality even because of
the peace that their lack of self-concern brought into their lives.
Because they really loved others they were not anxious about
self-concern that might keep them awake at night and thus
take away their vitality, peace, playfulness and sense of humor.
Of course, each father would have this own simple monk's
clothing and his own books which, however, he would be
careful with and not messily mark up because after he used
them they would belong to the community as all goods did.
The vital exercises of the moral virtues and the practice of
poverty built up a sociality and lack of defensiveness and
negative reactions that let the monks be affirmative to us
and taught us not to take offence at others but to love them.

Agape and *Hesed*

I,4.3   Nourishing Agapeic Eros with Chastity

Since the Monks and the priests they trained were not married
the vow of chastity meant a vow of celibacy and for some
keeping the vow was easy and for others it was very difficult.
Fourteen of us entered the seminary in 1951 as first year students
and only one of us became a priest and I suspect that with
five or six of us the main problem was that of sexuality.
The main purpose of celibacy was that we might have a totally
loving dedication to serving God and his people as St. Paul
in imitating Christ explained in his first letter to the Corinthians.
But as we know from Plato's *Phaedrus* and the Buddhists not only
priests take this vow for the practice of celibacy can initiate
the purification process of catharsis and the mystical ascent.
In the seminary we learned about Courtly Love in the Middle Ages
and we learned that just as a poet loves a lady that he might sing
the better so a knight loved a lady that he might fight the better.
We read some from Dante's *Divine Comedy* and we saw how
he had a celibate love for Beatrice that gave him inspiration.
As I have said I had great problems with sexual sinning
and then all of a sudden in some mysterious way when
Father Ambrose became my confessor I was able to be celibate.
In the summer when I was back at Sun Valley with all the
pretty girls I would have trouble again but then getting back
with Father Ambrose and the seminary environment I was healed.
One of the values of celibacy seemed to be that it could build
up a strong vitality such as Father Ambrose had and it could
be so powerful that it could give me a new vital energy and passion.
Plato already explained this so well in the *Phaedrus* when
he described the sublimation of *eros* with the myth of the charioteer.
But with Christianity there is an added element in that
a celibate *eros* could energize *agape* and aid the Christian loves
in going out to all with an inspirational power and presence.

I,4.4 Nourishing Agapeic Friendship with Obedience

The Mt. Angel Community was made up of about 100 Monks and
I would guess there were about 70 fathers and about 30 brothers.
When we focus on the vital as distinct from the spiritual, the
intellectual and the physical we can see that it is intimately
connected with the communal for no man is an island and we
are all part of the main and we greatly help each other to grow
as the Monk's helped us by taking us into their community.
The vow of obedience in its deepest essence was a vow of
humility for the Monks and the future priests they were teaching
would be obedient to their superior and humbly do whatever
the Abbot or prior or Bishop might think best for them.
Just as pride is the root of all evil so obedient humility
can be the root of goodness in a community and give it
and its members a love that contributes to vitality and
a vitality that lets the members grow in a more vibrant love.
The Benedictines, in addition to vows of obedience, chastity and
a community of goods, took a vow of stability, which meant
they would not leave the monastery without their abbot's permission.
It is obvious that the vow of stability was part of the vow of
obedience and the idea of permission indicates how being obedient
lets Monks and priests be childlike in the way that Jesus
wanted his disciples to be like little children who obey in joy.
A special kind of friendship was nourished in the community
for some things can be learned only in a community or family.
The social dimension of life corrects our craziness and helps
us mature for in listening to the perspectives of others we can
come to see how limited our attitude and view of others has been.
In the community of Mt. Angel healing was there for many
for we often learned how someone who had gone through
tragedy or crisis could attest that God is present through
the kind eyes and tender touch of the Monks and seminarians.

Agape and *Hesed*

I,4.5 Nourishing Agape with the Moral Virtues

In the seminary our whole life was centered on practicing
the theological, intellectual and moral virtues which were
meant to increase our love, light and life by helping us
to prefer nothing whatever to Christ the logos become flesh.
Up until the incarnation and resurrection of God become man
there was a deep down pessimism about the world of matter.
Humans thought of themselves as fallen into the body and
the whole purpose of life is to eventually be freed from the flesh.
But with Jesus the four moral virtues while remaining
in a position of central importance get a whole new meaning
as do even the ten commandments and all other moral systems.
As the new love of *agape* which loves all persons and even
enemies gets worked out it will remake the moral virtues and
they will add a richer concrete content to the unknown depths
of that *agape* which keeps becoming further revealed through history.
St. Paul in his letter to the Galatians begins to show how
moral virtues and moral systems get a new basis and meaning
with the self-scarificial *agape* of Jesus that joyfully suffers for others.
Paul says in Galatians that in Christ there are no longer
Greeks or Jews, male nor female, master nor slave for now
all persons are of equal worth and my neighbor is now everyone.
The Greeks and the Jews each had a self-realization ethics and
the whole purpose of practicing the moral virtues was to perfect
myself and my people for all humans were not members of Christ's body.
I had to a great degree been brought up by my father with
a self-realization ethics which said get a good education that you
might get a good job and have a good life but the seminary changed that.
From our Benedictine teachers we learned about the four moral virtues
but each of them was now rooted in a universal *agape* for everyone
and when practiced each of them could give to *agape* a new passion
and a desire to practice the virtue for others ever better and better.

Part Two: Seeking Their Causes

I,4.6   Nourishing Agapeic Affection with Justice

Justice is the key idea of Plato's *Republic* and is the virtue that
lets the Republic exist for without justice communities self-destruct.
Aristotle sees the moral virtues as means to the end of happiness.
For him there is a retributive and distributive justice for we must
give others their due and if we fail just retribution must be paid.
There are goods that belong to the community and these must be
distributed in a just way depending on the merits and deserts of each.
But once we come to Christianity we see in Paul's letters a new
kind of community of goods in which the poor are especially loved.
Given Jesus' new love for all there should no longer be slavery.
For Jesus said to those who would follow him that they should
sell all that they have, give it to the poor and come and follow him.
Jesus had a special affection for all whom he loved as his brothers
and sisters and for whom he became man and for whom he died.
This kind of *agape*ic affection was especially with St. Francis
who with a sense of justice loved sister sun and brother moon.
His new spirituality came into being especially out of love for
the poor of the new cities who were in need of a new justice.
With his affection he tamed the wolf of Gubbio and then that wolf
taught the people of the town of that very affection of St. Francis.
The Benedictines had this kind of affection for us and it was
grounded in a kind of justice for all which they were constantly
teaching us for Father Bernard often used to say that the door
swings both ways and if we with a sense of justice could not
follow all the rules and live according to the ideals then it was
evident that our vocation was not to imitate Jesus as a priest.
So what *agape* does for affection is to universalize it and to get
self-love well-ordered in accord with justice for if I love my family
as more important than others then my affection is not *agape*ic.
First I must love all people with affection as my brothers and
sisters and then I can have a special affection for my own.

Agape and *Hesed*

I,4.7 Nourishing Agapeic Eros with Temperance

The mysterious relation between temperance and vitality is presented in Plato's *Phaedrus* 245 and following when the person who is not able to be temperate meets just the right person and is converted to the vitality of celibacy. When I first read this it was real to me because I had struggled to attain *self-control* over my irascible and sexual appetites and even with great effort and constant confession I just could not get the vital energy to be pure in thought, word and deed and to have no angry outbursts. Then when I started talking about this with Father Ambrose the vitality and energy of his peaceful wise celibate being somehow started vitalizing me so that while I was with him for those last three years at Mt. Angel and he was my confessor I was able to practice a temperate *self-control* of my passions. Plato describes this sublimation of *eros* almost as if it came as a give or kind of grace for in just meeting that right person one is inspired to channel all that sexual passion into one's creative life style and energize the intellectual and theological virtues. Paul was perhaps energized in this way when he beheld Stephen being stoned and yet joyfully praying for his enemies. In *Galatians* Paul writes about becoming freed from the flesh and freed for the gifts of the spirit: love, joy, peace, patience, and *self-control* which free us to lovingly serve all others. That is the very essence of Jesus new *agape* according to Paul. Augustine was converted to an *agape*ic celibacy when he was reading Paul and Dante, Kierkegaard and Nietzsche tell of this experience of becoming so vitalized by meeting Beatrice, Regina and Lou Salome whom they continued to love with erotic *agape*. In the seminary we learned of a prudent fortitude that let us keep trying for temperance until we received its new vitality.

I,4.8 Nourishing Agapeic Friendship with Prudence

When I was in my fourth year of High School I became
special friends with a man by the name of Paul White.
He had been a professional golfer and received his vocation
after he had already gone through university and became
quite successful going from city to city playing in golf tournaments.
He was one of the judges of a speech contest in which I got up
and gave a talk extemporaneously on a freshly announced topic.
Afterwards he told me that if I worked at it I could be a good
speaker and he would be willing to help me as my couch.
In a way he was like my father and Father Ambrose who
both encouraged and helped me to do better with my studies.
However, he was different in that he too was still a student
and was more like a friend than a mentoring father figure.
I gave a written talk on Liberal Education with which he helped me.
He suggested that I memorize the 23rd Chapter of Matthew's Gospel.
Virtue has to do with practice, practice, practice, and he and I
did that with that speech getting the mood, the tone of voice, the
inflections and all the nuances just right and I won the contest.
Fortitude is the virtue that helps us acquire virtuous habits with
practice, practice, practice and prudence is the moral virtue
that according to Aristotle is the practical wisdom with which we
get just the right balance of the golden mean by not going to extremes.
We have to keep cool and not over-react but we do need to act
and not just be indifferent for virtue is the excellence of action.
Paul White was a man who deeply believe in excellence and
living in the most excellent way possible and that is why he
gave up a successful golf career because he saw the life of
the Benedictine Monk as the most excellent he could imagine.
He picked me out as a special kind of friend and we ate our
peck of salt together with practice, practice, practice trying
to be excellent first with speech but then with other thing too.

Agape and *Hesed*

I,4.9   Nourishing Agapeic Mourning with Fortitude

The three great secret things of sex, death and religion continued to evolve for me year by year in mysterious ways. As I practiced celibacy it seemed as if there were a build up of sperm and semen that gave me a new energetic and refined spirituality, intellectuality and vitality and death or mortality seemed to be conquered by a new kind dynamic vitality. As we worked away on practicing the vital exercises with the moral virtues I did seem to move away from the mortal sin of sexual intemperance to the vitality of a new celibate purity. Just as growth in *agape* brought with it a new affectionate justice, a new erotic temperance and a new friendly prudence so also growth in *agape* allowed for a new kind of mourning which let our fortitude become a new hopeful persistence. One day in class a single bell began to ring out the death knell. Father Gerard, our professor, said "It must be Fidelis." and we got down on our knees and said "Hail Marys" for the repose of his soul until the bell stopped ringing—one gong for each year of his life—and then we asked him to pray for us. Fortitude is a kind of courage in the face of difficulty and in the face of death and within the context of *agape*ic love which lasts forever and is stronger than death our courage gave to our mourning a belief that death has lost its sting and that it is but a process into a fuller and eternal life. My father as a child of five had gone through a successful mourning process with his mother and sisters when his father died and they got in touch with him and the spirit world. That shamanic awareness of the spirit would enable him to bond with my mother whose parents had each lost a parent. From the time I started learning my prayers at the age of five I identified with their loving belief in the spirit world and the seminary with its reverent celibacy increased that belief in me.

I,5 Growing Physically in that Seminary Seed-bed

I,5.1 *Nourishing Agapeic Health, Happiness, Wisdom, Holiness*

Deeply embedded in the Benedictine Motto of "Ora et Labora" is
the insight into the interflow between body, mind, soul and spirit.
Within the context of Jesus' loving incarnation and resurrection
the flesh gets a new everlasting value and the task of building
healthy bodies is right at the heart of all Catholic education.
Even when practicing the "Ora" of their prayer the Monks were
doing the "labora" of their work and getting good physical exercise.
For they would genuflect many times a day and thus build up
leg muscles and balance and when kneeling they kept their
back straight and they would pray and sing while standing
and sitting and bowing and kneeling and that was healthy.
We learned to do that with them and each morning before Mass
with the Monks we lined up two by two in silence and then
walked to the Monastery Church and we prayed while we walked.
And a prayer walk is a wonderful way of combining the
physical and the spiritual and I still practice that habit today.
We often did work together in the shop doing carpentry together
or raking leaves out in the wood and bringing them in bags
by the truck load to be used as mulch for the monastery garden.
But our physical work was also physical play for we did
play football, basketball and volleyball and we did play tennis.
That physical play did build up vitality for we did it together
and we learned how to perfect team work and even to be
good losers together and appreciate and learn from our opponents
who might beat us so that even as losers we were win, win winners.
With the constant physical exercises of right diet, hygiene and sleep
we built up virtues or good habits that we could perfect throughout
the rest of our lives and as priests teach to our parishioners.
With good physical health and strength we could do more for others
and we could live more vitally, think more wisely and love God better.

Agape and *Hesed*

I,5.2 Nourishing Agapeic Health with Physical Exercises

The Community of Mt. Angel Abbey focused on the values of health, education and welfare and many Monks and the priests whom they educated as a result lived to a ripe old age with joy and vitality. To a great degree they were able to avoid heart problems, cancer, Alzheimer's and many sorts of physical weakness because they took care of their health with many types of physical exercises. They were motivated not to be lazy, not to smoke, not to drink to excess and not to live only a sedentary life even though they spent a great deal of time reading, writing and giving spiritual advice. Their *agape*ic desire to spend their lives serving others and being a good example who could inspire especially the young but also persons at each stage of their life's way motivated them to exercise each day until they would get their second wind and perspire out their impurities. The very life style of the monastery and seminary got them to practice but also to reflect upon right diet, right hygiene and right sleep. Father Ambrose also told me that the physical exercises were very important in helping one live the celibate life style for working out could help you sleep well and not eating meat could help sublimate the sex drive and Buddhists knew of these secrets. So if ones concupiscible and irascible passions were strong one could exercise well, eat well and sleep well and one could become an inspiring teacher of sublimated and powerful passion. No wonder of it that modern societies spend great political effort and many tax dollars taking care of hospitals and the health system, and schools and the education and people on welfare. The Benedictines gave their lives that by promoting spiritual, intellectual, vital and physical exercises many people might be so graced that they learn the good habits to keep them off welfare.

I,5.3 Nourishing Agapeic Health with Physical Work

During the Summer before I went to the Seminary I had already
started the practice of hard, physical labor for my father got
his garbage route and I helped him clean up the town and we did
work up a good sweat getting it on the truck and getting it off.
My father was a very hard worker and had grown up working
on farms so the work life of the Benedictines was natural to me.
One of the vital aspects of physical work was becoming friends.
For as Aristotle puts it you become friends by eating your
peck of salt together so as you lick your salty perspiring
lips when working together you do eat that peck of salt together.
Working with someone over time does let you know each other.
We each do have our strange idiosyncrasies and they become
evident in working together so that familiarity can breed contempt.
But working with some can let you know especially if you have
an *agape*ic attitude that their good points outnumber their bad ones.
Whether you are doing dishes together or sweeping and mopping
the dormitory floor there are different ways of physical work.
So not only does the work help build a strong, healthy body
but it can also build moral virtue as you learn from each other
and overlook the other's faults without showing any irritation.
Of course, learning self-control while working also builds up
prudence and practical wisdom especially in the seminary
where the whole point was to practice love and growth in love.
Father Mathias, the scripture scholar, who was said to be
the smartest of all the monks would be seen doing physical work
outside at least five days a week and Father Method our Latin
and Algebra teacher was in charge of keeping the garden beautiful.
So the spiritual and intellectual exercises alone could be
dangerous because they were too sedentary but the spiritual
included the physical and the "*labora*" was stressed with the "*ora*".

Agape and *Hesed*

I,5.4 Nourishing Agapeic Health with Physical Play

Getting our physical exercise was not only a matter of work
but also it was a matter of play and in fact our best workout
came on the basketball court at the height of playful competition.
Father's Ambrose and Louis used to play football with us and one
time Father Ambrose went out and caught a pass but a student
by the name of James Kalberer closed the gap of about ten yards
in about two seconds and Father Ambrose got a laugh out of it.
We only played touch football and not tackle but still blocking
and protecting the quarterback could be very physical and while
basketball gave us the best workout each team sport did help us
develop certain skills that helped to develop parts of the body.
In my fifth year there in my first year of college we moved
from a class dormitory to a room with two persons and my
roommate was a young man named Brendan Mallon and he was
an excellent athlete who could especially really pitch softball.
Just as we did not play tackle football but touch so also we
did not play hardball but softball with underhanded pitching.
Brendan and I as we lived together in the same little room
for nine months became very good friends and we had
our own first college teams that would compete with High School
teams and the logicians, the philosophers and the theologians.
Living and working and praying and studying and playing
together makes for friendship throughout life and into eternity.
Each morning on my rosary prayer walk I still pray for
the community of Mt. Angel; for Father Ambrose, Father Method
and Brother Fidelis; Father Ambrose, Father Method, Brother Fidelis
please pray for me and all of mine, I pray for you and all of yours.
I pray for Father Bernard, Father Louis, Father David,
Father Athanasius, Father Edmund, Father Cosmos, Father Hugh;
I pray for Pat Carney, Ray Heuberger, Brendon Mallon, and
Glen Uelencott and for the entire community of Mt. Angel.

I,5.5 Nourishing Agapeic Health with Team Sport

Team sports seemed to have a kind of emotional contagion about
them that moved out from basketball to football to baseball.
In the Little Gym where we played in a small space our team
would have a prayer huddle before the game and we said
our "Hail Mary" that we would play well, be good sports and win.
Already the energy was high for we had warmed up and were
ready to go right from the opening tip off and on our little team
of five class mates in first year college we depended on each other.
The concentrated intensity of the team working together and for
each other led to great physical exercise as we ran up and down
the floor passing and catching and jumping and shooting and
perspiring profusely even as we guarded and tried to stop our
opponents from getting, passing, catching and shooting the ball.
So our physical exercises especially in team sport greatly
contributed to our vital exercises for excellence in basketball
meant excellence in prudence, justice, fortitude and temperance.
We had to be prudent in letting the substitutes play as much
as the starting five for that meant not only justice but also
it could mean winning and not letting someone get too tired
or to save him from fouling out or to use him strategically.
Team sports such as basketball really developed one's fortitude
for you had to have courage and keep working as hard as you could,
and that physical game which developed our physical health
also developed temperance or *self-control* for we learned
to think ahead and fool the opponents and not just do
what we might want to do on the spur of the moment.
But the intellectual and spiritual virtues were developed
in that little gym also for we came to see how a healthy body
would provide no distractions and peace as we did our studies.
And, of course, we not only prayed before and after the game
for its intensity developed more intense love between us.

Agape and *Hesed*

I,5.6 *Nourishing Agapeic Health with Track and Tennis*

When I was a senior in High School Carol Thiel, a first year
college student from Idaho Falls asked me if I would like to go
running in early Spring and get in good shape for the track season.
I liked the idea because my dad had been a first class runner.
So we went out on the roads below the Hilltop and ran for a mile
and after a couple of weeks we were going even faster for
two miles and by track season I could easily run for five miles.
Carol was a pious young man and we would say the Rosary
together as we were running and we would always get our second
wind and our bodily heart and our loving heart each grew stronger.
That May I ran the mile, the Quarter Mile, the 100 yard dash
and the High Hurdles and I won all four of them and came
in second in the High Jump and we knew that Bill Parkes
a philosopher would be leading in the Mile because he had
won it as a front runner with ease for the last two years.
I stayed just behind him until there was about 200 yards
to go and then passed him and just kept going faster and faster.
Paul White talked with me after the race and said that he was
happy to see that I worked as hard with running as I did in speaking.
He told me that he would teach me how to play tennis if I
were interested and he said that you could really keep in good
shape if you played tennis with some good partner all year.
So we started playing tennis and, of course, I was no match
for him but with fortitude we kept at it week after week.
He taught me how to serve and hit backhand shots and
forehand shots and I became his partner so that he
could keep up his game and get a good work out even though he
always beat me because he was a professional style athlete.
Track and Field does have many one man events but still
Carol Thiel and I always worked out together and tennis is
a very vital as well as physical game as you come to know your partner.

I,5.7 Nourishing Agapeic Health with Right Diet

In the Seminary the Monks taught us to be conscious of our
health in terms of what we took into our bodies and I don't
think any minor seminarian ever smoked a cigarette and
at table I remember one morning at breakfast asking another
seminarian why he had a cup of coffee each morning and he told
me that unless he did that he got constipated and I wondered why.
Every Friday we would not eat meat and during the forty days
of Lent we practiced fasting and abstinence which means that
we had one normal meal a day and two half meals and we
did not eat meat except on Sunday and since we were still
growing boys they told us not to fast unless we wanted to.
All of that got us to thinking about a healthy diet and we
began to see the dangers of hamburgers and hot dogs and
all kinds of so called junk food and we ate a lot of fruit and
vegetables which the Monks grew on the farm and we had
oat meal many times a week and we had a lot of brown bread.
Jimmy Maple who was a year ahead of me was well known
for eating his apple a day for it would keep the doctor away.
So there were not only the physical exercises of running faster,
jumping higher, throwing further and even boxing better
but we knew that right eating and drinking was also very
important and I was always naturally skinny and did not
have to worry about putting on too much weight in the least.
In the class below us there was a big fellow whom we
called Moose Elkington and he was so much stronger than me.
Father Louis had us fight each other in a three round
boxing match and so in front of all the students here was
this two hundred pound strong man and the 100 pound weakling.
I remember sitting on the John asking how my dad would
fight my grandfather who was built like Moose and I
kept moving very fast so he couldn't hit me and I kept hitting him.

Agape and *Hesed*

I,5.8   Nourishing Agapeic Health with right Hygiene

As soon as we would arise in the morning we would go
to the sinks to shave, brush our teeth and comb our hair.
We got in the habit of brushing our teeth four times a day
and once that habit is there it carries you along just as any
of the physical habits do and I would not confess it if I missed
running or working out for a few days or missed eating fruit
or missed brushing my teeth but I would feel guilty and correct it.
We put clean sheets and pillow cases on our beds each week
and there was a special fold used at the two bottom corners
and one year Father Bernard asked me to teach the first year
students and the new students just how to make their beds.
And in the seminary everything was neat and clean and we
had to polish and brush our shoes for inspection each Saturday.
We sent our dirty laundry home in special laundry boxes
which we mailed home and would get back in a couple of weeks.
I do not ever remember there being any lice or bed bugs
for an ounce of prevention is worth a pound of cure and
we were taught little sayings like that to help keep us healthy.
One saying that we all knew was: "Early to bed, early to rise
makes a man healthy, wealthy and wise." And we were always
early to bed and early to rise and yet we got our eight hours sleep.
There was also a saying about drinking eight glasses of water
a day and even with three glasses of milk a day I am not
sure I had five glasses of water but we were thirsty after a good
work out and could easily get dehydrated so we did drink
regularly and build up the good habit of flushing out toxins
not only with perspiration but also with good things to drink.
In my fourth year someone brought the flu bug back
at thanksgiving vacation and about seventy percent of us
were very ill with high fevers and we stayed in bed or
tried to starve it and sleep it off and we did finally succeed.

I,5.9 Nourishing Agapeic Health with right Sleep

Sleep like anything else could be done as a vice with not enough
or too much or as a virtue with just the right golden mean.
For nine years in the seminary the bell would ring each morning
at 5:30 am and we would go to bed each night at 9:30 pm
so that we got that right amount of eight-hours sleep.
As I got to know myself in the seminary I found that
there was a relation between right sleep and celibacy for
during my first three years before Father Ambrose helped me
to become celibate I found that I had a hard time going to sleep
after a month or so of sperm and semen build up so working
out and being ready to go to sleep at once also helped with celibacy.
I learned how to say the Jesus prayer when going to sleep
for instead of counting sheep I just prayed "My Jesus
Mercy" over and over again and after a bit I was asleep in peace.
Sometimes I would dream and maybe even have a sexy
dream and then I strange new event took place that I could
rely upon for when we had the flu there was a young first
year student in bed next to me by the name of David
Kavaleski and as I looked at him sleeping I said to myself
"How beautiful he is!" And I fell in love with him even
though I never told him and if I were having temptations
I would think of him and in his presence I could sleep.
Another time about four of us had to spend a few days
in the infirmary with a bad case of poison oak which
we got when we were helping Father Method pick leaves.
Next to me in bed was my class mate, Jerry Smith,
and again he was so beautiful that I fell in love with him.
And he is the only one of the fourteen who started out
in 1952 that went on to become a priest and he became
a Benedictine and took the name of Father Edmund and
he is still one that I pray for with a special love each morning.

Agape and *Hesed*

I,6 Growing in Excellence with the Liberal Arts

I,6.1 In 1ˢᵗ Commandment Obedience with better Reading

We did examine our conscience in terms of the Ten Commandments. In our first year we would read them and think and talk about them. In Exodus 20:1, the first one said:

> I am Yahweh your God . . .
> You shall have no gods except me.
> But I show kindness to thousands of those
> who love and keep my commandments.

At first this commandment seemed pretty easy to keep for I never had the slightest temptation to even think there could be another God. There was no doubt that we should love the Lord our God with our whole heart, mind and soul and our neighbor as ourself. But as we became better readers things became more complicated. After all Jesus was put to death because the Jews saw him as breaking this commandment by claiming to be the Son of God. God could be kind but God could not be *agape* or the love between the Father, the Son and the Holy Spirit for surely to worship a triune God is to put strange gods before the Jewish Yahweh. Who is this Yahweh and would the Israelites believe in Him? As we continued our education in the liberal arts of reading, writing, speaking, listening, dreaming and thinking we saw that the oral tradition of the Hebrews was written from four viewpoints and the Israelites did not see God as Yahweh. Each year as we read Latin, English Literature, geography and history we came to read with more insight and everything not only the Ten Commandments took on a new, richer meaning. Especially Father Method talked to us about a liberal education that could free us from the slavery of ignorance and open us to the riches of truth in its many different kinds and details. One time he took a few of us to Portland to hear Mortimer Adler and I bought an autographed copy of his "How to Read a Book".

Part Two: Seeking Their Causes

I,6.2   In 2nd Commandment Obedience with better Writing

Reading and writing complement each other for you learn how
to write well by reading great writers and the practice of writing
brings you to carefully study a greater variety of writers.
It is very helpful to comparative religion, comparative literature
and comparative philosophy to notice not only what they have
in common but to notice especially the differences in world view.
Reading the histories of religions, literatures and philosophies
helps the writer to know just what he needs to be writing about.
Father Method had us memorize the Prelude to Virgil's *Aeneid*
in Latin and in my sixth year Father Athanasius who taught me
Greek asked me if I would like reading poetry in Greek and Latin
with him and from him I learned the joy of memorizing poetry.
And with him I first memorized a poem of Gerard Manley Hopkins.
I wrote an early paper on Liberal Education for a speech contest
and writing was becoming more and more important for we knew
that we would have to write out sermons and speak them at church.
Being a good public speaker was a very important part of a priest's
life and the liberal art of writing which was helped by reading
could greatly help one to be excellent at the liberal art of speaking.
As I read more I found that writing helped me to better understand
what I was reading and we often wrote essays on what we read.
As I read and wrote and listened and spoke I became more and more
mystified by the second commandment at Exodus 20:7:

> You shall not utter the Name of Yahweh
> your God to misuse it.

I knew that I should not take the name of the Lord my God
in vain and yet I continued and still do continue to swear.
Did I get this deep seated habit from my father through both
heredity and environment and if from heredity how does that
work for I am no better today than I was fifty years ago?
Can my writing ever help me learn how to keep this commandment?

Agape and *Hesed*

I,6.3 In 3rd Commandment Obedience with better Speaking

Arete, the Greek word that is translated as virtue or manliness
means excellence and excellence in the liberal arts was meant
to help us to acquire the theological, intellectual and moral virtues.
Of course, the monks lived according to the three vows of poverty
chastity and obedience and obedience meant humility before one's
superior and as the opposite of pride it is the root of all virtue.
The third commandment at Exodus 20:8 said:

> Remember the Sabbath and keep it holy.

Of course, that again like the first commandment was no problem
because for us every day was like the Sabbath which we kept holy.
By praying the Mass twice a day and parts of the Divine Office
and saying the Rosary together during Mary's months of October
and May we really loved to have every day be a holy day.
Of course, praying out loud together and singing all involved
public speaking and that involved a loving voice that was
melodious, nuanced, and slow and fast and soft and hard
at the right times and places giving different voices to different persons.
Better public speaking did much for keeping the Sabbath holy
for that holiness was a reverence of praise, love, worship
and adoration and the public voice had to be trained in all of that.
Each day at lunch and at supper we would often listen to a book
that one of the students read over the microphone and in my last
two years Father Bernard asked me to help the students with reading.
So one would read for a week and we would practice the art of
reading together so that all could enjoy not only the book but also
the way in which it was read with grace, dignity and even humor.
Moses himself was a great public speaker and not only read the Ten
Commandments to himself but spoke them to others most properly.
Moses was God's spokesman and each Sabbath the Jewish priest
or Rabbi would be God's spokesman and it was their great task
to keep the Sabbath holy in a way that would invite others to do it too.

I,6.4   In 4th Commandment Obedience with better Listening

I am most thankful for my parents who began teaching me most
of all the liberal art of listening from my earliest childhood.
My mother would read to me in her beautiful voice from my Mother
Goose Nursery Rhyme book and from my Bible Story book.
Already at the age of three I started learning some of the Nursery Rhymes.
My father began teaching my prayers to me when I was five
and I listened very carefully as he began teaching me how to fish
and how to hunt and I really wanted to do these things with him.
So again obeying the fourth commandment was natural for me
and I always believed it as well as kept it for it said at Exodus 20:12:

> Honor your father and your mother so that
> you may have a long life in the land that
> Yahweh your God has given to you.

If one has very loving parents who deeply love each other it
probably does give him or her the opportunity for a long and happy
life for the trauma of divorce might greatly wound the child.
It is natural to love and honor your parent if you learn love
from them because emotional contagion is a powerful way of listening.
One of the aspects of being a good listener is to be a good questioner.
It is good to be obedient without questioning one's superior or
without questioning God and his commandment but the more we
learned in the seminary the more questions would arise.
In a way being a good listener who questions may lead to
a questioning of oneself such as with me when I wondered why
commandments two and six were so hard and the others so easy.
Being a good listener is also very much a part of being a good lover.
I did not only listen to my parents but they listened always to me.
Friends are those who grow in listening by listening to each other.
Lovers want to know each other Biblically and listen to every nuance
of love making's secret sounds and to know each other completely.
Growth in affection, friendship, *eros* and *agape* depends on listening.

Agape and *Hesed*

I,6.5 In 5th Commandment Obedience with better Dreaming

As our Alma Mater, the Benedictine Community of Mt. Angel, nourished
us year after year we found that our dreaming too could be a liberal art.
I first started talking with Father Ambrose about dreaming when
I told him about my sexual dreams and he told me about Jesus
taking the Sixth Commandment further by saying that you have
already committed adultery if you even desire a woman lustfully.
Of course, he said, we are not responsible for what we dream but
we discussed St. Augustine who in his *Confessions* no longer had
any problem with sex after his conversion but did dream about it.
I wondered if even our dreams could mature into a total celibacy.
It also began to occur to me that Jesus' thinking could also
apply to the fifth commandment at Exodus 20:13, which said:

> You shall not kill.

Again I never thought of this commandment as being problematic.
I never wanted to kill anybody and I never thought that I would.
But, wasn't my getting angry at people and swearing on an
habitual basis a committing of murder just as thinking about
a girl sexually already was a type of adultery according to Jesus.
Examining our conscience in terms of the Ten Commandments
was meant to develop a more sensitive conscience within us
In fact, the goal was to change our fundamental attitude which
which could even transform our dreaming and make it creative.
I heard from different scholars that when they were very involved
in writing they did not remember dreaming and often they would
awaken with new ideas for their writing as if they dreamed them.
I found this to be very intriguing and I wanted to nourish the art
of dreaming so that the dream day experience of my writing
could develop further and very creatively even while I was sleeping.
The liberal arts of reading, writing, speaking and listening
could all be greatly aided even by our dreaming if we would
transform our dreaming by being scrupulous about the commandments.

I,6.6 Growing in 6th Commandment Obedience with better Thinking

The whole point of growing in that seed bed was to become like Jesus.
One's thoughts, words and deeds at the conscious level are directed
by one's attitude, mood and feelings at the pre-conscious level.
We aimed at getting his *agape*ic attitude so that our thinking would
clearly see the good in the other even if there was a lot of bad.
We aimed at spontaneous affirmative reactions so that we would
see the other as more important than ourself just as Jesus did.
Instead of negative reactions of ressentiment we tried to build up
a thinking of proactive affirmations for all persons, places and things.
The sixth commandment at Exodus 20:14, which said:

> You shall not commit adultery.

was the one that made me think most of all for the priesthood
demanded that we be celibate that we might be free to serve
widows, orphans and aliens as did Jesus and even be the Servant
of 2nd Isaiah with Jesus in offering our lives as a sacrifice.
Of course, we grow in the liberal arts of reading, writing, speaking
listening and even dreaming the more clearly and coherently we think.
The spiritual, intellectual and moral virtues as well as physical
excellence all depend on right thinking whose standard is the truth.
If our minds in their thinking conform to the way things are
then we will have a healthy, happy, wise and holy thinking.
It is always very easy for us to fool ourselves and tell ourselves
lies that we believe because it is more convenient and self-serving.
But a priest cannot get away with that because people can see
through you very easily and they will just leave the church if
it is not at all times teaching humankind's highest affirmation.
Everyone can speak and think of love and say that all religions
have in common the golden rule but without thinking clearly
and deeply about love in the world religions and really paying
attention to their most basic differences one is not engaging
in right thinking and anyone can easily get a sense of that.

Agape and *Hesed*

I,6.7 In 7th Commandment Obedience with better Wonder

As the Monks nourished our thinking we came to discover wonder.
For it is a big part of our culture that we should think within
the limits of reason alone and in our pride forget any mystery.
We always thought about mystery: the Joyful, Sorrowful and
Glorious mysteries and not only the mystery of the infinite and
the eternal but also the mystery of the finite and the temporal.
We believed that all that God created is good and that if we only
developed our wonder we would appreciate the mystery.
In the communal life of our Alma Mater there was a wonder
that naturally grew out of the vows of poverty, chastity and obedience.
Being obedient to the seventh commandment at Exodus 20:15:

> You shall not steal.

was once again no problem if you followed Jesus and Paul and
the Early Church in having communal but no personal property.
There is something mysterious and wonderful in the way Jesus
renewed and gave a further meaning to each of the Ten Commandments.
Already it is some kind of wonderful that the First Commandment
once Jesus renews it sees God as the Love between the three persons.
That Love and what it implies for human persons is already
humankind's highest affirmation in that it loves each person
as having equal dignity, each as unique and all as interpersonal.
That is already the basis for communal living and should
promote a system of health, education and welfare for everyone.
If we saw each person as wonderful there would be no more stealing.
In fact each of the commandments flow from the meaning of the first.
If we do not think merely within the limits of reason alone but let
faith and reason work together we could begin to get beyond modernity
which with its faith alone or reason alone does not appreciate
the wonder that the heart has its reasons the mind knows not.
If we do not in our pride close ourselves to wonder we will be
able to have faith in a love that wonders at all things.

I,6.8 In 8th Commandment Obedience with better Gratitude

Thinking is at the heart of each of the liberal arts which help us to grow in the excellence of the theological, intellectual, moral, and physical virtues which it was our task to cultivate at Mt. Angel. Heidegger writes of "*Denken als Danken*" of "Thinking as Thanking" and that brings us from another angel to the wonder of thinking. Sometimes we would mention to one of the priests that so and so is really a problem lately and he would listen to us and we would talk about him but in the end he would say: "He is not a problem but a gift." Heidegger is concerned with the technical thinking of our present age which gets caught up in problems, causes and solutions and forgets that each existing being is a gift of Being or as the Monk would say: "of God." In that seedbed the spirit of gratitude was constantly cultivated by our prayer life for prayer is adoration, repentance, thanksgiving and petition and our main petition was that we and all of ours might love the better, repent our lack of love and be thankful for our love. As modern scientists and technicians become more specialized there is the danger that they can forget the big picture and with a lack of wisdom begin to suffer from a thinking lacking in gratitude. The spirit of wonder for the monks even had to do with miracles. A miracle is an event that science cannot explain and there can be healing miracles or all sorts of miracles that are evidence for saintliness and that is why miracles help a saint be canonized. *Mirare* means to wonder and such words as admire and miracle come from it and the saintly life as distinct from the scientific life has to do with a thinking that is full of wonder and of gratitude. Of course, scientists should be full of wonder too for they work with the miracle of life and of existence and the scientists in the Monastery took delight in teaching us about the marvels of the heavens that we would look at through a telescope or the marvels of an amoeba which we would behold with the microscope. Deep down in a person's faith is a wonder at the universe.

Agape and *Hesed*

I,6.9 In 9-10*th* Commandment Obedience with better Empathy

Besides teaching us to think with wonder and thanksgiving the Monks cultivated within us a spirit of empathy which goes beyond sympathy and its compassion to listening to the feelings of another about his or her inner self so that you come to know and feel them from within. Feeling another from within is different from feeling with another in that in empathy you might understand others better than they understand themselves so that for the spiritual advisor empathy is a very helpful sort of intuition that the more mature person can have. Once again as we meditated on the Ten Commandments bearing false witness against my neighbor did not seem to be a problem for me. But if somebody were to bear false witness against me the Monks taught me that my first reaction should be to pray for them. Even if they were trying to get me fired I should know with a kind of empathy that the sword they were trying to plunge into me would have to go through their own body first many times before it could ever touch me and then I should even be grateful for them, because a trial to be gone through can be a gift rather than a problem. To love the one who bears false witness against us can be a gift for all in that love is a giving of gifts and many can see the love also the ninth and tenth commandments at Exodus 20:17:

> You shall not covet your neighbor's house
> or your neighbor's wife or servant
> or anything that is his.

This sort of envy or jealousy could be quite a problem for me because I could easily desire or covet any beautiful female and it was as if the project of being celibate only increased the passion. As we try to think about Jesus and the women who followed him with empathy could we say that his sublimated *agapeic eros* let him love them in their own unique femininity and that they in turn loved him with an *agapeic erotic* empathy that let their emotional contagion go out and infect others with love for him?

II. With Jewish Postmodernists

II,4   Derrida's Ethics as First Philosophy Demands

II.4,1 Improving Demonstrations with deconstruction

As we begin to understand the nature and role of Derrida's ethics
as first philosophy so that we can see how his metaphysics of excess,
his epistemology of nominalism and his logic of mixed opposites
arises out of it, it will be helpful for us first to see how all of
his major ideas fit together systematically in an interrelated whole.
Ethics for him has to do with pure giving and the impossibility
of that since we will always receive returns for our giving.
As we think through the interconnected meaning of his ideas
we might build it all around his example of the hedgehog
in *Che cos'è la poesia? What is this thing called poetry?*
A new highway was built through the territory of some hedgehogs,
and one Spring day Mr. Hedgehog was called across the highway
by Miss Hedgepiggy and he started to cross the road at once
to respond to her call but busy cars and trucks were speeding by.
He halted in fright right in the middle of the road and rolled
up in a ball projecting his quills as he always did to protect himself.
He had to make his decision over the abyss of indecidability.
Should he go forward or retreat or just stay still in his ball?
This poetic possibility is there for each of us when we are called
to the responsibility of pure giving and Derrida seeks to clarify it.
Traditionally philosophical thinking proceeded with the four D's
of demonstration, definition, distinction, and dialectical reasoning.
In accord with the metaphysical excess that ethical decisions reveal
Derrida must improve upon each of these with his own four D's
of deconstructing demonstration by disseminated definitions
differencing distinctions and showing the double dissymmetry
that is involved in the dialectical testing of demonstrations.
If we seek to be wise and know the truth about the becoming
of our decision we should demonstrate that they are right.
But because of the complexity of each event this is impossible.

Agape and *Hesed*

II,4.2 Improving Definitions with Dissemination

In traditional philosophy as you were proving your point or demonstrating your thesis you would define your terms with essential, causal, descriptive, and etymological definitions so that all could agree upon the precise meaning of the various terms. You could argue, for example, that the human is a rational animal and show that what she or he does proceeds from certain kinds of material, formal, efficient and final causes and you could describe their vegetative, animal and strictly human activities. If I wanted to demonstrate that it would be valuable for a person to habitually perform spiritual, intellectual, vital and physical exercises I could use the various definitions of each term in order to help demonstrate my thesis to those whom I am addressing. Derrida shows, however, that the disconcerting law of dissemination keeps any definition from being adequate because there is a gap between any addressor and any addressee and any addressor and his words for anything we try to define is so complicated that no universal term will ever express all of it completely. in *A Derrida Reader, Between the Blinds*, edited by Peggy Kamuf, Derrida explains that on pages 87–90, and all the ideas we treat here will be found in that excellent reader. In 1972, Derrida published his book *Dissemination* and the chapter called *Plato's Pharmacy* is in *The Reader* pages 112–39. In Plato's *Phaedrus* 274e, Socrates tells Phaedrus the story of how the God Theuth gave to Thamus the art of writing and he said: "My discovery provides a recipe for memory and wisdom." The word recipe is a translation for *pharmakon* which is a drug that can both heal or addict and Thamus the King goes on to say that this is a pharmakon not for memory but reminder for memory will be weakened and it is not for wisdom but the conceit of wisdom for even fools who read might get superficial wisdom. So the work Pharmakon is disseminated with opposite meanings.

II,4.3 Improving Distinctions with Differance

By becoming a skeptic Socrates developed an ethics which moved from pride to humility, from pretension to honesty, from pondorosity to humor, from pomposity to health and Derrida's ethics as first philosophy is doing that too with its four D's. Derrida is always concerned with bringing about less violence. The Pharmakon shows us the logic of paradox or mixed opposites. It is both a remedy and a poison and Derrida shows how this brings us to decisions over the abyss of undecidability just as the hedgehog faced when he wanted to cross the road to give gifts. In developing his ethics of the leap over the abyss of undecidability Derrida deconstructs Levinas infinite other, Malebranche's morals and knowledge, Socrates' aporia, Plato's Pharmakon and Rousseau's dangerous supplement throughout *The Reader*. Ethics for him treats the question of violence and the question of responsibility and in treating the response he deals with the metaphysics of excess and dissemination especially by treating Husserl's shading or signs, Heidegger's time, Hegel's prefaces and Nietzsche's perspectives to show that each of them treats a similar idea be it: "writing, trace differance, supplement, hymen, pharmakon or parergon." He discusses this list of similar terms on pages 65 and 275. So connected with his notion of dissemination complicating every definition as the poison complicates the remedy there is his notion of differance that complicates all our distinctions. In *The Reader* on pages 65-66 and pages 569-70 he shows how differance improves our practical usage of distinctions by demonstrating that each here and now is distinguished from other heres and nows by intervals of space and time and that there are unlimited intervals within each here and now so that no distinction is complete so that we much always leap. Every decision is an aleatory throw of the dice full of possibilities.

II,4.4 Improving Dialectics with a Double Dissymmetry

When traditional philosophers demonstrate a thesis they give arguments for it and then dialectically answer objections to it. They consider the antithesis to their thesis and answer the arguments against their own arguments so that this dialectical reasoning is a key element of any demonstration as it was for Plato and Hegel. A Platonic Dialogue is structured dialectically in that Socrates is always arguing back and forth with his opponents and while the dialectics of the later Plato differ from the dialectics of the early and middle Plato we do not have to consider that here. Modern philosophy mostly because it did not consider the history of ideas did not argue dialectically but Hegel fully recovered that. He had his famous method of a thesis, then an antithesis and then a synthesis which was a new thesis calling forth a new antithesis. Because dialectical reasoning is a movement of thought from the one to the many of distinction and then the many to the one of definition it is fraught for Derrida with the double impossibility coming from the dissemination of definition and the play of differance. The trip of Derrida's hedgehog is unlike that of the Platonic dialectic out of the cave and that of the Hegelian Dialectic up the staircase because the gaps of dissemination and difference are a bad infinite that cannot be stopped up with a fully present simple and stable good infinite whether as *arche* or *telos*. We may wonder why uncertainty is an improvement on certainty. But if as Derrida shows any decision we make will have outcomes that are complicated and of mixed blessing then it is honest for us to admit that and it is humble and healthy also. To be honest and humble is already an ethical attitude and if it can lead to better health and even to humor then that Socratic ethical attitude which Derrida espouses is good. Once the hedgehog becomes uncertain about getting across the road he can at least be honest and humble about the facts of life.

II,4.5 Improving Decisions with Indecidability

Indecidability could take ethics into nihilism and relativism
but an ethics of indecidability protects the singularity of the ethical
subject with the absolute non-historical events of his or her free
creative decision which could not be free and creative if calculated.
An ethics of indecidability valorizes the worth of others as hedgehogs
can choose to respond to the call of the other with the leap of faith.
An ethics of indecidability can let the gap of the abyss open into
the space of freedom letting one say yes and amen to any result.
The road the hedgehog chooses to cross is an abyss of indecidability.
Derrida's hedgehog gives the other a pure gift which is not mutual.
In Buber's I-thou relation the hedgehogs would both cross the road
for each other but it would still be the abyss of indecidability.
Only in an I-it relation could things be objectively calculated.
The hedgehog in the context of Levinas' *Totality and Infinity*
would be called by the faces of widows, orphans and aliens
to cross the abyss of indecidability without any reciprocity.
There is no argument that widows orphans and aliens or anyone
for that matter should help me for it is a one way responsibility.
The hedgehog of *Totality and Infinity* is much like Derrida's.
But with the coming of the third and philosophy of justice
in *Otherwise Than Being* the hedgehogs are responsible to each other.
However, as suffering servants they can give the gift of death
and the sacrifice of their own lives as with Derrida's hedgehog.
Socrates' aporetic ethics took him beyond the fear of death.
As the wisest man in Athens who knew that he knew nothing
his ethics could become a self-realization ethics of the "know
thyself" so that over the abyss of indecidability he could be humble.
But Levinas and Derrida with the hedgehog Socrates lacks
have instead another realization ethics which is more Jewish.
How different are Levinas and Derrida and is Derrida's
deconstructive philosophy a wisdom of love in the service of love?

Agape and *Hesed*

II,4.6 Improving Desires with Donation

The Greek ethics of self-realization was based upon the desire
for happiness and virtues such as justice were means to that end.
So Greek ethics was one of desire and Jewish ethics one of donation.
The Greek loves of affection, *eros* and friendship were loves
of desire that wanted to possess and have the best possession for
my family, my beloved and my friend and this desire implied
a built-in exclusivity for I would love mine more than others.
The Hebrew loves of *hesed* and *ahava* were altruistic rather than
egoistic for I should love the Lord, my God, with my whole heart
mind and soul and widows, orphans and aliens as myself.
So just as Levinas is improving upon the metaphysical desire
of Plato for the Infinite with his altruistic asymmetrical giving
so Derrida's four Jewish D's even though they are also Socratic
are Jewish ways of explaining the donation that exceeds desire.
The wisdom of *hesed* and *ahava* teach Levinas' hedgehog
as he sees the face or hears the cry of the other to become
the suffering servant and to sacrifice himself for the other.
Does Derrida keep more of the Greek love of wisdom as he explains
his philosophy in terms of the donation demanding deconstruction?
When asked "What is this thing called Poetry" Derrida responds
on page 223 of *A Derrida Reader*,

> In order to respond to such a question—in
> two words, right?—you are asked to know
> how to renounce knowledge. And to know
> it well, without ever forgetting it: demobi-
> lize culture, but never forget in your learned
> ignorance what you sacrifice on the road, in
> crossing the road.

Derrida has renounced Greek objective knowledge with his 4 D's.
He has demobilized the Greek culture and he never forgets it.
For he knows that on the road he is sacrificing demonstration
definition, distinction, dialectics and defending desire.

II,4.7 Improving the Death of Debt with Divine Redemption

Once Derrida deconstructs the Greek ethics of desire from
the point of view of the Jewish ethics of donation he comes to
the problem of atoning for our injustice, paying our debts
and making up for what we fail to give from our hospitality.
Marko Zlomislic in his book *Jacques Derrida's Aporetic Ethics*
on page 44 quotes Derrida:

> I'm not sure there is pure hospitality.
> But if we want to understand what
> hospitality means, we have to think of
> unconditional hospitality, that is,
> openness to whomever, to any newcomer.

This ideal is impossible to practice politically for who would
be so foolish as to welcome the good and the bad without any
thought about who might harm us and who might not?
If the hedgehog has an ethics of going across the road
in hospitality to anyone who calls him he could be far
more threatened than just by the cars that might kill him.
Derrida develops an ethics of the impossible pure giving
and it is always going to leave the giver guilty for never
being totally helpful to even the enemy who calls out to him.
No matter how hard he tries to be of service to the other
he will always fail to do total justice with total hospitality.
Derrida says that deconstruction is justice and it does help
us to see the difference between desiring and giving justice.
But within the hospitality of pure giving there will always be
differance and a complexity of mixed opposites so that we will
hurt some no matter how hard we try we will be unjust.
The Christian ethics of Kierkegaard and Nietzsche will let
Jesus redeem this death and with his death bring death to debt.
So as we proceed we will have to see how Derrida's God helps.

Agape and Hesed

II,4.8 Improving Delirium with Dream Work

As the hedgehog tries to cross the highway he can be traumatized.
In the second paragraph on page 223 Derrida writes:

> I am a dictation, pronounces poetry,
> learn me by heart, copy me down, guard and
> keep me, look out for me, look at me,
> dictated dictation, right before your eyes:
> soundtrack, wake, trail of light, photograph
> of the feast in mourning.

Just as Derrida works with many deconstructed themes of Plato
so Freud is a central figure in the many voices of his thinking.
Freud's psychoanalytic approach to healing madness or delirium
has a lot to do with the mourning process and the talking cure
that aims at getting our dream work to bring us to affirmation.
As the hedgehog practices the pure giving of his hospitality
that brings him to his trauma how can he not go crazy?
As the hedgehog rolls up in his ball of fear and trembling,
in his ball of dread and despair he does receive by way of
a kind of inspiration this traumatic fixed idea that will haunt him.
He has learned this by heart and it could continue to horrify him.
As he begins his mourning process he is shocked and angry.
He feels like cursing these cars and trucks but he has to keep
his cool and maybe by being still they will be able to miss him.
He does learn this trauma by heart and it will be with him
forever but it might remain negative or it might become a feast
or a festival of mourning which will add to the gift he is giving.
This hedgehog trauma is an event of unconditional hospitality
and it can destroy the hedgehog and also the other hedgehog.
But the right kind of dream work and the right kind of mourning
process can become a talking cure that will sublimate this
horror into a most beautiful and holy poem for the other.
The donation of the four D's are all part of Derrida's dream work.

II,4.9 Improving Destiny with Densite

Derrida is as much a Nietzschean as he is Platonic and Freudian.
As he explores his Jewish ethics of unconditional hospitality
that has traumatized so many Jews he sees how Nietzsche
has improved upon the Platonic and Freudian sublimation process.
Nietzsche was a brilliant bipolar misfit who in August of 1881
received a poematic inspiration about the eternal return of all.
He saw himself to be enchained by the mania and the depression
of his illness but all of a sudden he learned how to dance
in his chains as his became a divine madness that let him
say yes and amen to all of existence and even to will the eternal
return of his own illness again and again for all eternity.
And that willing of the eternal return of his own sick self
let his become a creative illness that made of him a genius.
Nietzsche learned how to dance with the density of his trauma
and the very weight of his trauma became a light hearted
and light footed dance of joyful wisdom that could take him
beyond the love of wisdom to a love of folly, the folly of Jesus
who in the Anti-Christ became for Nietzsche the creative child.
The Drama of Zarathustra moves from the Camel of Christian
Platonism to the Lion of the Enlightenment to the Lioness
of Romanticism to the all loving child who affirms all.
Derrida knew well of what Nietzsche called: "Mankind's
highest affirmation" and his hedgehog lives out this affirmation.
But still the Jewish Derrida is not the Nietzsche who reports
on the death of many God's opening the way for Jesus.
Derrida's writing, like Nietzsche's, loves to laugh and play
and dance with is honest, humble, healthy humor.
So now it is our task to see just how Derrida is a postmodern
like Kierkegaard and Nietzsche and Hopkins and yet how
he makes a conscious point of being different as Jewish.

Agape and *Hesed*

II,5 What it Means that Love as Pure Giving is Impossible

II,5.1 Jewish Altruism seeks to give the Pure Gift

The Jewish duty love of *hesed* and the felt love of *ahava* are both excellently symbolized by Derrida's hedgehog who is called to give a pure gift without concern for self to the hedgehog across the road. If we think of Levinas this hedgehog is the symbol of the one who says, "Here I am." to the calling face of widows, orphans and aliens and the Suffering Servant who lovingly responds even to enemies. Derrida calls this Jewish non-reciprocal response a pure giving. We give purely when we do not desire any reward for our gift. He argues that this is the very nature of what we mean by gift. As Derrida writes on page 12 of *Given Time;*

> For there to be a gift, there must be
> no reciprocity, return, exchange,
> countergift, or debt. If the other
> gives me back or owes me or has
> to give me back what I give him or her,
> there will not have been a gift.

As the two kinds of love develop through the history and theology of the Hebrew Bible there became more and more emphasis upon a loving that did not expect to be reciprocally loved in return. Derrida's hedgehog makes a mad leap over the abyss of indecidability. He shows us that a distinction between the giving and the gift can be made for while there can be no pure gift there can be a pure giving that madly leaps with an unconditional hospitality. Even if the hedgehog thought that it was his duty to respond his giving would not be pure for that would give him self-realization. As we ponder Derrida's two books: *Given Time* and *The Gift of Death* we will try to see if he does distinguish a possible pure giving from the impossible pure gift and we will have to see what the significance of this impossibility is for his thinking.

II,5.2 Which can be Traumatic and Joyful Folly at Once

On pages 51–52 of *Given Time* Derrida discusses the response
of Jean-Luc Marion to his own thinking about pure giving.
Marion shows how Husserl and Heidegger both treat the given.
Husserl begins thinking with the givenness of things themselves.
Heidegger thinks we are called by Being not to forget Being and
to give ourselves over to the call of Being by responding to it.
However, Marion like Levinas argues that this call comes
from the Father and not from things themselves nor from Being.
At the bottom of page 52 Derrida quotes Marion who writes
that both the Jew and the Christian have their source in the

> Hear O Israel: The Lord our God is one Lord.

So Derrida is very clear with Marion about Jewish, Greek
and Christian conceptions of the call to give and on page 54
he begins to discuss the madness of any transcendental call
to us to give in the Husserlian, Heideggerian Greek way, or
the Jewish with Levinas or the Christian with Marion for

> [t]he transcendental question or rather
> the question *on* the transcendental
> gets complicated, it even goes a little mad.

This madness begins when the distinction is made
between a given thing and the condition for that giving.
A Lady may want to give her time to a charitable institution.
Her given time makes it possible for her to give this or that
concrete gift such as teaching a girl or giving her a dress.
Levinas would have her look at the face of the girl
which calls out to help her with her reading and with a dress.
But there is also the transcendent dimension of the call
in which the Father, the Lord our God, calls Levinas as
a Jew to respond to the call of widows, orphans and aliens.
This complicated calling takes one from the wisdom of self
realization to the mad folly of a leap into a pure giving.

II,5.3 *The Pure Gift of Giving our Time is Impossible*

As Derrida thinks through the madness of the gift he writes on page 55 of *Given Time*:

> All these questions concern a certain madness of the gift, which is first of all the madness of dissemination of the meaning "gift."

Derrida focuses on giving because love is the giving of gifts. The *ahava* and *hesed* of the Hebrew Bible especially as Levinas interprets them call upon us to give without expecting any return. However, Derrida wants to show that the decision to give is a mad leap over the abyss of indecidability and this shows the distinctive character of Jewish love and its responsibility. Any decision has pros and cons and while Descartes thinks we should decide only when we know we are doing the right thing Derrida argues that that is impossible because of the *aporias* of never enough knowledge, never enough time and never enough precedents prevent us from ever getting any kind of certainty. If Levinas decides to care for an alien he can never know for certain that his particular way of caring is the best thing to do. Trying to get sufficient knowledge would be a decision to decide against the decision to meet the urgency of the others need. Taking more time would result in a procrastination that again prevent one from taking the mad leap of giving. Previous precedents even by Jewish holy ones will never be clear enough because each situation is new or unique. Even though the gift is disinterested and unmotivated there still must be the intention to give as Derrida writes on page 123:

> There is no gift without the intention of giving ... what would a gift be in which I gave without wanting to give and without knowing that I am giving, without the explicit intention of giving.

II,5.4 As is the Pure Gift of Giving our Life

We can imagine Levinas or Derrida's hedgehog intending to give
their time to another just as the lady would who gave her time
to work at the home for girls and this wanting to give is part of giving.
Maybe the lady will want to give all of her time to the girls just
as one might want to be a Rabbi and give his life to others.
But while intending to give some of our time or our whole life
is necessary for the giving Derrida shows that too is problematic.
While we must intend to give if there is to be giving still giving
takes place in a mad leap in which we do not know all that is
involved and thus there is something about the gift that we can
not intend because we do not know what will result from the gift.
As Derrida puts it on page 23

> Everything stemming from the intentional meaning
> also threatens the gift with self-keeping,
> with being kept in its very expenditure.

So if the lady wants to give of her time and the Rabbi wants
to give his life Derrida says that that threatens the gift
with self-keeping for the gift must be involuntary and intended.
He says:

> these two conditions must—miraculously,
> graciously—agree with each other.

When he says the gift must be involuntary he is saying that
I cannot will or intend all that will happen for I do not know that.
What happens Derrida refers to as the event and that event
can have a life of its own with all kinds of unknown possibilities.
So while the pure gift might be an ideal it is impossible
because there will be all kinds of returns that will come back to me.
I want to give the gift and yet much of it is involuntary for
I have no control over what it will bring to me and to others.
The Rabbi intends to give his life but that is threatened by a
self-keeping that might give him a wonderful life which he receives.

Agape and *Hesed*

II,5.5 As is the Pure Gift of Giving our Death

In *Given Time* Derrida discusses Marcel Mauss' work on giving. It is in the nature of any gift that there be something non-mutual about it for if I only give to you that you might give to me it is not really giving but a kind of trading or mere exchanging. Every gift should have something pure about it and especially the Jewish giving to which the Lord calls his people should be pure. Mauss according to Derrida gives many examples of how giving is really a reciprocal exchange and on page 37 of *Given Time* Derrida writes:

> Mauss is describing the potlatch. He speaks of it blithely as "gift exchanged. But he never asked the question as to whether gifts can remain gifts once they are exchanged.

After showing how giving gifts and giving time and giving our life should be pure but never are in his book, *Given Time*, Derrida goes on to *The Gift of Death* to see if Abraham's sacrifice of Isaac might be a pure gift in which Abraham gets nothing back. If God calls upon Abraham to sacrifice his son, Isaac, and Abraham offers the gift of his son's death is that not pure? Is not giving the gift of death pure in that we don't get life back? However, on page 129 in *Given Time* Derrida begins to address this question by showing how giving is related to mourning:

> I pretend to keep the dead alive, intact *safe* (save) inside me . . . to love the dead as a living part of me . . . as happens in so-called normal mourning.

If Abraham is a man of infinite resignation and gracefully offers the gift of his son's death to God then he can get Isaac back a second time by successfully mourning his death. The normal process of mourning again makes the pure gift impossible for I am giving that I might get his life in me.

II,5.6 How Derrida does not Catch Up with Kierkegaard

Derrida's ideal is that the giving of the gift be non-reciprocal
or pure so that the giver is not getting anything back in return.
His main idea is that this ideal is impossible for no matter
how self-sacrificing our giving is we always do get returns.
As we move to his analysis in *The Gift of Death* we will have
the opportunity to spell out how he differs from Kierkegaard.
The main point of distinction we must focus upon is the leap
as it stands at the very center of each of their existential philosophies.
As we have seen any event of giving for Derrida is a mad leap
over the abyss of indecidability because we know so little about the gift.
However, as Kierkegaard explains in *Fear and Trembling* Abraham
can perform a double movement leap in his sacrifice of Isaac.
As a Knight of Infinite Resignation he is willing to sacrifice Isaac.
But God has promised him land, nation and name for his family
will have a land flowing with milk and honey and he will be the
father of a people more numerous than the sands of the sea and the
stars of the sky and his name will be a blessing to all peoples.
If Isaac, his son, is taken away this promise will not be fulfilled.
Therefore, Abraham is willing to make the mad leap of sacrificing
Isaac but he also believes by virtue of the absurd that he will
get Isaac back a second time so pure giving is not Kierkegaard's ideal.
Kierkegaard does not have to worry about the impossibility of
the pure gift for giving the gift is only one half of his belief.
He believes that God loves him and will give him gifts for any
gift that he might give, not that he has merited them but
rather Jesus the Son of God who has sacrificed has merited them.
Kierkegaard does not have to believe in his own pure giving for he
believes that God has loved him with a pure giving that brought
him into being and that has redeemed him and all that he does.
If Kierkegaard as a grain of wheat falls into the ground and dies
it will bring forth many returns because he follows Jesus.

Agape and *Hesed*

II,5.7 And How Levinas Deconstructs Derrida

After Derrida deconstructed Levinas' *Totality and Infinity* Levinas went on to write *Otherwise Than Being* and avoid the logical, psychological, epistemological, Metaphysical and ethical pitfalls that Derrida had made clear about Levinas' inconsistencies. In the meanwhile Derrida got into his serious obsession with pure giving and spent several hundred pages showing its impossibility. Ideally our giving should be non-reciprocal but there are many kinds of return that accompany every act of love's pure giving. In response to this Levinas develops his notion of the third who can give to me just as I give to the other so true love of the other does not have to exclude all receiving from the other. Self-love and love of neighbor can be compatible and that is why the commandment says: "love your neighbor as yourself." Derrida is right in pointing out the many types of self-love that are involved in any attempt to practice *hesed* and *ahava*. Buber is right that an I-thou relation is mutual and Levinas moves toward him with his notion of the third and Derrida is right in pointing out that the pure I-Thou will always have something of the impure I-it for its the melancholy of our fate. On page 151 of *Given Time* Derrida considers the third party in a conversation between a debtor and his creditor and he says:

> The third party is excluded by the secret of the dual scene. The two of them, and only two, are talking in a tête-a-tête.

If there is to be pure giving I should try to keep it secret and not get praise from a third or be loved by that third. Derrida thinks that the spontaneous giving to widows, orphans and aliens should be like the giving of the hedgehog and have its special secret and if he becomes the suffering servant who gives his life for the other being seen by a third is nothing.

II,5.8 With a Justice of the Third Beyond Deconstructive Justice

In *Force of Law* Derrida argues that deconstruction is justice.
The aporias of deconstruction bring us to honesty and humility.
If the hedgehog's decision to give is so complicated that he must
make it in a mad leap over the abyss of indecidability then
looking at that decision honestly and humbly can increase its justice.
Derrida makes it clear that pure giving is impossible and so
trying to be just to others is always a matter of the mysterious.
Being aware of the dissemination of definitions and the differance
in each distinction which results in deconstruction brings a self
awareness that can help the one trying to be just to be more just.
But Levinas is not worried about pure giving and a pure justice.
In *Totality and Infinity* and up through *Otherwise Than Being* he does
argues that the face of the other calls me to a non-reciprocal pure giving.
But the gigantic meditation of Derrida on the impossibility of pure giving
does not enter into Levinas' thinking perhaps because he stresses
the wisdom of love rather than the love of wisdom which brings Derrida
to being primarily a philosopher who wants to work out clear thinking.
Of course, as postmodernists Levinas and Derrida both treat ethics as
first philosophy and so just love for others is their starting point.
Derrida's criticism of Levinas in *Violence and Metaphysics* was
primarily a criticism against the logic of exclusive opposites,
and metaphysics of presence, and the epistemology of certitude.
Levinas took Derrida's deconstruction to heart and in *Otherwise
Than Being* worked with a logic, epistemology, metaphysics and
psychology that was more in line with his ethics of Jewish justice.
Levinas treatment of the third and its wisdom of love and its kind of
justice could be read as also deconstructing Derrida's impossibility
of pure giving for, of course, its' impossible but that is alright.
Substitution is the real possibility of putting oneself in the place
of the other and it is not impossible any more than is my receiving
gifts of loving justice from a third who can respond to my face.

Agape and *Hesed*

II,5.9 So that the Impossible Pure Giving is not Necessary

Derrida gives an excellent account of the Jewish loves of *hesed* and *ahava*. He explains the non-reciprocity of the mad leap each time I am called by the other who is wholly other be it either God, man, or animal. When I take the responsibility for the other with an attempted pure giving I find that it is so complicated that pure giving is impossible. Derrida thinks that when we are giving we should not be getting. And in his book on *The Gift of Death* he thinks that Kierkegaard agrees with him and he interprets Kierkegaard's Knight of Faith as being like Abraham who is willing to renounce all in sacrificing Isaac and thereby sacrificing all that he loves in this world. But Kierkegaard clearly states on page 49 of *Fear and Trembling*

> By faith I do not renounce anything.
> On the contrary, by faith I receive everything
> exactly in the sense in which it is said
> that one who has faith like a mustard seed
> can move mountains . . . By faith Abraham
> did not renounce Isaac but he received Isaac.

On page 64 of *The Gift of Death* Derrida asks if this Knight of Faith who is willing to sacrifice Isaac is Judeo-Christian-Islamic? He concludes that:

> The sacrifice of Isaac belongs to what one
> might just dare to call the common treasure,
> the terrifying secret of the *mysterium tremendum*
> that is a property of all three so called
> religions of the book, the races of Abraham.

While Derrida has only the single movement leap of faith Kierkegaard is very clear throughout his whole philosophy about the double movement leap of faith by which the Knight of infinite resignation gives everything up and the Knight of faith gets it all back again. God had made the promise of land, nation and name to Abraham and so he had faith in the promise and thus in getting Isaac back.

II,6 How Kierkegaard might Deconstruct Derrida
II,6.1 Who Deconstructs him by Ignoring Agape

If Kierkegaard were to read Derrida's treatment of his philosophy of love in *The Gift of Death* he would point out that Derrida reduces his conception of *agape* to his own Jewish conceptions of love and thus misses everything that is new and unique about Christian love. At the core of Kierkegaard's philosophy of the existential dialectic is his conception of the four stages of our journey on life's way, which are the aesthetic, the ethical, religiousness A, religiousness B. The religious for Kierkegaard consists of two stages in which I get beyond the collisions between the aesthetic and the ethical by making a double movement leap of faith first by absolutely loving the absolute and then with Jesus relatively loving the relative. Right at the heart of the philosophies of Levinas and Derrida are the collisions between the aesthetic love of self and the ethical love of others. They both say "Here I am" to their absolute God with a leap of trust and thus their religious love is the basis for their Jewish ethics. But Derrida only sees a single movement leap in Kierkegaard. So what we must understand is how Kierkegaard's double movement leap lets aesthetic self-love and ethical altruism be compatible. Kierkegaard understands religiousness A as a higher level of the aesthetic and religiousness B as a higher level of the ethical. Kierkegaard's *agape* in its aesthetic dimensions is a felt love somewhat akin to *ahava* and in its ethical dimension is akin to *hesed's* duty love and it is this distinction that Derrida misses. Even though Kierkegaard only has the one term *agape* he always distinguishes its two stages and shows how they can be compatible. On the other hand in the Jewish tradition there are the two terms of *ahava* and *hesed* but Levinas and Derrida do not use these to show how aesthetic self-love and ethical altruism can be compatible and Derrida goes so far as to always stress the impossibility of pure giving because there will be self-love.

Agape and *Hesed*

II,6.2 Which Hates Preferential Love

Problem two in *Fear and Trembling* is entitled *Is there an Absolute Duty to God?* and much of it has to do with Luke 14:26

> If anyone come to me and does not hate
> his own father and mother and wife and
> children and brothers and sisters, yes, and
> even his own life, he cannot be my disciple.

The *agape* of Kierkegaard's philosophy which Jesus introduced is a love for all persons who have equal worth, for each person as unique and for all persons in their interpersonal relation in Christ's body. On page 34 of *Fear and Trembling* Johannes de Silentio writes:

> I am convinced that God is love; for me
> this thought has a primal lyrical validity.

Kierkegaard knows that this great truth from John's first letter has to do with the three persons of God loving each other and that it is the foundation of the notion of personhood in Christianity. But a great task is implied if we are to love God absolutely and all persons with an equal love for there is a self-love in the three natural loves of affection, friendship and *eros* and we have to get rid of this preferential love so that we might love all equally. This passage from Luke about hating our beloved ones has to do with this process of purifying our hearts and coming to a true *agape*. The pseudonym, de Silentio, treats this theme of hatred at length in *Fear and Trembling* and Kierkegaard takes it up himself and explains it fully in *Works of Love* starting on page 108

> Therefore Christianity teaches that the Christian
> must, if it is to be required, to be able
> to hate father and mother and sister
> and the beloved—in a sense, I wonder
> that he should actually hate them.

Kierkegaard well knew from Luther about the self-love that can be in our natural loves and he shows how this must be purified.

II,6.3 In Order to Absolutely Love the Absolute

Both Jewish and Christian love believe in loving the Lord your God
with your whole heart, mind and soul and your neighbor as yourself.
But Levinas and Derrida stress the non-reciprocity of Jewish love.
I do not love God or others that I might get anything out of it
but I love them even if I am tormented and not rewarded in the process.
So soon as Levinas looked at Kierkegaard's *agape* he detected
a reward for Kierkegaard thinks that any good I do will be rewarded.
Whatever I do for God or for others will make heaven better for me.
But Derrida is more sympathetic toward Kierkegaard then is Levinas.
Given the impossibility of pure giving Derrida is not so harsh
with Kierkegaard but he does not appreciate how Kierkegaard
has the purification of love at the core of his understanding of *agape*.
That is the entire point of how Kierkegaard interprets the passage
from Luke 14:26 about hating all those loves that involve self-love.
Kierkegaard does not mean that I should hate any of my dear ones
but he does mean that I should hate the spontaneous, preferential
love which is a self-love which absolutely prefers mine to others.
With this passage from Luke Jesus has shown us what we must do
if we are to move beyond *ahava* and *hesed* to his new *agapeic* love.
As Levinas and Derrida make clear we should have a love
that is a pure giving but *agape* is purified giving rather than
a pure giving for Kierkegaard has a both/and rather than an either/or.
If I do go through the *agapeic* process of cooperating with
the grace Jesus' teaching gives me and do not love my own
more than I love the other then by hating self-love I will be able
to absolutely love Love itself which is God and then my neighbors.
If I obey the command of love and love all my neighbors equally
then I will absolutely love Love as I should love all universally.
That is the new character of *agape* that with it there is no longer
Jew nor Greek, nor master nor slave, nor male nor female
for we are all persons and we should universally love all others.

Agape and *Hesed*

II,6.4 And then Relatively Love the Relative

Kierkegaard spells out how to purify love with his analogy of the house in terms of which he explain the four stages of love on life's way. Our life is like living in a house with a basement, first floor and second floor and we can only live in the aesthetic basement where we immediately love others without reflecting on any ethical implications. However, we can move up to the ethical first floor and love all others out of duty and then we can go to the religious second floor and absolutely love the absolute or love God with heart, mind and soul. However, what the God-man teaches us to do is live on all floors of the house at once so that we can also relatively love the relative. After the purification process of hating our affection, friendship and *eros* which each have a built in exclusivistic self-love for I love my child more than other children, my friend more than other persons, my beloved more than other persons, I can come back after a universal love to a special love and relatively love my own with a spontaneity that is secondary to my true love. This is the main point of Kierkegaard's philosophy of love and getting a pure love for others with a secondary self-love for my own is his conception of loving my neighbor as I love also myself. Levinas and Derrida strangely seem to distort the second command. In the realm of natural love it is possible that my child or my friend or my beloved could be like God for me whom I love like an idol as if they were my absolute whom I love and adore absolutely. I must constantly practice this hatred of a false absolute love in order that I might come to a purity of heart and will one thing which is to love in the true way of love itself and thus love all with a right order that gives to God, to neighbor and to my special ones their own kind of love which Jesus has revealed. The God-man helps me to rightly love the eternal and the temporal.

II,6.5 *That he Loves a Self-Love that is not Pure*

Kierkegaard's use of the hatred command lets him purify false love.
There is not only the false love of loving my own and myself too much
but there is also the false love of not loving myself and my own enough.
By promoting the pure gift and the pure giving Derrida does not
have an adequate self-love that the second commandment orders.
By promoting the ideal of pure giving he finds that God's world
is not what it should be for pure giving turns out to be impossible.
The idea that he promotes turns out to be self-contradictory
as he shows in both *Given Time* and *The Gift of Death* and
Kierkegaard's philosophy of *agape* shows what is wrong with his
understanding both of *ahava* and its felt love for others and
of *hesed* and its duty love for others which exclude any reciprocity.
Kierkegaard loves *agape* which secondarily is a self-love which
is not pure for after it absolutely loves the absolute it does
relatively love the relative and lets me love myself and my own.
In fact it does not only let me love myself but it commands
that I love my neighbor as I love myself as if self-love is even
the standard for loving others or giving and getting is the way
God has always wanted it even in the world of *hesed* and *ahava*.
Buber is much closer to Jesus and Kierkegaard than are Levinas
and Derrida even though Buber also fails to understand Kierkegaard.
Deep down Levinas and Derrida must think that Jewish love
must be non-reciprocal because of the vast gulf between God and man.
God might initiate a covenant with Moses and his people but it is
not really a reciprocal relation because it is gift on God's part
and mostly failure on man's part even though it should be reciprocal.
When God gave his promise of everlasting merciful *hesed* to David
he knew that David would often break his law and David would
be punished but still the non-reciprocal *hesed* would last forever.
By becoming the God-man Jesus did become a mediator between
God and man and thus *agape* is a reciprocal God-man love.

Agape and Hesed

II,6.6 In Primarily Loving all Others and Secondarily his Own

Kierkegaard's *agape*ic formula is to absolutely love the
absolute and to relatively love the relative and we can
understand what this means in terms of Derrida's hedgehog.
The hedgehog can be called across the abyss of indecidability
by a great variety of voices calling out for his gift of help.
There might be Levinasian widows, orphans and aliens calling
out for a non-reciprocal pure giving and it might even be
an enemy calling out for the suffering servant to give of his life.
It might even be miss hedgepiggy who would simply like a
a good time of impure fornication or of King David like adultery.
There is no question of pure giving if she is like Bathsheba bathing.
On the other hand, the call might come from a family member
or a beloved or a friend so that the hedgehog has a spontaneous
preferential love of affection or friendship or *eros* for them.
It is this kind of love that concerns Kierkegaard and the
purification process of hating one's own self-love that we might
come with a purity of heart to love Love as Jesus taught us.
From this variety of motives that might call the hedgehog across
the road we can see how differently Derrida and Kierkegaard think
about pure giving and how Derrida totally misses Kierkegaard's points.
Kierkegaard's process of hating impure loves so that one might get
one's loving attitude right is not even thought of by Derrida.
Derrida does not consider the impurity of fornication and
adultery and he does not consider the self-love in natural love.
The hedgehog for Kierkegaard should respond to any voice
because it comes from a person and then distinctions need
to be made for if she wants adultery that is a poison gift
and a prayerful love for her should be given that wants to help her.
Once the hedgehog goes out to every person with an equal
neighbor love then he can care for his own especially.
This love is good even though it is not pure in Derrida's eyes.

II,6.7 Because Unlike Abraham God did Sacrifice his Son
Derrida is very helpful in explaining clearly the Jewish ideal
of love that is a non-reciprocal pure giving and is impossible.
His hedgehog does take responsibility and respond to any call
with a mad leap which has to do with not knowing what will happen.
The event of loving widows, orphans and aliens and of being
willing to be the suffering servant can make the lover suffer.
Besides being so clear and helpful about all of this in *Given Time*
and in *The Gift of Death* Derrida is also an extremely good
philosopher in showing how this pure giving is impossible
by distinguishing the many ways in which self-love contaminates
any attempt to practice the Jewish ideal love of pure giving.
Derrida brings us to think about Jewish love as a *Praeparatio*
Evangelica or a preparation of the Good News of Jesus' *agape*.
Many Church Fathers, theologians and philosophers have thought
about the ways in which *The Hebrew Bible* prepares the way for
the Gospel especially with the central idea of love in both.
The God of the Jews is the creator, the King and the Judge
whom we should love with our whole heart, mind and soul
and we should love our fellow Jewish neighbor as we love ourselves.
But when out of love for us the creator became a creature and
the King became a servant and the Judge became our brother
the new *Agape* came forth out of the preparatory *hesed* and *ahava*.
Jesus the God-man practiced a pure giving for all creation.
As God by his incarnation, suffering and death all for love
of us he received nothing in return as the perfect God.
And yet by revealing that we are all members of his body
and that we are all interpersonal persons he showed that true
love need not be so pure that it ought not to help the lover.
Because we are all connected it is natural that when I love
another I also love myself and thus as long as I love all
persons equally I can love my own even in a self-loving way.

Agape and *Hesed*

II,6.8 Out of Love for Us

The great problem for Levinas and Derrida is to show how
Jewish altruistic love can be compatible with egoistic love.
They know any affection, *eros* or friendship involves a self
love and Levinas tries to make them compatible with his notion
of the third which allows the other other to love me as I love the other.
Derrida does not accept Levinas solution and he just wants
to be utterly honest in showing that any altruism involves egoism.
We can clearly see in Derrida's treatment of Kierkegaard in
The Gift of Death just how far Jewish love goes in preparing
the way for *agape* and just how far it does not go in loving.
With the coming of the God-man as Kierkegaard explains there is
a new notion of purity of heart and of altruistic-egoistic love.
Becoming a fully loving person and developing a purely loving
heart is for Kierkegaard a life-long process of growing in true love.
Kierkegaard makes it so clear that there is a great self-love
in my affection for my family, in my *eros* for my beloved
and in my special friendship for my few special friends.
It is a life-long process to hate these spontaneous, preferential
loves which prevent *agape* from being a universal love for all.
But, insofar as throughout my life I see the problem and
keep purifying my heart then I will be able to perform
the double movement leap of loving faith in which I first
absolutely love the absolute and then relatively love the relative.
With the coming of God-man there is no longer anything
wrong with self-love so long as it is done with purity of heart.
Natural loves of affection, friendship and *eros* can easily become
self-destructive and by becoming a loving person and having
it as the task of our love to help others we become loving persons.
Once we love all altruistically even our own then loving our
own in a special way first of all as a person and a neighbor
but then as our own can be a good thing as a new pure giving.

II,6.9 Which Gives us a Pure Love that is Possible

With God as Jesus has revealed him all things are possible.
In fact The Law and The Prophets can become much more
consistent once *agape* comes to fulfill their *hesed* and *ahava*.
It is very obvious that the second commandment says that
we should love our neighbor as we love ourself and yet
Levinas and Derrida think that neighbor love should not
involve any self-love that would negate its asymmetrical purity.
Their main point is that when we give to widows, orphans and
aliens we should keep on doing it even if we get nothing in return.
That is clear and the suffering servant need not expect anything
in return but with the coming of Jesus and *agape* the idea
of self-love greatly changes for now even God loves himself.
With the arrival of Jesus' love it becomes obvious that God
is love and that the Father, Son and Holy love themselves in
loving each other and since God has self-love it is all right.
As we examine the history of *hesed* and *Ahava* throughout
the history of the Hebrew Bible we will seek to be clear about
the main issues to which Levinas and Derrida have alerted us.
Of course, we will see as much war and hatred going on
as we will see peace and love and all of this is part of
the progressive revelation by which we slowly come to
understand love and which is clarified qualitatively with *agape*.
The main point that comes with *agape* is that there can be
a pure self-love just as the three persons of God can purely
love each other and themselves in an egoism for three.
Once we behold the Trinity and see that all persons are
of equal dignity, that each is unique and that all persons
are interpersonal and in relation we can see that in loving
an other we will always love ourself because we are connected.
Of course, there is the great task to love with a new purity
in which I truly do love all my neighbors as I love myself

III With *Hesed* and *Ahava*

III,4 The *Ahava* of the *Shema*

III,4.1 What is this *Ahava* with which we should Love Yahweh?

As we begin to study the second kind of love in the Hebrew Bible, namely *Ahava*, we might begin with it as it is revealed by God. In Deut 6:4 we read the famous "Shema Israel":

> Listen, Israel: Yahweh our God is the one,
> the only Yahweh. You must love Yahweh
> your God with all your heart, with all
> your soul, with all your strength.

In *The Soncino Chumash* a Hebrew Pentateuch with English translation, we are told on page 1022 that we should:

> Obey His commands from love and not from fear.
> *With all thy heart.* The Hebrew word *lebab* and
> not *leb* is used to inidicate that God has to be
> loved with both the good and the evil inclinations.
> Heart denotes the mind.
> *With all thy soul.* Even at the sacrifice of
> your life. Soul denotes desire.
> with all thy might. With all thy property.
> To the utmost of thy power.

So this *ahava* is very different from *hesed* in that *hesed* is a duty to do good to the other whereas *Ahava* is a felt desire to be with and is what we mean by all the various kinds of love such as affection, friendship, *eros* and *agape* with their feeling. The root *ahava* is used well over 200 times in the Hebrew Bible and is an emotional feeling that is contrasted with any hatred. As we see in the Shema quotation it has to do with one's heart soul and strength and in Hebrew that is connected with one's passions for good and for evil, one's mind and with desire and one's energy. The scope of the concept of love in the Old Testament is very broad and as we shall see includes fifteen different meanings. All of these examples can help us ponder how we should love God.

III,4.2 It is Related to Fifteen Kinds of Ahava

In the *Theological Dictionary of the Old Testament* in volume one, pages 99–118 there is an article by Gerhard Wallis in which he shows how the scope of *Ahava* in the OT is very broad. From pages 104 to 107 he shows how the term *Ahava* has fifteen meanings: (1) affection of members of the opposite sex for each other; (2) conjugal intercourse; (3) intimate bond between father and son; (4) between mother and favorite child; (5) daughter-in-law and mother-in-law; (6) between men like Saul and David; (7) Jonathan and David; (8) teacher and disciple; (9) servant and master; (10) between a people and their military leader; (11) love for one's fellow men; (12) pouring out of one's heart to a stranger; (13) of Yahweh for his people; (14) of men toward God; (15) for sanctuary. And he argues that emotional experience is the germ cell of all *ahava*. We might notice as we begin that there can be *hesed* and *ahava* between the same parties and so as we begin with the *Ahava* between God and his chosen people we can see that it would have been there before *hesed* which is an action rather than a feeling. *Ahava* is thus like love in any religion or culture in that most of the above fifteen types are pretty universal and yet insofar as God will love his people with this kind of love and he wants them to love him this way its unique to the Jews. By loving Yahweh with their whole mind, desire and power the Jews become a God centered people and their primary task is to be a loving people who see love as good and worthy of all effort. *Hesed* is a piety that does the right thing but the great commandment to love God above all is not only a spontaneous feeling but is also a task to develop the attitude that gives rise to that spontaneous feeling for Yahweh at all times and circumstances. Like *hesed*, *ahava* will have secular and theological usages and again we will have to explore in order to see if in the Hebrew Bible the theological is the basis for the secular usage.

III,4.3 Wallis Explains the Secular Uses of Ahava

From page 107 to page 112 of his twenty page article Wallis goes to many *ahava* texts and explains four major types of what he calls the secular or non-theological use of the term. So *ahava* like *hesed* will have both secular and theological uses. On page 107 Wallis points out how some scholars relate *ahava* primarily to the realm of sexual love, of physical desire, of lust and even of sensual pleasure but as Wallis puts it:

> The emphasis suggested by the word *ahava*
> is not really on sexual love, but more on
> experiencing and desiring love.

After making this distinction he divides secular *ahava* into four types and gives many examples of each from the Hebrew Bible and the four types are: (1) the *eros* between man and woman (2) the affection within the family and between friends (3) the socio-ethical behavior (of the community) and (4) the love for enemies and for neighbors and this does begin to relate to religious love. So *ahava* has to do with the value of loving and it is as if we are born to be lovers and there is nothing we want more than love and to live lives of love and continued personal growth. As children we love to be loved with the *ahava* of affection. We begin to extend this *ahava* to our friends and to feel it for members of the opposite sex and we discover its many failures. Love can turn to hate and we have to take responsibility for love Wallis on page 110 shows how the Book of Proverbs points out how:

> Genuine love and friendship remain true
> especially in times of adversity
> because of their unselfishness.

When it comes to love of neighbor and love of enemy we are coming into the realm of the religious for this is prompted by divine arrangement (Lev 19:18) and as we will see the love of enemy will have certain pre-Christian restrictions.

III,4.4 And the Theological Uses

The theological usage of *ahava* according to Willis has to do with God's love for man and man's love for God and then man's love for neighbor and this notion appears quite late in the Bible. As Wallis puts it on page 112:

> The feeling of security in Yahweh's guidance
> of the individual may be understandable
> by a consciousness of his fatherly love.
> But the affirmation that God surrounds the pious
> or the righteous with love is evidently late.
> It is primarily the Deuteronomist who has
> considered Yahweh's deeds in behalf of
> the patriarchs a work of love (Dt. 4:37)

Wallis does discuss the theological message of the prophets and Hosea's treatment of *ahava* does arise long before the Deuteronomist wrote about God's *ahava* for man and the command that man should love God with all of his being. So as we go along we will have to examine if it is feasible to think that the *ahava* in Hosea between God and Israel is the sort of love that is commanded in the Shema oh Israel. Wallis also discusses the theological critical messages of Jeremiah, Ezekiel, Second Isaiah, and Third Isaiah and he writes about what he calls the paranesis of the Deuteronomist. He also discusses love for God in the cult and the prophetic criticism of the cult and all of these are theological uses of *ahava*. As we consider how to explore all this it seems that in Hosea there is a developed treatment of *ahava* on the one hand and a developed treatment of *hesed* on the other so this deserves a detailed exploration to clarify each and to relate them. Also we will have to treat the second great commandment that we should love our neighbor as ourself with a double *ahava*. But now we need to understand God's and our *ahava* for each other.

Agape and *Hesed*

III,4.5 The Deuteronomist and God's Ahava for Israel

The *Ahava* that Yahweh commands his people to give him is the same *ahava* or love that he has showered upon them. Wallis writes on page 114 that the Deuteronomist uses;

> the concept of genuine love, apart from
> the figure of marriage, extensively, and
> enlarges on its theological and ethical significance.
> That which Israel has is Yahweh's gift.
> Yahweh gave it to Israel because of his love for them.

Again on page 114 Willis writes that, for the Deuteronomist

> Yahweh's love is the prototype for love in general . . .
> The Deuteronomist's concept of love differs
> from that of Hosea, which was derived from
> the background of sexual love and marriage,
> and here he has made a notable advancement
> in the OT concept of the knowledge of God.

So to focus on the heights and depths of *ahava* we need to see how the Deuteronomist describes God's love for his chosen people. God's love for his people is greater than the best husband's love for his wife and as Wallis writes on page 116:

> Yahweh's love for his people and
> Israel's love for her God are interwoven.
> But Yahweh is always the one who
> take the first step in love, and Israel
> must actively respond to this love.

So Yahweh is primarily a loving God and he does forgive and start over if Israel does not respond with her *ahavah* to him. Whereas *hesed* is first given in the Davidic Promise *ahava* is an activity of God experienced by his people and began with his creation and continues with each act of love for them. God's freely given love to his people is the paradigm for all *ahava* and we can explore the various kinds of *ahava* in terms of it.

III,4.6 Which should be Reciprocated by Isreal's Ahava

So now we come to the *ahava* of the Shema for God has commanded man to "love" him (Deut. 6:5) and the Psalms contain testimonies of obedience to that commandment. On page 115 Wallis writes:

> The question has been raised as to how such love as this can be commanded. However, if love is not merely an emotional feeling for a person or a thing, but also involves a behavior that is becoming to love, then it is possible for Deuteronomy to elevate this behavior to the level of a commandment.

A commandment to love God as he loves us cannot be completely responded to at once for it is a lifetime task for each individual and an historical process for the people of Israel. Of course it is a matter of behaving and living according to all of the commandments but it does involve doing that with love. There is an interplay between a loving attitude and our thoughts, words and deeds and also out emotions, feelings and passions. God can command his people to love him with their whole heart mind and soul and if that becomes the central project of our lives we will be able through constant practice to develop loving feelings as we develop loving thoughts and speak loving words and do loving things for others and thereby love God more. As Willis continues to write on page 115:

> Yahweh tells his people to love,
> to keep his commandments out of love,
> and to subject themselves to him in obedience.

Jesus was obedient unto death and Christians will take vows of poverty, celibacy and obedience and even though Jews believe in attaining wealth and in family values they do get the notion of obedience going and it primarily has to do with obeying in love.

Agape and *Hesed*

III,4.7 So all Fifteen Dimensions of Ahava are Commanded

So as God's chosen people tried to obey his command and
and build within themselves a heart, mind and soul of *ahava*
they could come to believe that God loves them with every kind
of *ahava* and they could come to experience loving him that way.
Hosea taught them that they and God should (1) love each other
as members of the opposite sex can love each other and that (2)
it should be like the feeling in sexual intercourse as a couple can
make love with each other and, of course, (3) it should be like the
love between a father and a son and they knew God as their father.
The maternal side of God's *ahava* was to become known and
his people would come to love him with a feeling such as
(4) a mother has for her favorite child and sometimes a mother-
in-law and daughter-in-law might have clashes but they can
(5) develop a special kind of feeling that God and his people could have
when (6) Saul and David loved each other and (7) David and Jonathan
loved each other there was a special feeling that God could be
discovered to have as one might cultivate that feeling for God.
Of course, there is also a special bond of feeling that can arise
between (8) teachers and disciples and another one between
(9) servants and masters and these can have great variety
and they could all be experienced between God and his people.
There can be a special kind of *ahava* between a people and
their military leader and it would only be natural that (10)
this feeling could grow between God and his people as they fought
their many wars with all the enemies throughout the years.
(11) There is a certain kind of love between one and all his fellow
humans and that could grow between God and his people just
as could a love (12) that is the pouring out of ones heart to a stranger;
and, of course (13) all this focuses on the love of Yahweh for his
people which (14) they can return to him especially as they
practice (15) growing in worship and adoration in the sanctuary.

III,4.8 And can be Learned by Attentive Listening

Yahweh said to his people "Shema Israel," hear oh Israel.
Listen and be attentive and you will learn of God's love for you
and you will learn of how you should have a full love for God.
Yahweh spoke through his prophets that they might learn to love.
But the priests also aided each person and the community
to come to a fuller practice of *ahava* and Wallis on page 116
treats of *Love for God in the Cult* and this has to do with
worship in the sanctuary and he writes:

> It was in Yahweh's sanctuary that man
> became aware of his love, and it was only
> in his sanctuary at Jerusalem that man
> could manifest love to him in return.

By going to the temple and praying with love, praise, worship
and adoration and by repenting, thanking and petitioning
one could cultivate *ahava* and come to love God more and more.
As Willis says on page 116:

> In the sanctuary where men call on
> Yahweh's name together, they concentrate
> on his presence and love . . . Love is
> made concrete by joy in Yahweh's
> public worship, by love for his sanctuary
> in Jerusalem, or by love for his name.

The entire purpose of life is to grow in love and the singing
of the 150 beautiful psalms lets one joyfully love loving praise.
Worship also had an historical dimension for in the temple
the people remembered that as Willis says on page 117

> God's love for his community is
> appropriately based on the concept of
> his love for the patriarchs in Deuteronomy.

Ahava gave rise to worship and worship in the prayer of music
song and remembrance gave rise to the continuing growth of *ahava*.

Agape and *Hesed*

III,4.9 Which Ponders God's Ahava always in the Heart

The Jews had a vocation to develop loving hearts in the
mind of the heart, the desires of the heart and with all the
possession of the heart because they knew the heart of their God.
They knew that Yahweh their God was the one and only Lord.
For no other people had a God who loved as did their God
and no other people was called upon to practice a love like theirs.
Their vocation demanded of them that they listen better and better.
Their private prayer and their communal worship were ways
of listening and even as one might shepherd his sheep he came
to know that the Lord is my shepherd and I shall not want.
Not only were the fifteen kinds of human *ahava* developed
in the heart toward God but even animal love made its contribution.
So the loving Jew knew God's love better and better as he loved
more and more and he knew that he must also love his
neighbor as he loved himself and thereby also love his God.
Developing a loving heart toward all his fellow Jews was also
commanded and without obeying that command one could not
properly love God for the first commandment implied the second.
So now as we get ready to study the command of *ahava* for
one's neighbor we have to clearly see the connection between
the two love command's for not loving neighbor is not loving God.
Wallis prepares us to understand this when on page 177 he
explains the prophetic criticism of the cult:

> In the cult God is present through
> his sanctuary and the ritual.
> Consequently, this form of love for God
> is always in danger of forgetting
> genuine brotherly love.

Just how this happens and what genuine brotherly love is we
must now explore for it is commanded that *ahava*
be cultivated for God and for neighbor even as for oneself.

III,5 The Command of *Ahava* for One's Neighbor

III,5.1 Jews are Commanded to Love One's Neighbor

Lev 19:18 says:

> You will not exact vengeance on
> or bear any sort of grudge against,
> the members of your race, but
> will love your neighbor as yourself.

As Wallis writes about *Love for Neighbors, Love for Enemies* on page 111 he begins by saying:

> In this sense, an act which grows out of
> love for one's fellow man is not humanitarian,
> but a deed prompted by divine arrangement.

This sounds very much like *hesed* for it seems to have to do with an action done out of duty rather than a felt love, however, the word here in Leviticus is *ahava* and so has to do with one's passion. The Jews believe that it is God's command that they get the right attitude and feelings and thoughts, words and deeds toward God, themselves and their fellow Jews and this has to do with *ahava*. It is often the case that persons do not properly love themselves. They can be masochists in some way or other just as they can be sadists to some degree or other but the Jew is commanded to protect his heart from all negative feeling toward God, self and fellow Jews. Again it may seem strange that one be commanded to produce the right kind of feeling and get rid of other kinds of feelings but this fits right in with Nietzsche's philosophy of avoiding any ressentiment. The religious life of the Jew aims at getting all reactions just right so that there are no habitual negative reactions toward God, self or neighbor but only spontaneous reactions of a loving heart. Loving neighbor as Wallis puts it on page 111 overcomes selfishness.

> In no case should one allow his own
> selfish interests to prevail when this
> would be harmful to his neighbor.

Agape and *Hesed*

III,5.2 And this is the Source of Jewish Ethics

On page 110 when Wallis is discussing *Socio-Ethical Behavior* (of the community) he writes:

> Love and behavior motivated by love
> are not to be separated from emotion,
> and yet they are not dependent on emotion,
> but require wise consideration.

So the Jewish individual and the Jewish community is commanded to cultivate religious love for God and ethical love for neighbors. This love is *ahava* and thus a love felt with one's heart and in one's emotions so ethics demand a training of the passions. We may not think of loving ourselves with an emotion the way we might have feelings for another but we do love ourselves egotistically insofar as our self-interest tends to be natural. True altruism is a difficult attitude to truly cultivate and attain. But that is the point of this second command that is formative of the Jewish people for the overcoming of selfishness is central to Judaism and as Wallis puts it on page 111:

> Genuine love and friendship remain true
> especially in times of adversity because of
> their unselfishness. Thus true fellowship
> is not something that is expressed in outward
> appearance, but something with real substance.

By following the command of practicing altruistic deeds even at one's own expense one can begin to develop a heart of loving feeling. So there is a kind of circular building process that the command initiates by producing the works of love that build a heart of love. Loving works can begin to produce loving feelings and in turn those loving feelings can motivate more loving works for others. So also the religious promotes the ethical and the ethical promotes the religious for God's love for us can teach us to love God and in loving God we should love his people and thus better know his love.

III,5.3 Together with Hesed as the Other Source

Just how the two religious and ethical loves of *hesed* and *ahava* are distinct from each other and yet how they might work together is our task to try and understand even with help from Levinas and Derrida and with further help from the Gospel of Matthew. It seems that *hesed* is the everlasting merciful love promised to David the anointed King and perhaps therefore has to do with Messianicity and the Messiah so that when Levinas and Derrida are talking about Messianicity they are talking about *hesed*. Do both loves motivate Jews to care for widows, orphans and aliens and even to accept the role of the Suffering Servant for others? Or is it primarily *ahava* that does that out of love for neighbors? When we think of the *agape* in Matthew's Gospel we find that there are not two words and two concepts of love but *agape* seems to play both roles so could we think that Christ's love has to do with *hesed* and that the love of Jesus is more of an *ahava*? *Ahava* is obviously ethical in demanding love for one's neighbor. But so far we have been calling *hesed* a duty love and *ahava* a felt love and in Nelson Glueck's book E. M. Good raises the question about the relation between the two as he writes on page 32:

> Good notes that in most of the Bible *hesed* symbolizes God's love for man and *ahava* man's love for God, but Hosea reverses this pattern by expressing Yahweh's love as *ahavah* and human reciprocal love as *hesed*.

We will study *hesed* and *ahava* in Hosea but for now we can see the different usages just as we saw very different views about *hesed* and that is because there were different usages within the Bible. But in any case they both have to do with Jewish ethics and love for the neighbor and with *hesed* there is a stress on loyalty of the stronger party for the weaker as towards widows, orphans and aliens.

Agape and *Hesed*

III,5.4 The Prophet's Ethical Criticism of the Cult

Loving one's neighbor ethically was such an important part of loving God religiously that care was taken to protect the ethical. As Wallis explains on page 117 Israel's love for Yahweh was made objective as they came to love the sanctuary with *ahava*. He says that

> This love for Yahweh in the cult was not
> considered to contradict one's love for neighbor,
> brother, stranger or even enemy . . .
> But this form of love for God is always
> in danger of forgetting genuine brotherly love.
> This sort of divine service induces one
> to limit love for neighbor to the narrow
> circle of his fellow believers.

This danger as Wallis explains called forth a prophetic criticism of the cult which makes good sense because fellow worshippers could develop a special *ahava* for each other which would not love all the other neighbors with an equal feeling and concern. As Wallis puts it on page 110:

> Favoritism and jealousy are the hostile brothers
> of love, and love does not enjoy constancy
> in all cases . . . Emotions are subjective and
> vacillating; one can hardly estimate what
> they accomplish.

And yet getting the right emotion of *ahava* so that I love all others as I love myself is the ethical genius of this commandment. It is the Jew's job not to show favoritism and not to feel as if those who worship with him are more lovable than those others. Loving every neighbor as oneself takes a lot of faith because one can hardly estimate what subjective emotions accomplish. But that very subjectivity in its most passionate inwardness is the essence of one's love that can never be objectively certain.

III,5.5 Shows how Hard it is to Love Others Equally

To be ethical for the Jew was a life-long task and the standard
was so high that individuals and the community would always
have room for further perfection in getting *ahava* for others just right.
The prophets were always speaking for God about the failures
of his chosen people for as we have seen loving God in the cult
could easily lead one into temptation not to love the less devout.
There was just one difficulty after another and the wisdom writers
as well as the prophets and the priests had as their main task
to get the wisdom of love just right as is the case with Levinas and Derrida.
Each individual has to have God as the love of his or her life
and then neighborly love could be made right in terms of that.
If someone loved another human as the love of their life then there
would be favoritism and such a love could easily be greatly hurt.
If such a love were not totally mutual then hell could have
no wrath like a scorned woman's fury and a heart would break.
The *ahava* that God had for his Jewish people and the *ahava*
that he commanded them to have for him and for each other
was unlike any other love that humans had ever dreamed of.
It is odd that nowhere is the love of children toward parents
mentioned. Rather, they are to honor, revere and obey and this
shows that *ahava* is not honoring, revering or obeying but more.
The two commandments of *ahava* demand that the Jews get the
right order of love and it seems that children should love even
their parents as they love themselves and should love their neighbor.
Parents might tend to love their children with a feeling of *ahava*
that is much stronger for their children than for other humans.
It could be very easy for them to love their children with even
a stronger love than they have for God or even for each other.
But again the right order of love as given in the two commands
can make all this better for parents should love God most
and love each other and their children as they love all Jews.

Agape and *Hesed*

III,5.6 But that is what True Ethical Altruism Demands

It might seem crazy that a husband and wife should love each other and their children without favoritism and equally with everyone else. But that is what true justice and ethics demands for it is unloving to favor one above the other even if that other by my wife or child. There can be a strong natural *ahava* between a man and a woman or of a parent for their children but as in a court of law where God is the judge true altruism for others must be held as the norm. True love for all neighbors was protected by the prophets when they criticized the religious cult that could tempt some to favoritism. So also there must be the protection of neighbors even against a natural familial favoritism for true *ahava* must always be just. So as we have seen fifteen examples of *ahava* are referred to in the Bible so that Jacob's love for Rachel (Gen 29:20) and Jonathan's affection for David (1 Sam. 18:3; 20:17) are both called *ahava*. But the love of neighbor as self goes beyond all of these and demands that Jacob love all his neighbors as he loves Rachel and that Jonathan loves others as he loves David with true *ahava*. In nature I am an egoist looking out for my own interests first. Naturally I love my child more than other, my beloved more than others and my friend more than others, but this command to love my neighbor as myself is supernatural and goes against my egoism. The Jew is called upon to go against nature and to love all of God's people just as he loves himself to show no favoritism at all. I as a Jew should first of all love the absolute absolutely or love God with my whole heart, mind and soul and then love all of God's chosen people as I love myself and after that I can care for myself and my own in a special way but only secondarily. The first three of the Ten Commandments show me how to love God and the next seven help me understand how to love my neighbor. My neighbor includes all Jewish people even strangers and my enemies and that makes the difficult command even more difficult.

Part Two: Seeking Their Causes

III,5.7 And to have Ahava for the Stranger as for Oneself

On page 111 Wallis gives us the following quotations:

> Love for one's fellow man is also to be
> extended to the stranger who sojourns
> in one's own native land.

If God is the love of the Jew's life then it is their ethical task
to obey him and love each of his chosen people with *ahava*.
All through the Bible the love for widows, orphans and aliens
is emphasized and as we know this is a key point for Levinas.
I may not even know the foreigner who might be a Samaritan
rather than a Judean but I am commanded to love that person
even as I love someone who is strange and thus Wallis goes
to Buber and Hillel to see how they interpret the golden rule.
He says that Buber translates the commandment as:

> "Love your neighbor and yourself alike" i.e.,
> "Behave toward your neighbor as you do toward yourself."

And then he says Hillel interpreted the "Golden rule" this way:

> "You shall not do to your neighbor
> that which is unpleasant to you."

Then Wallis writes:

> It is true that both of these interpretations
> give this command a negative form,
> but they have correctly understood its meaning.

It almost seems that these interpretations are taking something
away from *ahava* for the neighbor who is a stranger for
they only emphasize doing things for them rather than have the
kind of feeling for them that you would have for your loved ones.
The interpretation that you should not do to a stranger what
is unpleasant to you still keeps some of the difficulty but it does
not stress feelings of love that when expressed could be pleasant.

Agape and *Hesed*

III,5.8 And Ahava for the Enemy as Oneself

Once more the command of Lev 19:18 says:

> You will not exact vengeance on
> or bear any sort of grudge against,
> the members of your race, but
> will love your neighbor as yourself.

So this definitely has to do with enemies upon whom you would like to take revenge and against whom you bear a negative grudge. The Jew is commanded to get rid of all this negativity toward his fellow Jew even when that Jew has done negative things to him. So toward one's fellow Jew *the lex talionis* of an eye for an eye and a tooth for a tooth has been commanded against by Yahweh and he not only says "Vengeance is mine" but he says be positive. This again is a gigantic command and a qualitative leap into something new and unnatural for we naturally protect ourselves. Wallis is helpful in understanding the reason for this as he again says on page 111:

> The OT quite clearly considered the "care" of one's own life and possessions to include maintaining the existence of one's own family and tribe.

It does make sense to have a wider view than the natural for in trying to build up one's enemy one is trying to build up one's tribe and one's people which is good in the long run. If one forgives and forgets and loves the enemy he can much more easily win him over and get him not to be an enemy. But if one acts negatively to one who has acted negatively then matters only get worse with a continued vengeance. So even though loving the enemy is difficult once you see what God is getting at as he gives this command it is wise. If the goal is that God's chosen people live according to the ten commandments then loving enemies is a means to that end.

III,5.9 These Neighbors, Strangers and Enemies are Jewish

Right in the commandment it says very clearly not to exact vengeance on or bear any sort of grudge against *the members of your own race* so the command of *ahava* extends only to Jews. There was a debate concerning *hesed* and its universality to all humans or not but it too seems to go out only to Jews..
Israel had many enemies down through the centuries for larger Kingdoms and Empires were always trying to take control of her. As Willis puts it still on page 111:

> Love for the enemy extended to the stranger
> but not to the "foreigner."

He quotes Schilling:

> Schilling correctly points out that love for enemies
> as it is expressed in the Wisdom Literature
> suffers because of religious tensions
> with heathen non-Israelites . . .
> Love for enemies is to be understood
> in a civic legal sense, non in a national sense.

So again in loving one's own one is loving oneself and thus the love of strangers and enemies insofar as they are Jewish makes good sense when one ponders God's command.
For Levinas widows, orphans and aliens would probably be Jewish and maybe even the Suffering Servant would not suffer for the heathen but have *ahava* and *hesed* for God's chosen people. The Jesus of Q1 in Matthew's Gospel will teach an unconditional love for all of God's children for the neighbor now means everyone. The two great commandments to love God and neighbor with *ahava* will prepare the way for loving them with *agape* but as Paul wrote to the Galatians in Jesus there is no longer Greek nor Jew, master nor slave, male nor female for we all are persons Now that we see the importance of *ahava* and *hesed* for *agape* we need to study and appreciate them more fully in the Bible.

Agape and *Hesed*

III,6 Jewish *Ahava* for Yahweh and *The Song of Songs*

III,6.1 Where Each Image Expresses a Quality of Ahava

Deuteronomy 6:4 commanded the Jews to love God "with all your heart, with all your soul, and with all your strength." The Jews were commanded to make their God the love of their life. What this love should be like can be seen in *The Song of Songs*. There we first meet a young lady who wants a man to love her as the love of his life because she loves him as the love of her life. She begins by singing at 1:1:

> Let him kiss me with the kisses of his mouth,
> for your love making is sweeter than wine;
> delicate is the fragrance of your perfume,
> your name is an oil poured out
> and that is why the girls love you.

Each of these images expresses a quality of *ahava* that shows the Jew how much he should love God to fulfill the command. This lover has a certain taste, a certain smell and even his name has a certain sound that makes all the girls want him as a lover. So also the very name of Yahweh should be like an oil that anoints the loving heart of the Jew and send throughout his body a flow of mucosity that is sweeter than wine and that name and that sweet flow should even let the Jew smell the Lord. The soul of the loving Jew wants to make love with God just as the girl wants to have this man for her groom and make love with him as his beloved bride with her adoring body. If the Jew really wants to love God with all his heart he will have to spend his life making *ahava* with God and as he does it and lets all his desire and passion seek God he will know all this. The Holy Jew would become pure of heart and his love for God would let him grow in purity of heart and if he ever should lust after anyone but his wife he need merely to think of Yahweh and of her and any temptation would flee his deeply loving mind.

III,6.2 For his Banner over me is Ahava

In *The Song of Songs* 2:3-4, we read:

> As an apple tree among the trees of the wood,
> so is my love among young men.
> In his delightful shade I sit
> and his fruit is sweet to my taste.
> He has taken me to his cellar
> and his banner over me is love.

For the Jew who loved God with his or her whole heart, mind and
soul God will be as special as this apple tree among other trees.
As the time of this *Song of Songs* there were many gods and
goddesses but Yahweh was different from all others as the God
of *ahava* who commanded total love from his chosen ones.
Other gods and goddesses were like various kinds of trees in the wood.
But Yahweh was like this apple tree and just as this young lady
loved to rest in the shade and protection of her bridegroom
so the loving Jew had great shade protection and comfort from
Yahweh and the more he loved God the more loving God became.
The lover took the beloved to his cellar where preserved apples
lasted through the winter and it was a wine cellar as well.
And as his banner over her was *ahava* so it was with God.
The loving Jew knew that Yahweh's banner over him was *ahava*.
When Evelyn Underhill in her book on Mysticism discusses
The Song of Songs and why the medieval mystics liked it so much
she writes on page 137:

> The mystic loved *The Song of Songs* because he saw
> reflected there, as in a mirror, the most secret
> experience of his soul.

The Jew who really spent his life loving God could have felt
this too and thus we will see how Hosea uses this metaphor too.
No wonder that the young lady says: "His banner over me is *ahava*."
She wants all to know how she loves him and how he loves her.

Agape and *Hesed*

III,6.3 And I am Sick with Ahava

In the *The Song of Songs* 2:5–6 we read:

> Feed me with raisin cakes,
> restore me with apples,
> for I am sick with love.
> His left arm is under my head,
> his right embraces me.

This image of being sick with love expresses how the Jew should yearn for God and for going up to his Holy Place to be in his presence. You can imagine how a young girl in love might desire to be with her lover, how she might yearn for his left arm to be under her head and his right embracing her even to the point of sickness. Young lovers want to be with each other more than anything and absence only makes the heart grow fonder once love is strong. Again on page 137 Underhill writes of

> The sense of a desire that was unsatiable,
> of a personal fellowship so real, inward
> and intense that it could only be compared
> with the closest link of human love.

For Medieval mystics such as Bernard of Clairvaux Jesus would be the bridegroom and the soul would be the bride but already with the Jews of the Hebrew Bible we can better understand their *ahava* for God because these images are found in many of the Psalms. And Hosea did want Gomer to love him this way just as God commanded such an *ahava* of his people for him in the Shema. He spoke to the depths of his chosen people's hearts and asked them to listen carefully for he would tell them how they should love him. When Israel was in the desert for forty years she and Yahweh came to love each other but then she did often fall in love with false gods. She could put strange gods before Yahweh and love them with all her heart so there can be true love and also it can turn false.

III,6.4 For Ahava is Stronger than Death

The epilogue at the end of *The Song of Songs*, 8:6, sings:

> Set me like a seal on your heart
> like a seal on your arm.
> For love is strong as Death,
> passion as relentless as Sheol.
> The flash of it is a flash of fire,
> a flame of Yahweh himself.

The *ahava* of human lovers is "a flash of fire, a flame of Yahweh." So as *The Song of Songs* comes to its concluding statement it does see that the best way to understand the passion of human love is to recognize that it is a flash of the fire of God's love in the lovers. And just as God is, was and will be so love is as strong as death. Love and death are great secret and mysterious things but even if your lover dies you could go on loving him just as strongly as ever. The woman in love here wants her lover to be a seal on her heart. Every beat of her heart whispers her lover's name within her breast. If her heart should go to Sheol, the place of the dead, she knows that even there love would pulsate in her heart so even though many Jews do not believe in life after death a strong *ahava* can get them thinking. Love is a desire to be with and God wants to be with his people just as the Bridegroom wants to be with his Bride and his people are commanded to want to be with God as the Bride desires the Groom. *Ahava* is here seen as a passionate desire like that of lovers to be more and more united in their kissing, their necking and their petting until they are totally one in a great orgiastic climax. This is the desired union of two to be totally one in a love making that really does make a union between them that will last forever. God saw his union with his people to be this kind of *ahava*. Lovers desire to come together and to be one in love and this is the kind of love that God commanded his people to have for him.

Agape and *Hesed*

III,6.5 And Many Waters Cannot Quench Ahava

Again in the epilogue at 8:7 we read:

> Love no flood can quench
> no torrents drown.
> Were a man to offer all his family wealth
> to buy love,
> contempt is all that he would gain.

Ahava is a living flame of desire for union and of delight in union.
This living flame of love is so strong that you could not put
it out by dashing water upon it for this love is like a forest fire
and even if torrents of rain came upon it it would continue to blaze.
This living flame of love that blazes in the hearts of Yahweh and
his people for each other could never be bought with money.
This love is so much better than any amount of money that
a lover knows that if someone wanted to buy his love it would be
totally ridiculous for love is a task and a spontaneity but not
a commodity to be bought and sold as if it were a mere thing.
St. Bernard in his sermons on *The Song of Songs* explains
how the living flame of love grows step by step and he begins
his commentary on the kisses of the mouth by asking what other
kinds of kisses there are and he explains first the kiss of the feet.
If one begins by kissing the beloved's feet with ten kisses one
on each toe while kneeling and adoring the foot the soul can be
delivered of the nine choirs of demons that may prevent true love.
Then there can be the kiss of the hands, again with ten kisses,
one on each finger while on one's knees adoring the beloved's hands.
This can fill the soul with the nine choirs of angels and bring
about a flow of mucosity in one's mouth and throughout one's body
so that one is ready for the kisses of the mouth so longed for
by the lovers knowing that after its ten kisses another kiss will come
and that will be the kisses of the beloved's breasts that finally
prepare one for the total union of the mystical love making.

III,6.6 For Yahweh's Conversation is Sweetness Itself

In *The Song of Songs* 5:16 we read:

> His conversation is sweetness itself,
> he is altogether lovable.
> Such is my love, such is my friend,
> O daughters of Jerusalem.

The Bride who is the symbol of Yahweh's chosen people always calls the Bridegroom "my love" for God is her love just as she is God's love and we must see what it means to be someone's love. It would seem that love is a verb and that we love somebody. But Israel came to see God as her love and his speaking to her must have had a lot to do with that for his conversation was heard as sweetness itself both in its tone and in its message out of all peoples Yahweh picked Israel to be his chosen people and he spoke to her the whole of the Hebrew Bible and it was sweetness itself to be directed in love by her Divine lover. The Bible as her lover spoke it to her through his prophets priests, kings and sages showed how he is altogether loveable. All of the *Ahava* in *The Song of Songs,* and it is the greatest of all songs because it is all about the deepest love in every word, is sweetness itself and it is all about the most delicious sweetness. The chorus sings to the Beloved in 5:9

> What makes your love better than other lovers,
> O loveliest of women?

As she thinks of other peoples and their gods she cannot imagine a luckier people who could have a more loving God. She herself is the most graced of all Beloved's and she knows her God is the best of all.

> My love is fresh and ruddy
> to be known among ten thousand.

She can imagine ten thousand different Gods but could anyone of them ever come close to being so lovely as her lover?

Agape and *Hesed*

III,6.7 And we Belong to each Other

In chapter 7:11 she sings

> I belong to my love
> and his desire is for me.

Yes, she knows that she belongs to her love for he created
her and then he called her to be his special lover and he
made a love covenant with her and made many promises to her.
She knew that that love was consummated and that they
belonged to each other as God and wife forever in total *ahava*.
Yahweh chose his people out of love and commanded them to love
him with all their mind, desire and power which would unite them.
They were to have a covenant like a man and wife in any marriage.
Throughout *The Song of Songs* as the Bride and the Groom sing
to each other they express in many ways how they want to and do
belong to each other only to grow in that happy union.
They want to do everything together as we see in 7:12–13

> Come, my love
> let us go to the fields.
> We will spend the night in the villages
> and in the early morning
> we will go to the vineyards.

They want to play together, work together, live together and make love
together that they might belong more and more completely to each other.
All of this love is a matter of faith for the Jews for they believe
that God made a covenant of love with Abraham and a covenant
with Moses and his people and gave them this command to love.
That there could be *ahava* between God and his people was the
main point of their faith which made them a religious people.
The religion of the Jews was a matter of faith in *ahava* with God
and a hope in that *ahava* that God would help them love him.
They knew that often they were not like the Bride with a full love.

III,6.8 And my Love's Desire is for Me

Chapter 6:3 says

> I belong to my love, and my love belongs to me.
> He pastures his flock among the lilies.

The Bride's lover is a shepherd and he is often out with his flock. While they do belong together and to each other they often desire each other not only for union when they are together but also when they must be apart and that happens frequently and desire is a big part of the *ahava* for their love is a thirsting for each other. It is almost as if they are in a dry desert and the flocks of the shepherd are thirsting and he is thirsting but he for his beloved. So many of the beautiful love songs are songs of longing and desire. At 4:16 she sings

> Awake, north wind,
> come, wind of the south!
> Breathe over my garden,
> to spread its sweet smell around.
> Let my love come into his garden,
> let him taste its most exquisite fruits.

She is a beautiful garden for him and she desires that he desire her and that he come and enjoy her fruits for she does bear the most exquisite fruit in her beautiful face, hair, neck, breasts, thighs, legs, feet, hands and arms that want to take him. He sings back to her at 5:1

> I come into my garden
> my sister, my promised bride,
> I pick my myrrh and balsam,
> I eat my honey and my honeycomb,
> I drink my wine and my milk.

God desires his people with an *ahava* that hungers and thirsts for them as if they were honey and wine and he commands them to love him with their desiring *ahava* that seeks him alone.

Agape and *Hesed*

III,6.9 And all my Desire is for Him

God has desired his people with *ahava* and he has desired them so much that he has commanded them to love him with a desire that is as great as the beloved's for her lover. It is obvious from her songs that all of her desire is for him. She is focused on him alone and no one else could distract her. A love such as hers is the ideal for the Jewish people and anything less means that they still have room for improvement. Once again the epilogue at 8:6–7 is a beautiful and perfect ending:

> Set me like a seal on your heart,
> like a seal on your arm.
> For love is strong as Death,
> jealously relentless as Sheol.
> The flash of it is a flash of fire,
> a flame of the Lord himself.
> Love no flood can quench,
> no torrents drown.
> Were a man to offer all his
> family wealth to buy love,
> contempt is all that he would gain.

God's *ahava* is a living flame of Yahweh himself and he has commanded that each of his people and the community of his people all have this desiring *ahava* for him that is as strong as death. Until their death this must be their burning, growing passion. But Israel will turn out to be a false lover and not love Yahweh with her whole mind, heart and power for she will seek other gods. This will bring us to the theological, critical message of the prophets. Once the tribes of Israel break away from Judah and set up their Kingdom in Samaria they will always have self-seeking kings. They take themselves away from the *hesed* promised to David and Hosea especially is critical of their *hesed* and their *ahava*.

IV With Matthew's *Agape*

IV, 4   Matthew's *Agape* Seeks First the Kingdom of Heaven

IV, 4.1 As the Son Reveals its Mystery in the Father

The central focus of Matthew's Gospel is the Kingdom of Heaven.
If we seek it first all other things will be added unto us.
As we come now to the third of his five parts on the Kingdom we
must ponder what is called the Mystery of the Kingdom of Heaven.
The Narrative section has a good deal of Q2 material about John
the Baptist and the Son of man as condemning his contemporaries
and lamenting over the lake town which will be harshly judged.
The Kingdom of Heaven is a mystery and is not understood by
the learned and the clever but is revealed to the simple and childlike.
Jesus gets to the heart of the mystery at Matt 11:26–27:

> Yes, Father, for that is what it pleased you to do.
> Everything has been entrusted to me by my Father;
> and no one knows the Son except the Father,
> just as no one knows the Father except the Son
> and those to whom the Son chooses to reveal him.

The Father is a mystery to all except the Son and the Son is a mystery
to all except the Father and the Father sent the Son to reveal him.
The Lord's Prayer shows how Jesus reveals the Father:

> Our Father, who art in Heaven hallowed
> be thy name, they Kingdom come, thy will
> be done on earth as it is in heaven.

The Kingdom of Heaven is the Father's Kingdom and to understand it
in its mystery we need to understand the Father in his mystery.
The whole point of Jesus coming is to reveal his Father's Kingdom.
But the Son is also a mystery and the father through his
Holy Spirit will reveal the Son through his words and works.
So far in Matthew's Good News Jesus has chosen his
disciples and he has proclaimed his Father's Kingdom
to them and he has preached it to them and the many.
Now he is going to delve into its mystery for them and all.

Agape and *Hesed*

IV, 4.2 By Teaching it Directly to the Disciples

At Matt 13:10–12 we read,

> Then the disciples went up to him and asked
> "Why do you talk to them in parables?"
> "Because," he replied, "the mysteries of
> the Kingdom of Heaven are revealed to you
> but they are not revealed to them."
> For anyone who has will be given more,
> and he will have more than enough;
> but from anyone who has not,
> even what he has will be taken away."

Matthew continues here with the strong judgmental attitude of Q2 which emphasizes that sinners will be punished with the rods of men for any wrong doing and that justice is primary. We have already seen what Jesus thinks of true disciples back at Matt 7:21–27:

> It is not those who say to me, "Lord, Lord,
> who will enter the Kingdom of Heaven,
> but the person who does the will of my Father
> in Heaven . . . " Therefore, everyone who
> listens to these words of mine and acts on them
> will be like a sensible man who built
> his house on rock.

Here Jesus spoke also to his disciples in parables about being true disciples and again those who will not do the will of his Father will not be able to enter the Kingdom of Heaven. And that is the main point here that he teaches his disciples directly and not in parables the mysteries of the Kingdom. If the disciples imitate and follow Jesus they will begin to understand him in his mysterious divinity as only the Father knows him and they will begin to know the Father with the Son. The disciples heard the call of Jesus and followed him at once.

IV, 4.3 But Through Parables to the People

When the disciples ask Jesus why he speaks to the crowd
in parables he responds at Matt 13:13 by saying:

> The reason I talk to them in parables is
> that they look without seeing and listen
> without hearing or understanding.

We must remember that Matthew is writing for a Jewish audience.
From the Jewish people came the first disciples for the first
Christians were Jewish and his followers thought he spoke
with authority in showing how the law and prophets were fulfilled.
Also speaking in parables is very Jewish for the Hebrew Bible
uses four kinds of expressions: the literal and the allegorical
which can be moral, mystical and typological and all three
of the allegorical are parables which explain something with a story.
The parable which is asked about here is the parable of the sower.
The sower's seeds can fall in four places: on the edge of
the path, on patches of rock, among thorns and on rich soil.
The seed will bear no fruit in the first three situations but in rich soil
produces a crop, some a hundred fold, some sixty, some thirty.
When Jesus spoke to the Jews some were like the edge of the path,
some were like patches of rock and some were like thorns and the Jesus
of Matthew knows that it will be like that for all people for all time.
If his words do fall on rich soil then there can be a whole spectrum
of believers, for some will produce one hundred fold, some sixty and
some thirty which means that that is how much they will understand
the mystery of Jesus, of the Father and of the Kingdom of his *agape*.
If Jesus just spoke with a literal explanation some would get
his point and become his disciples but he does try to
lure others into understanding the mystery of *hesed* and *ahava* as
it is fulfilled in *agape* and that is why he uses these parables.
Here Matthew's Son of man speaks out of frustration because
even if he uses the best of parables many have no ears to hear.

Agape and *Hesed*

IV, 4.4 With Hope that they will Understand

After Jesus explains to them why he speaks to them in parables because they look without seeing and listen without understanding Matthew goes on to show how this fulfills a prophecy of Isaiah and thus Jesus says further at Matt 13:14–15,

> So in their case this prophecy of Isaiah
> is being fulfilled which at Is. 6:9-10 says,
> "You will listen and listen again,
> but not understand
> see and see again, but not perceive.
> For the heart of this nation has grown coarse,
> their ears are dull of hearing
> and they have shut their eyes
> for fear that they should see with their eyes,
> hear with their ears
> understand with their heart and be converted
> and be healed by me."

Even though they resist him Jesus does keep trying to get through to them by appealing to them and speaking to them in parables. They cannot know the Father nor his Kingdom directly but with faith they could get in touch with his mystery and begin to know through a glass darkly but they will not trust Jesus. Jesus who knows the Father tries to open them to the mystery but they will not listen to him for their heart has grown coarse. Jesus even appeals to them by quoting their own Isaiah to them but Isaiah is right and they do not listen to him either. Jesus tells them how their hearts have grown coarse and he knows that many of them will not listen to him. But a few have and he hopes a few more will so he keeps trying parable after parable with hope that they will begin to get faith and love and maybe begin to hope with him.

IV, 4.5 And be Converted and Healed

Many seem to fear the mystery of the Kingdom of God and
they do all they can to avoid giving themselves to God's will.
Isaiah already saw this and Matthew's Jesus is here on earth
for one reason: that he might lead people to do God's will and
not their own so that they might be converted and healed.
Once again at Matt 13:15 we read,

> For the heart of this nation has grown coarse,
> their ears are dull of hearing,
> and they have shut their eyes,
> for fear they should see with their eyes,
> hear with their ears,
> understand with their hearts
> and be converted
> and healed by me.

It was not only this way with the Jews of Isaiah's time and
with the Jews of Jesus' time but it is this way with many
of us at all times because we do not want to stop sinning.
We do not want to do God's will as Jesus teaches it to us,
give up our sinfulness and be converted and healed by Jesus.
This is the mystery of the Kingdom that we are afraid of.
Jesus wants us to have faith and trust in his Father who
is wholly other than anything we can sense, perceive and know.
Why should we give up our sinning which we like so much
for some mystery which we cannot understand but only believe?
Not only is the Kingdom of the Father mysterious which Jesus
is telling us about, but Jesus himself as the God- man is mysterious.
Why if he were God would he become man and suffer for us?
Why would he teach of a God who steps back and lets us be
free, knowing full well that we will sin and not do his will?
So he wants us to believe in his mystery that we might then
begin to believe in the mystery of his Father and his Father's will.

Agape and *Hesed*

IV, 4.6 For this Mystery of the Kingdom is Joyful

The very next words of Jesus at Matt 13:16–17 after he quotes Isaiah are:

> But happy are your eyes because they see,
> your ears because they hear!
> I tell you solemnly, many prophets
> and holy men longed to see what you see
> and never saw it, to hear what you hear
> and never heard it.

So the disciples who at once follow Jesus do start to know of the Kingdom of Heaven and they are not only converted but healed. And right away they begin to understand him when he tells them that their eyes and ears are happy because of what they see and hear. The first mysterious aspect of the Kingdom is that in doing the Father's will as Jesus reveals it they do discover a new type of joyful mystery. The joyful mysteries of Jesus are theirs as they are reborn in him. Their first joyful mystery is the annunciation when Jesus proclaims to them the Kingdom of Heaven and the second is the Visitation. As they listen to him preaching the Kingdom they visit it more and more with him and they begin to see and hear its mystery. Then they have their third joyful Mystery of the Nativity when they are reborn and faith, hope and love are fully alive within them. And now Jesus tells them that they are blessed among humans. Their fourth Joyful mystery is the Presentation for they go with him to Synagogues and soon they will go with him to the Temple up in Jerusalem and he will present them to be dedicated to the Lord. Their fifth Joyful Mystery will be the finding in the Temple for they will become proclaimers and preachers and teachers of the word about the Mysterious Kingdom of Heaven and they may seem lost but you can always find them being about their Father's business. So the mystery of this Kingdom of Heaven has to do with letting the Father's will be done in your life so you can be happy with him.

IV, 4.7 Even Though it is Sorrowful

The disciples will come to know of the mystery of the Kingdom
of Heaven by knowing more and more of the mystery of Jesus.
Heaven is a place of happiness and great joy and beginning
to enter it is a joyous event but there is also mysterious sorrow.
Peter, for example, was called by Jesus and he was married
and had a mother-in-law whom Jesus healed but in following
Jesus he had to leave his wife and become a celibate who
would no longer satisfy his desire for women, wealth and freedom.
Even though his wife too must have become a disciple and
encouraged Peter to follow the master there was some suffering
for both as they left the world, the flesh and the devil to follow
Jesus and to live for the Kingdom of Heaven and preach it to others.
In the next part on the church, first fruits of the Kingdom
of Heaven at Matt 16:24–26, Jesus makes this clear,

> Then Jesus said to his disciples,
> "If anyone wants to be a follower of mine,
> let him renounce himself and
> take up his cross and follow me.
> For anyone who wants to save his life
> will lose it; but anyone who loses
> his life for my sake will find it."

This takes us more deeply into the mystery of the Kingdom.
It will be a Kingdom of happiness and joy and we can begin
to experience that here and now on earth but there is also sorrow.
Peter will be with Jesus when he takes up his cross and
Peter will die on his own cross in Rome nailed upside down.
He will know of Jesus' five Sorrowful Mysteries: the Agony
in the Garden, the Scourging at the Pillar, the Crowning
with Thorns, the Carrying of the Cross, and the Crucifixion.
All of this sorrow that can also be joy has to do with *agape*
which will love the enemy even more than the self and one's own.

IV, 4.8 For it is Glorious

So Matthew's Jesus proclaimed the Kingdom and
then taught of the mystery of the Kingdom directly and in parables.
As we behold God's glory we further know him in his mystery.
In the Septuagint the Hebrew words for glory: *Kabod* and *Shekinah*
were translated into Greek as *doxa* and so in this third volume
we are doing a doxology of reconciliation by pondering how
glory has to do with the loving, forgiving, reconciling heart of Jesus.
The Greeks and the Hebrews used the word *doxa* in opposite ways.
For Plato *doxa* meant opinion as distinct from the truth.
But as Levinas so nicely put it for the Jew it means the
manifesting of the unmanifest even in its unmanifestness.
The unmanifest is the very essence of mystery so that
as we behold God's glory we further know him in his mystery.
Again in the next part of the Kingdom becoming manifest in
the Church Peter had a key role to play at the Transfiguration
for at Matt 17:1–8 we read,

> There in presence he was transfigured;
> his face shone like the sun and his clothes
> became as white as the light . . . .Then
> Peter spoke to Jesus. "Lord," he said,
> "it is good for us to be here . . . "
> Suddenly a bright cloud covered them
> with shadow, and from the cloud there came
> a voice which said, "This is my Son,
> the Beloved; he enjoys my favor.
> Listen to him."

So the Father is revealing the mystery through the Son and the Son
and his mother with their five Glorious Mysteries of the Resurrection,
the Ascension, the Descent of the Holy Spirit upon the Apostles,
the Assumption of Mary into Heaven and the Crowning of Mary
as Queen of Heaven and Earth will gloriously turn sorrow into joy.

IV, 4.9 In Manifesting the Unmanifest in its Unmanifestness

In his sermon on the parables which he gave in parables we read
at Matt 13:34-35,

> In all this Jesus spoke to the crowds
> in parables; indeed he would never
> speak to them except in parables.
> this was to fulfill the prophecy:
> from Psalm 78:2,
> I will speak to you in parables
> and expound things hidden
> since the foundation of the world.

The entire Hebrew Bible is an expounding of things hidden since
the foundation of the world and this mystery about God and
his creation is now being more fully revealed by his Son.
The Jews following Moses stressed an atonement justice theology
and suffering was often seen as punishment for sin but now
with Jesus our suffering can be a love that is offered for others.
Even Good Friday can be Christmas Day because of Easter Sunday.
The glorious mystery of the Resurrection from the dead expounds
things hidden since the foundation of the world for death had
its sting and it seemed to end everything here that we wanted forever.
But Jesus is the new Moses and the *ahava* that Moses commanded
us to have for God and for neighbor can now mysteriously last forever.
With David and God's promise of an everlasting merciful *hesed*
we did get the beginning of an incarnational love theology and
that did become clearer when Jesus became the incarnate Son of God.
Jesus is also the new David and the Davidic Kingdom now has a new
meaning as Jesus the Messiah, as Christ the King, loves his servants
by becoming their suffering servant and dying for them on the cross.
Jesus as the new Moses of *ahava* and the new David of *hesed* is the
fulfillment of both of those loves for Matthew with his *agape*.
Jesus' love revealed so much about the mystery of the Father's love.

Agape and *Hesed*

IV, 5   And His Righteousness

IV, 5.1 Matthew alone Stresses Seeking God's Righteousness

Matthew as a Jew and in writing for the Jews is very concerned
about righteousness which is obedience to God's will in every way.
Thus Luke 12:31 has Jesus say, "Seek first his Kingdom"
while at Matt 6:33 Jesus adds, "and his righteousness."
The Law and the Prophets all demanded righteousness of the Jewish
people and a good example to start with might be all the details that
they had to get just right for the first and all the subsequent Passovers.
In Exodus 12, Moses is given all the rules that he and the Jewish
people must get just right and righteousness is just that, getting
everything right and with justice so that it is always just right.
In order to begin entering the mysterious Kingdom of Heaven
each person and the people must do God's will and that means
that they must seek righteousness which is to try to do God's will.
The theme of righteousness is announced at the very beginning
of Jesus' ministry when John says he should be baptized
by Jesus but Jesus says at Matt 3:15,

> "Leave it like this for the time being;
> it is fitting that we should, in this way,
> do all that righteousness demands."
> At this John gave in to him.

In Latin the word for righteousness is *justitia* and in Greek
dikaiosune and both words in English mean justice.
So righteousness does mean getting justice just right and
it was no doubt the Father's will that John baptize Jesus so at Matt 3:17
the Father could say: "This is my beloved Son who pleases me."
For the Kingdom to come God's will must be done and the task for
Jesus is to be totally righteous in order to reveal his Father's will.
Thus Jesus' commands often go beyond those of Moses saying
for example that if a man has impure desires for a woman
he has already committed adultery and is not righteous.

IV, 5.2 For Partial Obedience will not Suffice

At Matt 6:33–34 Jesus tells us in his Sermon on the Mount,

> Set your hearts on his Kingdom first,
> and on his righteousness, and all these
> other things will be given you as well.
> So do not worry about tomorrow:
> tomorrow will take care of itself.
> Each day has enough trouble of its own.

The main point about righteousness is that it is a purity
of heart that wills one thing, namely, the will of the Father.
Jesus tells us that we cannot serve two masters for we will
either hate the first and love the second or treat the first with
respect and the second with scorn for we cannot be a slave
of both God and money and being a capitalist is a temptation.
If we worry about life and food and clothing we will not be
free like the birds of the air for our Father will look after us.
If we are partially obedient to God's will and only love our own
and not our enemy then we will not love with righteousness.
Our faith in God should let us trust with a little child's trust
and everything will go wonderfully well for us and others
even if many a day should be a Good Friday for us in which
we carry our cross with Jesus in loving obedience to the Father.
The main point about the total obedience of righteousness is that
we can never go wrong and any suffering is a joyful love for others.
Jesus was totally obedient to his Father even when he said
"Not my will, but thine be done" as he carried his Cross up
Calvary, and on the Cross when he prayed "Father forgive them, for
they know not what they do," as we read at Luke 24:34.
And we should obediently imitate Jesus.
Matthew's Jesus fulfills the Law and Prophets with total obedience.

Agape and *Hesed*

IV, 5.3 Either in Jewish Ethics

At Matt 5:7 the fourth of the eight Beatitudes says,

> Happy are those who hunger and thirst
> for righteousness; they shall be satisfied.

God the Father revealed to his people not only the moral
law with the ten commandments but about 500 rules and regulations.
Jewish morality was very demanding much more so than for
any other religion and the righteous Jew would focus his life
around God's law and being totally obedient without question.
Much of this is relaxed by Matthew's Jesus but much is also
made more stringent for often the Rabbis did not permit divorce.
But at Matt 5:32 Jesus says:

> Everyone who divorces his wife
> except in the case of fornication,
> makes her an adulterer.

So a wife who hungers and thirsts after righteousness could
be happy if she would divorce her husband if he were an adulterer.
But if one in his heart got angry with another or lusted or
hated an enemy then the law of like for like would come
back to haunt him for what you do to others you do to yourself.
That is the law of righteousness that Jesus now made clear.
At Matt 7:12 Jesus tells them of this golden rule,

> So always treat others as you would like
> them to treat you; that is the meaning
> of the Law and the Prophets.

This law of Justice or righteousness is like the law of Karma for
the Hindus and the Buddhists for you do always get what you give.
The Jewish Law and Prophets always taught this righteousness.
But now with Jesus we are told to love others as we would have them
love us and our heavenly Father will judge in accordance with our love.
Seeking the righteousness that Jesus teaches demands total obedience
for any little failure will bring us to suffer for it.

IV, 5.4 Or in Jewish Good Works

Matthew's Jesus demanded a very strict obedience not only
to the letter of the law but to its spirit for he was focused on
not legalism but the morality that governs human
relations as we see at Matt 5:44, 45, 48:

> But I say to you: love your enemies
> and pray for those who persecute you;
> in this way you will be sons
> of your Father in heaven . . .
> You must therefore be perfect just as
> your heavenly Father is perfect.

For us to start entering the Kingdom of heaven here on earth
we need to practice a righteousness that takes into account
Jewish morality and Jewish good works and goes beyond them.
Thoughts and desires are now as important as words and deeds.
As we have seen, Jesus not only condemns the act but
even the desire for murder (5:21–26), for adultery (5:27–30)
and for retaliation (5:38–42) and here he demands that
we be perfect as our heavenly Father is perfect in loving enemies.
Besides a powerful morality that is at the heart of Judaism
there is also a stress on good works as we have seen in Levinas.
Care for widows, orphans and aliens and being the Suffering Servant
for others, even those who persecute us, are strong Jewish ideals.
But Matthew's Jesus stresses a righteousness that takes good works
much further because that becomes the very point of the disciple's life.
The righteousness of good works will bring Jesus' disciples to feed
the hungry, clothe the naked, visit the imprisoned and welcome
strangers into one's own home and if one fails to perform these acts
of mercy he or she will invite condemnation on Judgment Day.
At Matt. 19:21 Jesus tells the rich young man who has
kept all the moral commandments to go and sell all that he has
and to give the money to the poor for then he can be righteous.

Agape and *Hesed*

IV, 5.5 *Or in their Code, Creed, Cult and Canon*

Matthew's notion of righteousness extends to getting every aspect
of one's religious culture just right in one's morality, one's beliefs,
one's religious rituals and in selecting the truly sacred texts.
We have just seen how moral righteousness for Jesus goes to
the spirit of the legal code and lets persons start entering
the Kingdom of Heaven by loving everyone even more than self.
Jesus is always proclaiming and preaching the mystery of a
Kingdom of love and the righteousness that it demands from all.
Also Jesus teaches a new creed that now believes in the Father,
Son and Holy Spirit and in Matthew's Good News the events of Jesus'
life that are listed in the Apostle's creed are all described in detail.
Credal righteousness is as all important as is codal righteousness
and Matthew's Jesus in teaching and in action makes sure we know it.
Jesus is also concerned with cultivating our relation with God in
righteous worship and so he drives money changers from the temple.
Preparations for the Passover Supper are made and he fulfills
the Law and the Prophets here too by the institution of the Eucharist.
At Matt 26:26 and following he turns the bread and wine into
his body and blood and tells them to eat and drink for this is
the blood of the new covenant and the righteousness of the new cultic
sacrifice will take persons ever more deeply into his Kingdom.
And finally there is the question of canonical correctness and
just what books are truly revealed and inspired so that they
belong to the canon of scripture and Jesus is the child of wisdom.
And Jesus and his disciples accepted and used all of the Septuagint
even those eight books which were not written in Hebrew but Greek.
Matthew himself kept away from any Gnostic interpretations
of Jesus and was well aware how they could lead away from
righteousness in morality, belief, ritual and the sacred canon.
Matthew always seeks to remain true to the Jesus of Q and of
Mark and of the eye witnesses he knew for the sake of righteousness.

IV, 5.6 And Jesus Embodies Righteousness

In teaching and living his new love Matthew's Jesus also teaches and lives out a new justice and that is the justice of righteousness. Justice is giving others their proper due and with Jesus we come to see a new worth in every person even if they are our enemy. In fulfilling the *hesed* and *ahava* of the Law and the Prophets Jesus also fulfills the Jewish notion of justice with his righteousness. There was the law of talion with its eye for an eye and a tooth for a tooth but Jesus new righteousness involves turning the other cheek and never paying someone back in retaliation. For Matthew's Jesus righteousness is a community responsibility. When we come to Matthew's fourth part on the church, first fruits of the Kingdom of Heaven, in section B, the discourse on the church, Jesus speaks explicitly of communal responsibility. As Howard Clark Kee puts it on page 141 of *Understanding the New Testament*:

> The way of righteousness is more than a matter
> of individual behavior; for Matthew it involves
> the life of the individual in the corporate
> experience of the community as well . . .
> Every true disciple is to be ever concerned
> for the welfare of the weaker members
> of the community.

And on the same page he writes about not offending the little ones and the Parable of the lost sheep, which Matthew uses as

> a warning to the Church to guard with care
> even the lowest of its members from harm.

The law of justice is right at the heart of the world religions and the great philosophies but for Jesus its meaning is new. There is the law of the like for like but with Jesus' *agape* that forgives the sinner and enemy there is a new righteousness and Jesus who embodies it is unlike any philosopher or religious founder.

Agape and *Hesed*

IV, 5.7 For Righteousness is Love in Action

Howard Clark Kee writes on page 144:

> The way of righteousness is not a path
> of legalism, by which the commandments
> are obeyed in order to "keep the rules."
> It is a way of life according to which
> the commandment to love is put
> into concrete action.

The word for righteousness could be translated into English as virtue.
And thus we are supposed to live a virtuous way of life which
for Jesus would have to do with habitually loving others in accord
with their needs and in helping them to become righteous also.
According to Jesus the most important thing for every human
is to seek first the Kingdom of God and his righteousness
and if we do that then everything else that we need will be
given unto us and any suffering we can offer for love of others.
A virtue is primarily a good habit and being with others who
practice the habit of a completely altruistic love helps us
to get into that habit also just as we can help others to live it.
This brings us to the Church which is the first fruit of seeking
the Kingdom of Heaven and its righteousness for the Church
is the community that helps each be fulfilled by righteousness.
They can help each other attain the habits of physical, vital,
wise and holy virtue together and as missionaries go out to
the whole world so that all might receive the gift of God's *agape*.
Jesus founded his Church in a very explicit way as we read
in Matt 16:13–20:

> You are Peter and on this rock
> I will build my church.
> And the gates of the underworld
> can never hold out against it.

Any community to be efficient needs a strong ruler with authority.

IV, 5.8 And it Helps Others in Reconciliation

For Matthew as we know reconciliation is the key to righteousness.
If you go to the alter and remember that your brother has something
against you go and be reconciled with him first and then offer your gift.
In the last paragraph of his discourse on the church Jesus gives
the Parable of the unforgiving debtor who was forgiven a debt
by the king but did not forgive the debt of a fellow servant whom
he had thrown into prison and his fellow servants told the king.
Jesus then said at Matt 18:34–35:

> And in his anger the master handed him
> over to the torturers until he should pay all his debt
> and that is how my heavenly Father will deal
> with you unless you each forgive
> your brother from your heart.

No one will be able to enter the Kingdom of Heaven until
they are reconciled with everyone and that is the purpose
of purgatory but we need to start reconciliation here and now.
So righteousness as love in action demands that we forgive
from our heart anyone who has trespassed against us and that
we seek reconciliation until we are forgiven.
Again this loving forgiveness and reconciliation is a key part of
the church and thus at Matt 16:19–20 Jesus went on to say
to Peter and the other disciples with them:

> I will give you the keys to the Kingdom of Heaven
> whatever you bind on earth shall be considered
> bound in heaven; whatever you loose on earth
> shall be considered loosed in heaven.

Here Jesus is instituting the sacrament of confession and reconciliation.
Peter and the Apostles and their successors have the all important
task of bringing about the righteousness of reconciliation and here
Jesus is giving them the special power to forgive when that
forgiveness is warranted and to hold back until it is warranted.

Agape and *Hesed*

IV, 5.9 By Being Humble like a Little Child

Throughout Matthew's Gospel there is a great emphasis on being like little children for the Kingdom of Heaven will be theirs. The Discourse on the Church at Matt 18:1–4 begins with the words,

> At this time the disciples came to Jesus and said
> "Who is the greatest in the Kingdom of heaven?"
> So he called a little child to him
> and set the child in front of them.
> Then he said, "I tell you solemnly,
> unless you change and become like
> little children you will never enter
> the Kingdom of heaven. And so,
> the one who makes himself as little
> as this little child is the greatest
> in the Kingdom of heaven."

What does this mean that righteousness is to become like little children in order to be the greatest in the Kingdom of heaven? This is obviously right at the heart of the message of Matthew's Jesus. Love, the Kingdom of heaven, righteousness, the church and now the little child all fit together at the foundation of the Good News. It would seem that the emphasis on "little" connects with humility. If pride is the root of all vice then humility is the root of all virtue. Peter was chosen to be a disciple and an apostle and the leader of the apostles and the church and he could become proud but we are being told here that to do his job he must be like a little child. There is also a special childlike love which we must now explore in order to understand the *agape* of Jesus and its righteousness. Somehow *agape* is like that of a child's love and righteousness or true virtue and justice must also have a childlike attitude. As we begin this exploration of *agape* in terms of the childlike we might note that children love with affection and not with friendship or eros primarily, so what is childlike affection or *agape*?

IV, 6 And thus makes Affection Righteous

IV, 6.1 For Affection can be Self-centered

Throughout Matthew's Gospel as Jesus reveals the mystery of
the Kingdom of heaven and of his Father and of himself the main
point is that his new love of *agape* is totally altruistic.
He does not love his neighbor as himself but as more than himself.
He does not only love his neighbor but all persons, even his enemy.
In fact he emphasizes especially loving those who kill him as he
prays for them "Father forgive them for they know not what they do."
Matthew's Jesus is very concerned about righteousness and getting
our love just right so that we can begin to enter the mysterious
kingdom of this mysterious love which is unlike any other love.
The mystery of this love is that it must work against natural
loves in order to fulfill them and let them become supernatural.
This is the basic pattern of Matthew's paradoxical vision of Jesus.
Matthew's Jesus works against the Jews to let them be fulfilled.
He works against sinners with punishment to let them be fulfilled.
Matthew's Jesus is the Q2 punishing Christ who can let the
Q1 all loving Jesus' mission eventually be accomplished for all.
In order to see how Jesus' *agape* can make the natural loves
righteous we must start with affection as Jesus himself did.
Natural affection is self-centered for in loving my child, or
my brother or sister or mother or father or anyone with
affection I am bonded to them in a preferential love and in
preferring mine to others I love myself and mine above others.
Jesus did not see affection with its self-interest as righteous.
This is the beginning of the mystery that he is revealing for he
step by step makes it clear that there is a better love than self-love.
Even *hesed* and *ahava* need to be fulfilled and made righteous
for they still have a preferential self-love in them in that
the house of David is not yet seen as universal and love
of neighbor as self is not as altruistic as Jesus will make it.

IV, 6.2 But Agape can Orient it to the Other

Matthew's Jesus can seem very contradictory if we do not see
the paradoxical way in which *agape* fulfills all other loves.
To make them righteous is to make them just so we must
see how justice might work in serving the cause of true love.
Jesus' new mysterious love even reveals a new mysterious justice.
Thus in Matt 10:34–36 we read that Jesus teaches:

> Do not suppose that I have come to bring peace
> to the earth: it is not peace I have come
> to bring, but a sword. For I have come
> to set a man against his father, a daughter
> against her mother, a daughter-in-law
> against her mother-in-law. A man's
> enemies will be those of his own household.

When you first read this you would think that Jesus is the devil.
But bringing the sword to a small-time peace can let it become
a big-time peace for love and peace go together and Jesus' message
is to turn a small-time self-centered love into a big time
universal love so that there can be eternal peace and joy for all.
That is the mystery of the Kingdom of heaven that Jesus proclaims
and it can only happen when all loves become righteous for if love
is not just and all inclusive then heaven will not be for all.
In the family of natural affection the Jewish commandment of
honoring your mother and father can be obeyed and peace will reign.
But there is a preferential self-centered love here for I love my
family more than other families and Jewish families more than others.
If Peter sets all aside to go and follow Jesus then his own
parents and his wife and her parents could become angry with him.
Of course, with his new *agape*ic affection he might love them
more than ever but without faith they would not know that.
It is easy to see how Jesus is bringing a sword between himself
and all those Jews who do not know of his more righteous love.

IV, 6.3 And Matthew's Child has Righteous Affection

As soon as Matthew comes to the mystery of the Kingdom Jesus
begins to speak of the little child as we read at Matt 11:25–26:

> At that time Jesus exclaimed, "I bless you,
> Father, Lord of heaven and of earth, for
> hiding these things from the learned and
> the clever and revealing them to mere children.
> Yes, Father, for that is what it pleased you to do.

For Nietzsche this notion of Jesus as childlike
was essential to his understanding of Jesus' love
as being able to say "yes" and "amen" to all.
The Drama of Zarathustra proceeds through its five acts of
spirit, camel, lion, lioness, and child which is Nietzsche's goal.
Nietzsche sees the child as innocent and playful and creative and
he does get right to the heart of Matthew's notion of the child.
Here in this first passage on the child Jesus contrasts the child
with the learned and the clever, and Peter and the other apostles
and his disciples are for the most part simple people like fishermen.
The learned and clever Jews thought that their righteousness was
far superior to that of Jesus and they saw him as anti-Jewish.
But simple people who are child-like can at once see that love
should be universal and that there is goodness in everyone that
can innocently and playfully be affirmed for a naïve child who
has been well loved will trust that everyone is loving and loveable.
A child might easily go out in playful, joyful, dancing love
without thinking I am better than you and be affirmative to anyone.
So family affection for the learned and the clever might be wonderful
in its self-centered, exclusivistic attitude of pride and superiority.
When Jesus comes to make this righteous it will seem to many
that he is bringing a sword and they will want to use it on him.
But the simple who have not learned of their superiority
might welcome him as he welcomes them with *agape*.

Agape and *Hesed*

IV, 6.4 *That lets Everyone be Brother and Sister*

Jesus as the Son of God knows that we all have one Father and
that we are all one great human family so if affection is
to be righteous we should have equal affection for everyone.
Matthew tells us that when Jesus was speaking to the crowds
his mother and brother appeared and were anxious to have a word
with him but at Matt 12:48–50 Jesus responds to the man who
told him this:

> "Who is my mother? Who are my brothers?"
> and stretching out his hand towards his
> disciples he said, "Here are my mother
> and my brothers. Anyone who does the will
> of my Father in heaven, he is my brother
> and sister and mother."

The Q1 sayings of the Jesus community in Galilee were
the source of this saying and many of the sayings about children.
And again we can feel the tension between Q1 and Q2 in this
saying for the ideal is that all love each other as members of
one family and those who do the will of the Father do that.
Of course, most people do not see that we should all have
a common affection and thus they do not do the will of God.
The people of the Q community went through three stages of
understanding *agape* and the mystery of the Kingdom of love.
The Jesus of Q1 taught that by loving enemies we could do much
to convert them to a righteous attitude but then the Son of man
of Q2 saw that whoever was not righteous would be punished.
Now in Q3 in these saying about the common family of man
and about true disciples being like children we get to the insight
in which atonement justice is helpful in bringing about forgiving love.
All of this is reflected in Matthew's Gospel and he wants a righteous
affection in which all see that they are brothers and sisters but if
people do not do the will of God there will be a helping punishment.

IV, 6.5 And lets Humble Little Ones be the Greatest

Jesus himself was the greatest for with the Father and the Holy Spirit
he was God but then paradoxically he became even greater by
becoming the child of Mary and by suffering out of love for us.
This is part of the mystery of the Father and the Son and
at Matt 18:1–4 he gets us thinking about it:

> At this time the disciples came to Jesus and said,
> "Who is the greatest in the Kingdom of heaven?"
> So he called a little child to him and set
> the child in front of them. Then he said,
> "I tell you solemnly, unless you change
> and become like little children you will never enter
> the Kingdom of heaven. And so, the one who
> makes himself as little as this child is
> the greatest in the Kingdom of heaven.

We already used this quotation as we started thinking about
agape letting affection become righteous and it is mysterious.
God in his *agape* became a little child and being reborn as a
child lets us imitate Jesus who became greater by becoming less.
The wise and the clever think of perfection as that which cannot
change for if God is pure perfection how could he become better?
But Jesus reveals God as three loving persons and their perfection
is greater than that of a God who is so perfect that he cannot get better.
The Father, Son and Holy Spirit are always loving and they even
grow in love for when the Son of God became the child of Mary
something new about love came into being and that is the
meaning of creation that lets something new come into being.
To really be a disciple and begin to understand this mystery Jesus'
followers have to experience this very same transformation.
This mystery of God out of love curtailing his own freedom
by stepping back and letting others be free is revealed by Jesus who
steps down as a child and he invites us to imitate him.

Agape and *Hesed*

IV, 6.6 For They are Dependent on Others

At Matt 19:13–15 we read,

> People brought little children to him for him
> to lay his hands on them and say a prayer.
> The disciples turned them away, but Jesus said,
> "Let the little children alone, and do not stop them
> coming to me for it is to such as these that the
> Kingdom of heaven belongs." Then he laid his
> hands on them and went his way.

The disciples are very slow to learn about the mysterious Kingdom.
They are learning that they too should lay their hands on infants
and bless them whenever the children or their parents want it.
It seems that these disciples would not believe in infant baptism.
In their thinking we have to be older and wiser and know what
we are doing before we can get a blessing that makes any sense.
But Jesus not only rebukes their protesting and he not only
blesses the children but he says the Kingdom belongs to them.
If we are not like little children we will not be in the Kingdom
of love for our love will not yet be righteous and holy.
Little children do not yet know friendship and *eros* for they are
only capable of affection and each disciple needs a love like theirs
which is humble and dependent upon the goodness of others.
God became like that when he became the baby in the manger.
The magi came to offer him homage for the Holy Spirit led
them with a bright starlight and disciples must be like them.
This *agape*ic affection for disciples must be a two-way street
in which like the Magi they love the little ones and they must be
like the little ones and love with the dependent love of the child.
Jesus was dependent upon Mary and Joseph and he learned
from them a human affection as he began to feel warmly and
playfully and joyfully loved by them he began to reciprocate
so that he loved them too with a child's affection.

IV, 6.7 And thus Live out Agapeic Praise

As a child grows in the constant affection of mother, father,
family and relations she or he is just bursting with praise.
It begins with the mother's breast so lovely at feeding time.
The child is totally dependent and she comes to laugh with joy
as others love to fulfill her every need in a playful affection.
As the child receives gift after gift he grows in appreciation and
feels with happiness how wonderful are the gifts and the givers.
Those who give also live in a spirit of praise for the child.
At Matthew 21:12 and following when he drove
the money changers from the Temple we read,

> There were also blind and lame people
> who came to him in the Temple and
> he cured them. At the sight of the wonderful
> things he did and of the children shouting,
> "Hosanna to the Son of David" in the Temple
> the chief priests and the scribes were indignant
> "Do you hear what they are saying?"
> they said to him. "Yes," Jesus answered,
> "have you never read this:
> By the mouths of children, babes in arms,
> you have made sure of praise."

This quotation comes from Psalm 8:2 (LXX) and from
Wisdom 10:21 and gets to the essence of the childlike spirit.
In an affectionate family there can be the spirit of praise
and thus for Jesus the disciple who is childlike will live
in the prayer of praise and that is the first of the four
important parts of prayer: praise, repentance, thanksgiving
and petition which every person should constantly practice.
Right affection as we find it with the child has so much to offer
to a righteous *agape* that should love God and others with a child's
praise for all that exists because it is a gift of beautiful being.

Agape and *Hesed*

IV, 6.8 And Agapeic Affectionate Gratitude

As we have seen Nietzsche made the child the apex of his Drama of *Zarathustra* and in the chapter called "The Three Metamorphoses" he writes,

> The child in innocence and forgetfulness,
> a new beginning, a sport,
> a self-propelling wheel,
> a first motion, a sacred Yes.
> A sacred Yes is needed my brothers,
> for the sport of creation.

Underlying all of this is a childlike spirit of gratitude. The child is dependent on others and is ever so happy when others delight in showering all sorts of gifts on the little one. For Nietzsche as for Matthew the clever and the intelligent are often caught in an attitude of ressentiment with its habit of having negative reactions to so many situations. To be able to have rather an attitude of *amor fati* or love of what fate brings us is the main point of Nietzsche's writings. The child in its innocence is able to say the Yes and Amen prayer to everything that comes its way and this is why Jesus who is childlike urges his disciples to be like children. The child can forgive and forget and not hold a grudge that can begin to change the attitude of ressentiment against existence. You might wonder what Nietzsche means by linking the child with the sport of creation and if that is connected with Jesus. According to the creation story in the first chapter of Genesis God created something on the first six days of creation and he saw that they were good and this is Nietzsche's main thought. What is, is good, and we should be thankful for it and the child does that and Nietzsche calls this the idea of eternal recurrence. If we have a spirit of gratitude we will say to each thing that is "let it eternally return" and that is creative gratitude.

IV, 6.9 And Agapeic Affectionate Petition

Jesus taught his followers to be like little children and he taught
them to pray *The Our Father* for God is our Daddy dear.
In *The Our Father* we pray to our Abba Father with seven petitions.
We pray 1) that his name will be hallowed, 2) that his Kingdom
will come, 3) that his will be done, 4) that he will give us
our daily bread, 5) that he will forgive us our trespasses, 6) that
he will lead us not into temptation, 7) and deliver us from evil.
So if we live like little children we will begin to make righteous
both our affection and our *agape* which can fulfill each other.
This mutual fulfillment is the main point of Matthew's Gospel.
Agape has been brought by Jesus to fulfill *ahava* and *hesed* and
if they allow themselves to be fulfilled then they can fulfill *agape*.
If we live like little children then our *agape*ic prayer life
will have a robust praise, gratitude and petition and that
can begin to fulfill our affection by letting it become altruistic.
It is very easy if we are learned and clever to be like the scribes
and the chief priests and really wonder what these children are
doing by looking at Jesus and singing "Hosanna the son of David."
Why should we love our enemy and how many people actually
do it for if we turned the other check to Hitler would he not just
take over the world and send every last Jew to the gas chamber?
Can we afford to be like little children and resist not evil?
So according to Matthew's Jesus we are first to seek the Kingdom
of heaven and God's righteousness and we need to make righteous
each of the natural loves and each of the religious loves.
We do need to "pray as if God does everything and work as if we do
everything" for we do need to be both innocent children and
responsible adults which is the mystery of Matthew's Kingdom.

Father Sullivan

The Entrance to St. Thomas Seminary

The Seminary Chapel at St. Thomas

Father Gus Front Row 3rd From Right

Father Hill Front Row First Left

Part Three

Receiving Solutions

Agape and *Hesed*

With Sulpician Spirituality

I,7 Faith Seeking Understanding at St. Thomas

I.7.1 Father Gustafson taught us the History of Philosophy

In September of 1959, at the age of twenty one I entered St. Thomas Major Seminary in Kenmore, Washington, a suburb of Seattle. There were nine Sulpician Fathers who taught about 150 of us through two years of philosophy and four years of theology. Father Sullivan, the Rector, was our main spiritual director and he gave us a talk each day developing a five point program of putting Jesus in our mind, in our heart, in our hands, in our vision and on our lips since that is our life's purpose. Each seminarian majored in philosophy and so in our first year we met three times a week for two courses: one on the history of philosophy and the other on a branch of systematic philosophy. Father Gustafson taught us all ten of our philosophy courses and I cannot imagine a better philosopher and teacher of philosophy. I liked him so much that I chose him to be my confessor and I was so inspired by him that I loved studying as much as I could. We started that year with ancient Greek philosophy and logic and the two dove tailed together and greatly supported each other. In logic we learned of the 4 D's: Demonstration, Definition, Distinction and Dialectical reasoning and we saw that reasoning was all about demonstrating a thesis with clear definitions and distinctions and raising dialectical objections and answering them. So right away as we began studying the history of the Greek philosophers we learned that philosophy (the love of wisdom) is the quest to know the truth about the becoming of all things. We were going to study the art and the science and the history of reasoning and we knew it would help us better understand our faith. We knew that philosophy could help us to help others to understand their faith and to grow in their faith and we were so excited. All of our six years work in the Minor Seminary prepared us for philosophy and then theology and life was beautiful and good.

I,7.2   In Love with the Greek's Love of Wisdom

Wisdom is perhaps the most important of the intellectual virtues
and finally after six years of preparation we were now ready
to start becoming philosophers and we entered into the quest
to know the truth about the becoming of all things and thus
to think about the big picture of all that is, was and will be.
Father Gustafson taught us about Aristotle's notion of physics
which had to do with the origin, process and goal of all becoming.
We began with the Pre-Socratics and their theories of origination
or how things came to be out of a source or first cause.
In simplest form philosophy was for them in its beginning
a conversation about five theories of origination or archeology.
All things could come from one source, or two, or a few,
or many or from unlimited sources and they began to think
that there was one material cause such as water, air, fire or earth.
Also some thought that in the beginning there could be only Being
and that all becoming came from that source of Being itself.
Then Heraclitus thought of the sun and from that all came
forth from its fire through a twofold process of peace and war.
For peace gave things warm life and war brought cold death.
Empedocles posited a few basic sources and thought of
water, air, fire and earth as formed into cosmos by *storge*
or loving affection and falling into chaos because of hatred.
Reason brought him to an interplay of a god of love and a god of hate.
Then there were the materialistic atomists who posited many
atoms falling through the void forming cosmos and chaos.
And some like Anaximander thought that the source of finite
things had to be infinite and a mystery beyond our mind's grasp.
For four months Father Gus taught us Greek philosophy
out of a wonderful history of philosophy book that I still have.
We learned about loving wisdom in terms of Empedocles and
affection, Plato and *eros*, Aristotle and friendship Plotinus and *agape*.

I,7.3 In Faith with the Medieval's Wisdom of Love

As young men we come to the seminary because we had faith
that the Son of God had called us to imitate and serve him.
I had seen his face in the face of my mother and father and
Father Heeren and in the face of the beautiful young nun who
taught me at Catechism school and talked with me about having
a vocation and told me how happy she was as a bride of Christ.
In the seminary we had faith that

> unless a grain of wheat falls
> into the earth and dies,
> it remains alone; but if it dies,
> it bears much fruit. (John 12:24)

By living a life of poverty, chastity and obedience and entering
into the passion of Jesus in order to serve others we could come
to see the face of Jesus with a new living, existential vision.
Father Sullivan and Father Morris explained to us how living
the passion of Jesus with him would help us to see the glory
of the face of God and let others see God's face in our faces.
As we studied medieval philosophy with Father Gustafson
we come to understand why Augustine would think that
"I believe that I might understand" and then go on to think
that I have "a faith that seeks understanding" for faith
in the God who is love lets us find what philosophers seek.
And then their philosophies can help us understand our faith:
Augustine, Aquinas and the Franciscans each gave their
reasons explaining why the Beatific Vision or seeing the Face
of God is that which can make us happy and so philosophy
fit in perfectly with helping priests understand their sacrifice.
Jesus' loving passion which reveals the glory of the face of God
has within it a great wisdom of love which helps us to
understand what Socrates, Platonists, Aristotelians, Stoics
and Epicureans are questing after and how they can help us.

I,7.4   And he taught us Systematic Philosophy

Father Gus taught us systematic philosophy from a Thomistic
Aristotelian point of view and so after learning logic we went
on to metaphysics and saw how philosophy is "a certain
knowledge of things through causes" which we studied in metaphysics.
From that we went to psychology, epistemology etc. in an orderly
fashion and all of this helped us to better understand our faith.
In Natural theology we studied the existence of God, the essence
of God, the Absolute attributes of God and the relative attributes of God.
In thinking about Aquinas five proofs for God's existence and
the essence of what God is we came to see even with reason alone
that God might best be understood as a God who out of love
brought forth our universe even with a creation out of nothing.
We came to see step by step how reason can contribute greatly
to faith and how philosophical love and wisdom can aid so much
in understanding even the Christian celibate love of Jesus and Paul.
Plato's treatment of erotic love in the *Symposium* helped us
to understand the ladder of love used by Christians such as
Theresa of Avila, St. John of the Cross and St. Bernard of Clairvaux.
But the *Phaedrus* was even more instructive and intriguing
as we saw the sexual energy of the Black Horse being channeled
into a creative energy for the white Horse and charioteer.
Already Plato knew of the values of celibacy and he showed how
it can be received as a gift by falling in love with the right person.
As I went to confession with Father Gustafson I again began
to have trouble with my masturbation and he said he had a hard
time understanding me because he never experienced this problem.
He asked me if I did this in a state of semi-sleep and I told him
no that I did it so that I could go to sleep and he told me to keep
praying and maybe I too would be able to receive the gift of celibacy.
I figured that I was more like St. Augustine and Father Gus was
more like St. Thomas and I prayed that I would receive the gift.

Agape and *Hesed*

I,7.5 Helping Jesus be in our Mind with Metaphysics

In our metaphysics class Father Gus thought with us
about the idea that "something cannot come from nothing."
Everything that comes to be needs a material, efficient,
formal and final cause and with Aristotle we saw why.
Aristotle explained the history of theories about the material
cause, that out of which something is made, by going to
the history of the Pre-Socratics and their five kinds of theory.
But they already began to see the need for an efficient cause,
that by whom something is made, and thus they posited
war and peace or love and strife as moving material things.
Plato clarified the notion of the formal cause as that which
lets a thing be a special kind of being or belong to a species.
Form is the source of species and existence and nothing could
exist unless it had the two intrinsic causes of matter and form.
Aristotle himself brought out the need for a final cause
for everything that exists has a purpose and is related
to other things in the cosmos in terms of ends and means.
So in his ethics, for example, Aristotle sees virtues as a
means to happiness and happiness is the goal of our existence.
This study of metaphysics in which we studied the principles
that go beyond physics and yet let physics and the other
branches of philosophy be sciences helped us greatly
in getting an orderly understanding of our faith, hope and love.
We believed that our purpose or *telos* or goal of our living
got us to meditate more fruitfully upon seeing the face
of Jesus and to let others see the face of Jesus in our face
that we might all behold the face of God for all of eternity.
Metaphysics got us into archaeology, physics and teleology
and that took us to eschatology, a study of the last things.

I,7.6 Helping Jesus be in our Heart with Psychology

Father Gustafson was an excellent Thomistic philosopher and
he helped us so much to appreciate Thomas' way of relating
faith and reason by seeing philosophy as the handmaid of theology.
He showed us how reason with its own effort can attain much
truth which we saw in Aquinas' five proofs for God's existence.
In our psychology class we saw how Aristotle proved
the immortality of the soul and we thought about freedom of the will.
In his psychology Aristotle used the principle of "action
follows being" and argued that whatever we can do implies
a power of being within us that can perform that kind of action.
Plants are different from inanimate things because they have
the powers of nutrition, growth and reproduction and so we
must think of a vegetative soul that can perform those actions.
The animal while having the vegetative powers also has
the powers of local motion and sensation for it can move
about and operate with the five external and four internal senses.
The human has the vegetative and animal powers but it also
must have an intellect because it can know immaterial
abstract ideas which belong to the spiritual rather than material realm.
Matter can be destroyed because it can be broken into parts
but the spiritual or immaterial is immortal because it cannot
be broken into parts or destroyed and so the human intellect is immortal.
Father Gus taught us that all so clearly that we could never
forget it and it will be part of our immortal life together.
But the freedom of the will was a different issue for while
material relations are determined we learned that because of
our immateriality our thoughts words and deeds could be free
and ethics would be meaningful as we would choose good or evil.
But my problems with masturbation made me wonder how free
I was and Father Gus talked with me about building up the right
attitude which could guide my moods and feeling helping me be free.

Agape and *Hesed*

I,7.7 Helping Jesus be on our Lips with Epistemology

Theoretical philosophy was very important and especially because
it was supposed to help us to get a good practical philosophy.
Getting beautiful, good, true and wise ideas in our minds
seemed to be happening for with Father Sullivan we could see
that seeking the see the face of Jesus and the face of God and
to bring that face to others was the purpose of a priest's life.
But to make those ideas of the mind real in the heart proved
to be most difficult for I could see the point of seeing the face
of Jesus by being the seed that falls into the ground and dies
that others might live for self-emptying is the way of *agape*.
But I just could not be totally celibate or even kind and peaceful.
I continued to have impure thoughts and uncharitable thoughts.
As a priest I needed to see the face of Jesus in others and my
face should reveal the face of Jesus to them and my mind
and my heart and my lips and my hands should all bring
the loving Jesus and the loving God to everyone I would meet.
Father Sullivan also explained to us how we should have Jesus
on our lips at all times by speaking with love and, of course,
our lips were a big part of our face that should smile with joy.
In teaching us epistemology or the theory of true knowledge
Father Gus helped us see into all of this more clearly for
understanding knowledge has to do with the problem of universals.
He explained to us how the concept or idea is the universal
sign of a thing for if we have the idea of horse it is meant
to extend to all horses in a way that is true to all of them.
As we will see there have been four theories of the universal.
Plato and the ultra-realists, Aristotle and the realists, Kant
and the conceptualists and Ockham and the nominalists.
Each understood the universal idea in our mind and the word
that expressed it on our lips in a different way and we came
to wonder about nominalism and the idea as only a name on our lips.

I,7.8 So that He might be in our Hands for Others

We would sometimes say a little prayer together that
expressed the Sulpician spirituality for priests:

> God be in my head
> > and in my understanding.
>
> God be in my eyes
> > and in my looking.
>
> God be in my mouth
> > and in my speaking.
>
> God be in my heart
> > and in my thinking
>
> God be at my end
> > and my departing. Sarum Primer, 1527

This prayer does not mention having God or Jesus in my hands
but for the priest that has to do with holding the Eucharist
and with having a hand that disperses blessings for all.
As Father Gus taught us more about the four theories of truth
we came to wonder more and more about the truest way of
having Jesus on our lips and in our hands for we saw that:

(1) Ultra realism (Plato, Augustine, Descartes) sees the universal
as a transcendent, eternal form, e.g., horses are only
appearances that participate as particulars in the form of horseness.

(2) Moderate realism (Aristotle, Aquinas, Locke) sees the universal
as having a foundation in the form common to things that
is abstracted from them so that this horse is real.

(3) Conceptualism (Stoics, Abelard, Kant) thinks that
singulars are universalized by formal powers of the mind.

(4) Nominalism (Skeptics, Ockham, Kierkegaard) is the theory
that the universal is not a transcendent form, nor an
immanent form, nor a form of the mind but it is only a
name on our lips for the single individual cannot be
adequately universalized but should be loved in its complexity.

Agape and *Hesed*

I,7.9 And always in our Vision with his Logic of Love

Philosophy as we learned it in our first year at the major
seminary was not only the handmaiden of theology but was
also the handmaiden of our spiritual life for she helped us
to see what kind of reality belong to Jesus and to all persons.
The idealism of Plato and Kant took away from the reality
of persons, places and things all of their lovely complexity.
Aristotle argued that this individual is not merely an appearance
but a reality in itself and he explained how we can get true knowledge
of each individual through an involved abstraction process.
Kant explained why and how the forms of things belong to our
minds and make our experience of things possible but again
this is not a basis for knowing and loving single individuals.
In the seminary we learned to appreciate Aquinas and
the Franciscans for Scotus followed Aristotle in explaining
philosophically this individual and he called individuals *haeccity*
or this and this individuality was made up of every relation
that the individual would ever have and thus no universal
concept could every grasp it so Ockham concluded that
we should always remember that the universal is never an
adequate concept but is only a name that we speak.
So the face of Jesus which we seek to see by emptying
ourselves with him out of love for others is infinite
as the face of God and will always be beyond us in its mystery.
That is why we have a faith that can never be reduced to
knowledge and that as Scotus and Ockham and later
Kierkegaard and all the postmodernists argued is a nominalism
which philosophy can work out and help us fully appreciate.
Once we get the face of Jesus in our vision we can understand
how we can truly know its reality but also we can see
how it is so rich that it will always be beyond knowing.
Aristotle and the nominalists helped us see a love beyond knowledge.

Part Three: Receiving Solutions

I,8 Believing that We Might Understand in the Seminary

I,8.1 *How Modernity separated Faith and Reason*

Father Gus taught us not only about the *fides quaerens intellectum*
the "faith seeking understanding" of Augustine but he also taught us
about his *credo ut intellegam*, his "I believe that I might understand."
There is much we want to understand about how things came to be
about how we might best live and about what there is after death.
The philosophers and the different religions offer many different
answers to these questions and many are content to live with
the faith of their fathers and not to explore the various options.
But Augustine did explore many philosophies and religions
and he came to greatly admire the mystic way of Plotinus with
its purification, illumination and unification but no matter
how hard he tried he could not practice the purification of celibacy.
Then he read the words of St. Paul and his conversion took place
for from then on he was able to be celibate and love God for
"you have made us for yourself, oh God, and our hearts are restless
until they rest in thee" and with his new belief he could understand.
His new belief let him understand happiness and freedom and
it appeared to him to be the most loving belief he could imagine.
That was his criterion for the truth of his new gift of faith.
It truly was humankind's highest affirmation and in all of his
studies he had never come across a more loving way of life.
Now he could spend his life trying to better understand his
new belief and his books on happiness, freedom and the two
loves that have built two cities were such attempts.
Faith and reason fit so well together for in his own experience
faith let him live out the best that reason could offer and
his belief could let him understand all the different truths.
Father Gus explained to us all of this and then he showed us
how modernity developed a logic of exclusive opposites with
Luther building on faith alone and Descartes on reason alone.

Agape and *Hesed*

I,8.2 With the Reformers choosing Faith alone

Father Gus explained to us all of this and then he showed us
how modernity developed a logic of exclusive opposites
with Luther excluding reason and Descartes excluding faith.
Luther tried to live the life of celibacy just as did Augustine
be he never could do it and the sublimation conversion process
that was a gift for Augustine never was given to Martin Luther.
He came to think that to know, love and serve God we do not need
the mystical way with its abnormal non-married dedication
and the philosophy and the philosophies that always accompany it.
He saw the Catholic tradition from Augustine onward as
corrupting the life of true Christian faith with a false paganism.
Of course, in our class on Modern Philosophy we were not that
interested in the new religion of the reformers although we did
study that very much in other courses on the history of Christianity.
It is intriguing that Modernity from its beginning worked with
faith alone in religion and reason alone in philosophy and perhaps
the philosophical thrust was a reaction to the strong protestant demand.
Descartes after all was a Catholic and had studied meditation with
the Jesuits and perhaps he wanted to show just what reason could do.
Also he was an Augustinian of sorts for Augustine had refuted
skepticism with his argument "Si fallor, sum" (If I err, I am).
That is a model for the "cogito ergo sum" (I think, therefore I am).
With pure reason Descartes thought he could establish the three
roots of the tree of philosophy: I am, God is and matter is.
Then he thought the human could reason out the trunk of physics
and then the three branches of medicine, mechanics and morals.
Of course, with reason alone he cannot prove that there is a God
who is a person and he cannot get a morality of self-sacrifice.
But, modern philosophy as it developed with the continental rationalists
and the British empiricists and then the Enlightenment with Kant
did show that reason has wondrous powers that should be affirmed.

I,8.3 And the Enlightenment Thinkers Reason Alone

Father Gus taught us the history of philosophy from a lovely
green book by William Turner which began with the Pre-Socratics
and went right up to the present day with Western Philosophy.
We used it for all four semesters first on Greek philosophy
then on Medieval, then on Modern and finally on contemporary.
I still have the book with notes in it from Father Gus' lectures.
I have used it down through the past fifty years when further
learning and teaching philosophy for it is an excellent survey
and it is so helpful to see what Father Gus said about things.
Once modern philosophy got rid of faith as part of the
philosophical method it was very interesting to see what happened
to psychology and ethics and the key ideas of love and personhood.
Descartes had a theory of innate ideas for in arguing:
"I think, therefore I am" he saw that this idea had a perfect
certitude that could not be doubted so there had to be an idea
of perfection or of God that let him know if an idea was certain.
Locke started the empirical method by arguing against innate
ideas and showing that all of our ideas begin with experience.
Hume also was an empiricist and Kant wrote his *Critique
of Pure Reason* to clarify the categories of our mind which
make experience possible for we humans have minds
that can produce universal ideas whereas mere animals do not.
In his ethics Kant argued that there are categorical imperatives
that demand that we treat persons as persons and not as things.
But Kant's notion of personhood did not stress the unique
complexity of each single individual and he did not stress
the interpersonal personhood of all persons in a community.
Kant approached religion from within the limits of reason alone
and thus he did not have a belief in seeking to see the face
of Jesus with the self-sacrifice of the grain of wheat that falls
into the ground and dies that others might have life more abundantly.

Agape and *Hesed*

I,8.4 Contemporary Philosophy puts them Together Again

Father Gus taught us about the inadequacies of the various
modern approaches to ethics from utilitarianism to Kant's
categorical imperative and he did praise the approach of Hume.
He showed us how the three social contract theories of Hobbes,
Locke and Rousseau were based on a conventional mad-made
contract in which humans are wolves to each other rather than
a natural community of the family of man with God as our Father.
Our wonderful book by Turner was published in 1903 and reprinted
in 1929 and I wouldn't be surprised if Father Gus and the Sulpician
fathers teaching at the seminary used it when they studied philosophy.
Because it was dated Father Gus told us about Kierkegaard,
Nietzsche, Max Scheler, Maritain, and Gilson and how they all
returned to philosophy as a combination of faith and reasoning.
He told us about Blaise Pascal a contemporary of Descartes who
taught that "the heart has its reasons that the mind does not know."
He said that to a degree Hume and Scheler built their ethics on
a moral sentiment theory in which the heart can intuit values.
Kierkegaard and Nietzsche went beyond modern philosophy from
Descartes and Hegel and were influential on philosophers like Sartre.
Maritain and Gilson were postmodern scholastics and greatly
appreciated the philosophy of Thomas Aquinas and also Bonaventure.
Father Gus knew these philosophers very well and he left us with
an enthusiasm to know them better for it seemed that we were
living in an exciting new age of believing that we might understand
and of a faith seeking understanding and we even heard the idea
of ethics as first philosophy and we had a course just on ethics.
Descartes had metaphysics as first philosophy and morals
with medicine and mechanics were branches on the tree of philosophy.
But with Hume and Scheler it seemed that you began with ethics.
and, of course, we were always studying scripture and various
spiritual writers and contemporary philosophy seemed to fit in with them.

I,8.5 The Dying Face of Stephen Reveals a New Ethics

Father Gus taught us ethics for a semester and showed us how
self-realization was the main point of most ethical systems.
Aristotle showed how practicing the virtues lets us be happy.
Aquinas took the moral and intellectual virtues of Aristotle
and placed them within the context of the three theological virtues
of faith, hope and charity and the love of neighbor or of all
humans became even more important than self-realization.
So with the study of ethics it became our task to put together
the philosophical ethics we learned from Father Gus and the
spiritual ideal that we learned from Father Sullivan of putting
the face of Jesus before our eyes that we might have him
in our mind, in our heart, on our lips and in our hands for others
just as the face of Stephen let Saul see the face of Jesus.
Saul was a persecutor of Christians because he believed that
they were blaspheming the law and the God of Moses but
as he watched the stoning of Stephen he came to see the face
of Jesus loving and praying for those who were killing him.
As Father Sullivan told us about this we clearly saw the new
ethics of the Sermon on the Mount and of loving our enemies.
There was nothing like this ethics of loving the enemy
in Judaism or paganism for it turned upside down any
self-realization ethics by offering my destruction for the very
one who is destroying me that he might be self-realized.
If Jews today saw the face of Stephen as did Saul they too
would move from being Saul to becoming Paul and even pray
at each holocaust meeting for Hitler that he too might be saved.
There in the Seminary this new ethics began to dawn upon us
and as we thought about our Sulpician teachers who practiced
poverty, celibacy and obedience that they might see the face
of Jesus and show us his face we realized that this was
happening and that we would forever be indebted to them.

Agape and *Hesed*

I,8.6 By Revealing the Vision of the Dying Face of Jesus

Father Gus taught us ethics for a semester and showed us
how self-realization was the focus of most ethical systems.
Aristotle showed how practicing the virtues let us be happy.
St. Thomas took the moral and intellectual virtues of Aristotle
and placed them within the context of the three theological virtues
of faith, hope and love so that the love of all humans as our
neighbors became the focal point instead of self-realization.
As we studied ethics it became our task to put together
the philosophical ethics we learned from Father Gus and
the spiritual ideal of putting the face of Jesus before our eyes
that we might have him in our mind, in our heart, on our
lips and in our hands for others just as Stephen did for Saul.
The *Imitation of Christ* as Stephen lived it out was so powerful
that it could convert Saul who was intent upon stoning him to death.
During Holy Week especially we thought about Jesus as the servant
who would suffer for others and we meditated on the four suffering
Servant antiphons of Second Isaiah such as the one at Isaiah 53:2

> He had neither beauty nor majesty;
> nothing to attract our eyes.

As Father Sullivan and Father Morris spoke to us about this Jesus
we could begin to see four different kinds of ethics: the self-
realization ethics, the ethics that loves the neighbor as the self,
the ethics that cares for with love widows, orphans and aliens
and the ethics that loves the enemy even as Stephen reveals
the enemy loving Jesus who prays for those killing him.
It was good to get all of this clear in our mind so that we could
see just how following Jesus would take us into a new world view
completely different from any other with its new love of enemy
and yet connect with them as the fulfillment of each of them.
Suffering joyfully for anyone afflicting us could bring us to
a new self-realization and to a love of neighbor and of the alien.

I,8.7 And the Logic of a New Cosmology

The four different ethical contexts had implications for cosmology. When it is asked: "Why is there something rather than nothing?" there can be a spectrum of pre-Socratic, pre-ethical answers but once we get to the self-realization ethics of the great Socratics: the Platonists, Aristotelians, Stoics, Epicureans and Sceptics there has to be a cause of the universe or cosmos that is adequate to account for things here so Aristotle would posit a prime mover. A self-realization ethics had a logic to it that was connected with a self-moving mover and a physics that thought of the world as an ordered cosmos given order by an ordering mind. This ethics and this ordered cosmos would stress the golden rule and the idea that we should love our neighbor as we love ourself. The third kind of ethics which can see the Jewish people as a suffering servant who care for widows, orphans and aliens implies a new kind of cosmology as we see in the first chapter of Genesis in which the loving God creates the cosmos during six days and sees that each created thing is good and humans are made in his image and likeness as being personal and good. Once we came to the fourth ethics of the loving face of Stephen and of Jesus forgiving and loving the very ones killing them there is a new world view in which the problem of evil is solved. In the pre-Socratic, Aristotelian and Jewish the Originating source or the Prime Mover or the creator God could be seen as good and it could with great urgency be asked why is there suffering and evil? Empedocles and Heraclitus tried to account for evil by positing an originary hatred or an originary war but if existence is seen as good as in the first chapter of Genesis then how can there be an all good and all powerful God who would permit evil suffering? The Suffering Jesus gives us a new cosmology because now suffering can be seen as a way of loving rather than as evil. Jesus enables us to see the face of God and his world in a new way.

Agape and *Hesed*

I,8.8 *By Revealing the Loving Face of God*

Throughout the Old Testament there are about a hundred references to the face of God and it was the goal of the devout Jew to see God's face by living out the idea of *hesed* and of *ahavah*. Moses was at first the friend of God and spoke with him face to face. But after the idolatry of worshipping the golden calf no human could see the face of God and live and Moses only saw the backside of God. But Jesus lets us see the face of God in a new way for by following Jesus we see the backside of God but by following him in his suffering we see the face of the loving Jesus and thus the face of the loving God who will suffer out of love for us. Philosophy as we studied it in the seminary was really an interplay between faith and reason and our faith did help us to understand God, man and the universe much better than we would have with reason for the first two kinds of ethics and their connected worldview belonged to reason alone but the next two world views were Jewish and Christian. Believing that we might understand already made our study of philosophy a kind of theology with ethics as first philosophy. By believing in the Jewish covenant and believing that we should obey the ten commandments and do the will of God and be just to all humans we knew of a world view that reason alone would never reach but which led to a very noble belief and practice. By believing in the *agape* of Jesus which fulfilled the *hesed* and *Ahavah* of the Hebrew Bible we came to a world view that was even contrary to reason in self-sacrifice even for enemies. What we would study in Theology for four years would differ from our ten philosophy courses because it would explicitly begin with scripture and faith and we would study the history of theology even as it went through the nine periods of history in the Hebrew Bible and we would study Aquinas, Augustine and others. But in philosophy we saw how theology let there be a better philosophy.

I,8.9 And the Logic of Its New Natural Theology

Our final systematic philosophy course besides logic, metaphysics, psychology, ethics and cosmology was natural theology which made clear the difference between Catholic philosophy and theology. In natural theology we studied four things: (1) The proofs for God's existence, (2) The essence of God, (3) the absolute attributes of God and (4) the relative attributes of God as a united whole. For our exam we had to know St. Thomas' five proofs for God's existence and show why we could only know God's essence and his attributes analogically and not univocally for our mind cannot fully know what God is but only that he is even though we can know some about him with reason. We found it wonderful to know these arguments because it helped us to have a stronger faith and we knew that this would be an excellent starting place to teach others about God. During my summer vocation after my first year of theology I had a discussion group with my fellow students at Ketchum and we discussed the five ways and enjoyed it so much that we did it once a week for more than two months. Again we came to see that natural theology could be understood from four perspectives given the four ethical views of the world. The God whose existence we proved with reason could again be a pre-Socratic source, an Aristotelian prime mover, a Jewish creator of a good world and the God whose face Jesus lets us see. Faith and reason seemed to support each other and the more we believed in the Jesus who offered his life for others the more sense it made for us to offer our lives for others and so faith and the practice of it supported each other but not only that. For that faith in the *agape* of the loving Jesus in showing us that God is love helped us expand the notion of the God of reason. The God who was all powerful and all-knowing and was greater than any creature it brought into being would suffer for love of the creature.

I,9 Believing Because it is Absurd in Theology

I,9.1 Father Dougherty Taught us Scripture in the Old Way

After eight years in the seminary we received our college degree
with a major in philosophy and now we were ready to study
four years of theology before we would be ordained as priests.
We did begin to receive the sacrament of the seven holy orders
already when we were in first theology and so I received tonsure
where they cut my hair in four places so show that I was not going
to live only in this world and I received the orders of lector and Porter.
The lector is one who will read at the liturgical services and the
porter is the one who will welcome people at the door of the church.
The study of scripture was a big part of our theological training.
During our first semester of our first year Father Dougherty gave us
an overview of the Old Testament and we learned that there were nine
periods of Hebrew history and we studied how the prophets, priests,
kings and sages transmitted the word of God to the people of God.
After the stores of the first eleven chapters of Genesis there was (2) the
Patriarchal Period (3) the Mosaic Period (4) the Period of Conquest and
settlement (5) the United Kingdom (6) the Divided Kingdom (8) the Exile
in Babylon (8) the Priestly Period of Return and (9) the Wisdom Literature.
Father Dougherty was a very pious man and really loved the
Bible and he would pray before and after each class and he wanted
us to love the word of God also but he was not a fundamentalist.
Right from the beginning he taught us of the four kinds of
interpretation that St. Augustine learned from St. Ambrose.
He always showed us how to read tests from a literal, moral
mystical and typological point of view and even with the help
of St. Paul he taught us the meaning of the typological sense
and of the moral and the mystical and so we applied philosophy
even to reading scripture and that made so much sense to us.
Father Dougherty had memorized all 150 of the psalms as he
prayed them each week and we looked forward to doing that too.

I,9.2 Father Hill Taught us Scripture in the New Way

In the Winter semester of 1960, we received our introductory course
on new Testament Studies from Father Hill who had studied with
William Foxwell Albright the author of *From Stone Age to Christianity*.
At this time Catholic Scripture Scholars were just mastering the
new methods of the Higher Biblical Criticism and one of Father Hill's
students Fr. Raymond Brown S.S. was fast becoming the leading
scholar of Johannine Studies and he came to St. Thomas and
spoke to us of his work and the new age of scripture scholarship.
While telling us about the Gospels of Matthew and Luke and how
they were based upon Mark but also shared many sayings of Jesus
in common Father Hill also told us about the Wellhausen theory and
how the Pentateuch was put together from the writing of J, E, D, and P.
We were fascinated by all this and loved to talk about it with
each other even during our recreation when on walks together.
To see how there was first an oral tradition both for the
first five books of the Bible and for the New Testament and
to come to see just when the different writings took place and
from what theological viewpoints was something we would want
to study for the rest of our lives and to teach our parishioners.
As we began to think of the historical Jesus and just what he
himself taught and then what his followers thought step by step
seemed exceedingly valuable even for our own spiritual lives.
To begin to see how Mark at about 70 and then Matthew
by about 80 and then Luke by about 85 and John by about 90
put their Gospels together under the Inspiration of the Holy Spirit
captivated our interest and it was so interesting to be taught by
Father Dougherty and then Father Hill and we discussed that together.
To think that there were seven authentic Pauline letters and
that the others were written by the Pauline school even helped us
to understand the Book of Isaiah and how 2nd Isaiah was
written about 250 years after First Isaiah by the school of Isaiah.

Agape and *Hesed*

I,9.3 Father Morris Taught us Moral Theology

Father Morris was another very holy man like Father Dougherty
and he gave us spiritual talks when Father Sullivan was away.
He was the living embodiment of a loving and sensitive conscience
and in Graduate School had been especially trained in Moral Theology.
Father Morris wanted us to be clear about the moral revolution
that was initiated by Jesus Christ and so he taught us about Jewish
law and the Stoic natural law and he showed us how the
*agape*ic morality went beyond both and also fulfilled each of them.
He explained to us how in the New Testament an act which is not
an act of love has no moral value in it since love is central.
He told us how in Matthew's Gospel the entire Law and the
prophets depend on these two commandments of loving God and
neighbor so that love is not only central but also the totality.
When one decided to become a disciple of Christ as we did in coming
to the seminary we became a member of Christ's body and do not
only imitate Christ but share in his passion and death for others.
Father Morris told us how according to Paul in Romans 13:8-10
we have no duty according to the law toward our neighbor except
to love him for the love of the neighbor is the fulfillment of the Law.
The love mentioned in the two commandments is not two loves
but one for what is done to the neighbor is done to Christ himself.
Father Morris really got me thinking when he talked about the place
of sexuality in moral theology and moral thinking in our present day.
He said that in the New Testament chastity was not a major theme.
Perhaps it started to take center stage with St. Augustine but in our
day sex receives more treatment than any other moral question.
I wondered if within myself and maybe not too many others, for I
did not want to generalize, trying to live the celibate life in the
seminary did not increase my sex drive and make women more dear?
Absence makes the heart grow fonder and the sound of a woman's
voice became so beautiful to me that I seemed to love all women.

I,9.4 Father Foudy Taught us Dogmatic Theology

Our study of theology was centered around the code, the creed, the cult
and the canon for we studied the canon of sacred scripture and
the code of law and of morality and the liturgical cultic practices.
Dogmatic theology was in a way the detailed study of the Apostle's creed.
Father Foudy taught us about The Father, The Son and The Holy Spirit.
We did a kind of biblical study of Christ's titles of King, Messiah
and Savior and then we looked at the servant of the Lord and Son of Man.
It was an unforgettable learning experience to see how the idea of
The Son of Man developed through the Old Testament and then to see
how it was used again in a developmental way in the New Testament.
But the idea that seemed most important for our own spiritual life
was that "corporate personality" which means that a group is
incorporated in the person of its leader as David incorporated Israel.
As the Servant of the Lord the suffering Son of God is the Messiah King.
In Luke 24:26 it is stated that the Messiah had to suffer in order
to enter into his glory and this was a distasteful notion to everyone.
We are members of Christ's Body when we suffer with him and
the notion of "corporate personality" reaches its apex here and is at
the center of the Christian revolution of an absolutely new love.
Isaiah 53:7 says that he opened not his mouth like a lamb
that is let to the slaughter and Jesus is the lamb of God who
is resacrificed at every Mass enabling us to unite with him.
Whether we studied philosophy or scripture or moral theology
or dogmatic theology we always reached that point of following Jesus
in his suffering and thereby seeing the face of Jesus and the face of God.
All of our studies were not only theoretical but most practical
in always bringing us to unite ourselves with the Sacred Heart of Jesus.
Jesus achieved his work by sharing deeply in the common experience
of humankind and of all flesh for we all suffer and pass away.
Identity with Jesus' suffering is first of all identity with Jesus'
loving and all loving beings who suffer do belong to his body.

Agape and *Hesed*

I,9.5 *Father Purta Taught us Canon Law*

Father Purta, a young priest of Polish background from Scranton, Pennsylvania, came to St. Thomas fresh from getting his Canon Law degree in Rome and we were his first class and we loved him. He was a wonderful teacher and loved to tell jokes even about the toilet paper in Rome which was so rough that you went over there a colon but came back with a semi-colon.
Just as lawyers are very important in helping modern society work so the priest must study the law codes of the Catholic church and help mediate between a person and him or herself, between members of families and between many persons and groups. Moral theology treats of the love we should have in all of our relationships but canon Law helps the priest deal with frictions. Very bright seminarians are often sent to study canon Law after their ordination and seminary training for that is an excellent training for future Bishops and Monsignors who are chancellors of the Diocese and help all the groups get along together. It is interesting that in my second year of theology when I had my Platonic experience of falling in love and becoming celibate Father Gustafson asked if he could talk with Father Purta about me and for a couple of months we thought about my vocation together. The person trained in Canon Law is taught to see the implications of a person's thoughts, words and deeds and to try to prevent trouble. Father Gus said that he did not understand me and Father Purta thought that I did not have a vocation because a priest cannot be falling in love with various girls and women in his parish or town. Canon Law taught us the practicalities that Lawyers have to know for every priest will have to deal with helping persons get along and there are innumerable problems that are always coming up. We learned of Justinian and his Law Code and again we thought about the scriptural roots of legalism and we studied the history of the great moments in the development of Canon Law in the church.

I,9.6 Father Desmond Taught us Public Speaking

We had an excellent training in public speaking in the minor
seminary and that had to continue at every step along the way
in the major seminary for giving sermons and reading and
speaking clearly and convincingly is a major task for Priests.
In class we would practice giving a homily or sermon and
the other students would say what they thought and Father Desmond
would help each of us get right every nuance of annunciation
and voice projection and all the techniques as well as giving a well
ordered talk with introduction, body and its parts and a conclusion.
He taught us how all the other branches of our study helped us
to give a good sermon and be a good speaker for philosophy, moral
theology, scripture studies, dogmatic theology and canon Law all
helped us prepare the message and be a good medium for that message.
The goal was to become an inspiring speaker and once again that had
to do with the power of love for love is not the power to dominate
but the power to communicate the self which begins with the incarnation
which is God's communication of self in the flesh of Jesus Christ.
Jesus is the communication both of the love of God for all flesh
and of the love all flesh for God even through the Holy Spirit.
So our prayer life came to be seen as a very important part of our
public speaking for those listening should be able to feel our love
for them and know even in the tone of our voice and all of our gestures
that we are praying for them unceasingly as their priestly mediator.
The priest must be like Jesus in bringing the love and word of God
to his people and of bringing the prayer of the people to God.
Father Desmond taught us not only public speaking but also
singing so we continued perfecting not only our Gregorian chant
but also some who were good were in the choir singing polyphony.
With Father Desmond we continued learning history as we looked
more and more into the history of church music and the kinds of
spiritualities which would give rise even to different kinds of oratory.

Agape and *Hesed*

I,9.7 *And We were Always Learning History and Sociology*

As priests we would have to be not only holy men and good lawyers and speakers but especially good psychologists so that we could understand the depths even of the preconscious problems and attitudes of each person who would come to us seeking guidance. In philosophy we studied psychology for one semester and we came to know of the history of psychology even as it moved into Freud, Jung and Adler and we also came to know of sociology. At the very time that I was studying in my first year of theology my sister, Bette Jo, was majoring in sociology at Gonzaga University. Father Bernard had already taught us a course in sociology at Mt. Angel and with the big changes to come very soon in the church with Vatican II sociology even became a subject that might replace philosophy as the best major for one studying to become a priest. It was a modern social science that gathered statistics as it sought to understand all sorts of social groups in their deep down physiology and habits so that there might be a way of helping delinquent girls, alcoholics, gang members and any sort of group member or person who needed counseling and guidance. Father Bernard and the Mount Angel community still shape my attitude and habit today and sociology as Father Bernard first taught it to us and as we continued to study it at Saint Thomas explains health, happiness, holiness and wisdom as well as their opposites. Each morning even today as I go for my prayer walk and pray the Rosary I still pray for the community of Mount Angel. I pray for Fathers Ambrose and Method and for Brother Fidelis and I ask them to pray for us . Then I pray for Father Bernard, Father Louis, father David, Father Athanasius, Father Edmund, Father Cosmos and Father Hugh. I pray for Pat Carney, Ray Heuberger, Brendan Mallon, and Glen Uelencott.
I pray for them and the entire community of my nourishing mother and I ask all of them to pray for me and all of mine.

I,9.8 And We had a Retreat each Semester

Each semester three days were set aside for a retreat that
we might meditate and concentrate upon various aspects of that
love which was the centrality and totality of our seminary life.
Often one of the Bishops from the seven Dioceses that sent
seminarians to St. Thomas would direct the retreat for us.
I have in my hand a little notebook, which is entitled
Bishop Leipzig's Retreat, April 7 (probably in 1960) and it says:

> As West Point is demanding in discipline, so is the seminary.
> Upon the day of our ordination we become an important person.
> Every move we make is observed by many people.
> We influence them and help send them to heaven or to hell.
> See what would happen if we should lose one family from the faith.
> We can all be Fulton Sheens in our own little parishes.
> Our life is our greatest sermon so we must be sincere.
> People judge us by how we say the Mass.
> They know when it is too fast or too slow.
> No priest should ever neglect the rosary.
> We cannot ask the people to say it if we don't.
> First things must be first.
> Be kind to a family when someone dies
> for this is what gets the people.
> Disappointments come often to the priest
> and we must carry our cross as Christ did.
> If we do not have trouble we will never rise to heights.
> Pray that we can meet these.

Everything in the seminary came around to following the suffering
Jesus and Bishop Leipzig ended his retreat by telling us
about St. Theresa the Little Flower who wrote: "How sweet is
the way of love! True, one may fall and be unfaithful to grace.
But Love knows how to draw profit from everything by consuming
what is displeasing to our Lord and leaving a humble peace."

Agape and *Hesed*

I,9.9 That We might Teach the Joy of Jesus' Suffering

The Rosary which Bishop Leipzig urged us to pray everyday
is a summary of Jesus's *agape*ic revolution for in no other religion
is there this loving mix of Joyful, Sorrowful and Glorious Mysteries.
The Buddhists come close in stressing that all life is suffering
but they want to get rid of it rather than undergo it passionately
in union with Jesus as a way of loving others and thus being joyful.
Isaiah is the originator of the three suffering servant poems
but there is no explanation as to how joy and glory might be
connected with them which is at the heart of Christian love.
When St. Paul writes about love he says "charity, joy, peace, etc.
and joy is the first reality that he connects with *agape* just as he
saw it in the smiling, loving face of Stephen as he was stoned.
In a certain sense just as the minor seminary at Mount Angel
was our nourishing mother so the major seminary at St. Thomas
was our directing father and so each day I pray for
Father Gustafson, Father Sullivan, Father Morris, Father
Thirkle, Father Desmond, Father Purta and Father Chirico
and for Father Tom Taylor and Father Jim Dunning.
Each morning on my prayer walk right after I say the
"Hail Mary" for the community of Mount Angel I still pray
also for the community of St. Thomas.
I pray for all those still living: for Father Dunning's
beautiful sister and for Michael Brodie, Bill Taylor,
Bill Wiegand, Jeff Sarkies, Carol Thiel and Bill Gould.
Then I say the "Hail Mary" for them and all of ours and
I ask the blessed dead to pray for me and all of ours.

Part Three: Receiving Solutions

With Levinas and Derrida

II,7   Derrida's *Praeparatio Evangelica*

II,7.1 With a Messianicity without the Messiah

Our main task in these millennial meditations is to understand just how *agape* came into the world, what it meant as it was first described in the New Testament and how it has developed since then. *Hesed* and *Ahava*, the two forms of Jewish love, prepared its way and Levinas and Derrida in our day can be very helpful in showing us just what that Jewish love is and how *agape* differs from it. Derrida sees love as the hospitality that is welcoming to others and he refers to the spirit of this hospitality as a Jewish Messianicity. Anyone who wholeheartedly takes responsibility for the needy has the spirit of pure giving and Derrida sees that as Messianicity. However, Derrida is very opposed to any concrete historical Messiah such as Jesus Christ for that kind of claim is the source of much hatred and bloodshed as he makes clear on pages 69–70 in *The Gift of Death* where he writes about Mount Moriah for the Jews as being the place for the grand Mosque of Jerusalem and the Way of the Cross for the Christian with:

> each claiming its particular perspective
> on this place and claiming an original
> historical and political interpretation of Messianism.

He goes on to write also on page 70:

> Isaac's sacrifice continues every day.
> Countless machines of death wage a war
> that has no front. There is no front
> between responsibility and irresponsibility.

Derrida's whole task is to set up this front between responsibility and irresponsibility and he thinks that believing in a concrete Messiah like Jesus is irresponsible because it will bring about much war between the Jewish, Christian and Islamic peoples. So according to Derrida as *agape* arises out of Jewish love it will be focused on Jesus Christ as a concrete historical Messiah.

Agape and *Hesed*

II,7.2 With a Responsibility without Celibacy

Derrida begins his book *The Gift of Death* with a chapter on Patochka's understanding of the history of Christian responsibility. Patochka says nothing about the Jewish preparation for *agape*. Rather he sees Christianity as growing out of the Platonism that had developed out of the orgiastic culture of irresponsible sexuality. In Plato's dialogues on *eros*, *The Symposium* and *The Phaedrus*, we see how he is intent on going beyond mere sexual pleasure to a sublimation of sexual energy that can use it creatively to take responsibility for a new freedom and a new goodness. Of course, Jesus was a celibate and Paul urged it for all ministers that they might be free to serve the Lord and to serve all people. Catholic priests and religious were celibate and Derrida wrote about Augustine's *Confessions* in which his mother, Monica was told by Ambrose that a child of so many prayers and tears would not perish. Derrida goes on to show that once Christianity grew out of Platonism according to Patochka it produced a responsibility for all persons with the notion of personhood becoming central. One is brought to wonder if the sublimation of the orgiastic might free one for a universal love once that Platonism meets the Jewish idea of love for others within Christianity. In the Jewish ethos there is no idea of celibacy and as Derrida helps us to see how Jewish love is a preparation for Christian love we see that it did not prepare for celibacy. Jesus was a celibate and many women were attracted to him. But the Jewish ethos always stresses the ideal of marriage and family life and, of course, Judaism is not a proselytizing religion that wants to go out to all persons and convert them. With his deconstructive reading Derrida presents Patochka so that we can think about these very different sources of Christianity. There is no hint of celibacy in *hesed* and *ahava* as they prepared the way for *agape* which takes celibacy seriously as does Plato.

II,7.3 With a Postmodernity without Modernity

As we get help from Derrida in analyzing just how and how not *hesed* and *ahava* are preparations for *agape* the next point has to do with his being a postmodern and not a modern thinker. Judaism and traditional Christianity saw ethics as first philosophy. But with the coming of modernity that changed for Descartes saw metaphysics as first philosophy as it proved the existence of my mind, God and my body and saw physics as growing from those roots and giving rise to medicine, mechanics and morals. Derrida like Kierkegaard and Nietzsche goes back to a religious ethics as first philosophy and then philosophizes from that starting point. Descartes, Hobbes, Locke and Kant tend to philosophize within the limits of reason alone as did the Greeks whereas *agape* is an ethical viewpoint like *hesed* and *ahava* beginning with faith. Postmodernity also works with a notion of persons in relation while modernity sees each person and state as being a rugged individual. Luther declared that "I stand alone before God." And the social contract theories off Hobbes and Locke assume that there is no natural bond between all persons so we have to produce a conventional bond. For the modernist every man and every state is an island and none of us are part of the main as each region has its religion. Derrida does write about persons as he writes about Patochka almost as if he is saying that within Judaism there is not an idea of person as you find it rooted in the trinity in Christianity. But still for Derrida the Jewish people do form a community and *hesed* and *ahava* which call for a responsibility of duty love and felt love for all Jewish persons and especially the needy. So Derrida is a postmodernist in his emphasis on ethics as first philosophy and with his notion of the covenant community. But while Kierkegaard and Nietzsche were both celibates in line with Plato, Plotinus, Augustine and Dante that aspect of postmodernity was not appropriated by Derrida.

Agape and Hesed

II,7.4 With a Spirituality without Organized Religion

Once Derrida decides to have ethics as first philosophy and thus
the idea of pure giving rooted in Jewish *hesed* and *ahava* that
decision will have implications for religion, logic, economics,
politics, psychology and a culture's health, education and welfare.
When ethics aims to take responsibility for others in all their needs
it can see the dangers of concrete Messiahs in whose names peoples
might wage wars based on a logic of exclusive opposites that we
are right and they are wrong and we should fight for the truth.
So to take responsibility for the good of all and for lasting peace
Derrida is opposed to this Messiah and that Messiah and he
wants a spirit of hospitality that stresses an open spirituality.
Just as he sees dangers in any concrete Messiah so he sees
dangers in any organized religion that also might set up
a logic of exclusive opposites between itself and other religions.
Derrida knows that Judaism, Islam and Protestantism tend
to go in that direction and not want to learn from any others.
All during modernity rugged individuals as persons and as states
fought against each other in religious, political and economic wars.
Derrida is aware of all the Holy wars that were fought
throughout the Hebrew Bible and of how the Sunnis and Shias
are at each other's throat and everybody else's and of how
as soon as Luther and Calvin got going these were religious wars.
While he is putting forth his theory of religion without religion
in many of his later writings in *The Gift of Death* he does
present the view of the Catholic Religion with its celibacy
that has proceeded with dialectical opposites instead of
exclusive opposites as it proceeded from the orgiastic
to the Platonic to the Christian with its openness to others.
Augustine was a Platonist Christian, Aquinas an Aristotelian
Christian, the Franciscans were Stoic Christians and the
Carmelites became Buddhist Christians with a logic of mixed opposites.

II,7.5 With a Logic of Mixed Opposites without Exclusive Opposites

Derrida is aware of four different logics of the opposites.
His ethics as first philosophy which is a Messianicity of
hospitality for all sees the violence of the first three logics.
The greatest danger for an ethical world view is that it think
in terms of a logic of exclusive opposites as those who
believe in the value of the orgiastic might think of Platonism.
Those who think that the highest value is to have sex with
one beautiful body and then many beautiful bodies as it says
in *The Symposium* and then with somebody with a beautiful
soul are going to exclude Platonic celibacy as a false value.
But with Platonism we see a logic of inclusive opposites for
differences are seen only as appearances and once we know
the truth all that is will turn out to be a part of the Good.
Plato with his ladder of love that takes us out of the cave is
going to indulge in what Derrida calls the violence of Metaphysics.
A Metaphysics is violent if it sees all the individuals of a species
as being basically the same and then sees all the species
as being different forms that all belong to the same Being.
Plato may think of that Being which is true because it is
beyond all becoming as the Good but really it is not Good.
That is why Aristotle criticized Plato because his logic
of inclusive opposites did violence to every individual.
The third logic is that of Hegel's dialectical opposites.
There is a thesis and then its opposite the anti-thesis but
it does not end there for next there is a synthesis but
it does not only get rid of difference for next there will be
an antithesis to the synthesis and so history will proceed.
Patochka as Derrida sees it has a kind of Hegelian logic
as he goes from the orgiastic to the Platonic to the Christian.
But Derrida wants a fourth kind of paradoxical logic
of mixed opposites in which the pure is an impossibility.

Agape and *Hesed*

II,7.6 With the Sacrifice of Economy without Heavenly Reward

In the last chapter of *The Gift of Death* in the chapter entitled "Every Other is Wholly Other" Derrida discussesthe passages from *The Sermon on the Mount* which have to do with giving.

> But when thou doest alms; let not
> thy left hand know what thy right hand doeth:
> that thine alms may be in secret;
> and thy Father which seeth in secret
> shall reward thee openly. (Matt. 6:1–4)

Jesus the Messiah preached a pure giving in which his people should love their enemy and give without expecting any return. But he also promised a heavenly reward for any good done here. So Judaism's love of widows, orphans and aliens and of those who torture the Suffering Servant prepared the way for the love that Jesus here teaches but it did not promise a heavenly reward. Many Jews such as the Sadducees did not believe in heaven and they kept the justice with its eye for an eye and tooth for a tooth. Love would not negate justice according to Jewish *hesed* and *ahava*. Derrida ends his book (p. 114) by going to Nietzsche who writes about "the stroke of genius called Christianity" in which we see

> God personally immolating himself
> for the debt of man, God paying himself
> personally out of a pound of his own flesh—
> the creditor playing scapegoat
> for his debtor, from love can you
> believe it? from love of his debtor!

The Christian Messiah with the grace of his love and suffering for us overcame the law of strict justice and teaches us to love our enemies just as did he and we will all be happy in heaven! So there is this great leap of *agape* beyond *hesed* and *ahava* in which the gift of the Messiah in his grace lets us believe that we can all be saved and rewarded in an eternal heaven.

II,7.7 With a Just War Politics without Non-Resistance

On page 102 of *The Gift of Death* Derrida quotes the Messiah Jesus:

> But I say unto you, that ye resist not evil
> but whosoever shall smite thee
> on thy right cheek, turn to him the other also.

On page 103 Derrida reminds us of how Patochka teaches that Christ teaches that we should obey those words:

> Love your enemies . . . pray for them
> which . . . persecute you. (Matt. 5:44)

Derrida says (p. 103) that it is important to go to the Greek and the Latin for as Carl Schmitt in chapter 3 of *The Concept of the Political* argues

> *Inimicus* is not *hostis* in Latin
> and *ekthros* is not *polemios* in Greek.

Derrida writes (p. 103) that Schmitt concludes from this that

> Christ's teaching concerns the love
> that we must show to our private enemies...
> Christ's teaching would thus be moral
> or psychological, even metaphysical,
> but not political.

Derrida says (p. 103):

> As he reminds us no Christian Politics
> ever advised the West to love the Muslims
> who invaded Christian Europe.

But Derrida (p. 104) does not agree with Schmitt and writes:

> It would seem difficult to keep the potential
> opposition between one's neighbor and one's enemy
> within the sphere of the private.

To make his argument Derrida goes back to (Lev 19:15–18) which says "thou shalt love they neighbor . . . as a member of the same ethnic group." and Jesus is going beyond this to all.

Agape and Hesed

II,7.8 With a Psychology of Loving ours Without Loving All

Derrida's main argument for being opposed to particular Messiahs is that they provoke war by claiming to be the chief authority. As we think with Derrida about how Jewish love helped prepare the way for Christian love he points out how Leviticus in saying "Thou shalt love thy neighbor as thyself" really did mean a member of your same ethnic group and not everyone. Derrida seems to be suggesting that a politics of Christian love which stresses non-resistance is impossible because there have to be just wars so that we can defend ourselves against those who always come along and want to take over the world. But what does Derrida think about a Christian psychology of *agape*? We have seen that he wrote on page 103 of *The Gift of Death*:

> Christ's teaching would thus be moral
> or psychological, even metaphysical,
> but not political.

What does Derrida think of the psychology of *agape* and its morality? If one did begin to fulfill the task of a psychological *agape* in which with my attitude and my feeling, I actually did pray for those who hate or are opposed to me and really do me harm and if I did come to love them is that an ideal. Derrida thinks that we should not love all our fellow Jews that way but should love Hitler or anyone who dislikes us. Does Derrida see the distinction between the political and the psychological beginning to collapse with Jesus' *agape*? If psychologically I should love even my potential enemies can I still fight against them with a defensive just war and yet pray for them and love them with feeling at the same time? I would think that this is a distinct possibility and that Derrida would see it as an hypocritical position that does not really love psychologically any more than it truly loves politically. Insofar as *agape* psychologically loves the enemy is it not immoral?

II,7.9 With a Metaphysical Rescue of my Cat but not all Flesh

Derrida writes on page 103 of *The Gift of Death*,

> Christ's teaching would thus be moral
> or psychological, even metaphysical,
> but not political,

But what does he mean by "metaphysical" when it comes to loving?
Moral Christians should love everyone especially their enemies.
Psychologically one should do that in one's attitude and feeling.
But politically a just war against aggressors should be fought
even though morally and psychologically we still love our enemy.
The physical has to do with this realm of becoming and its possibilities
here and now for each thing and even and the metaphysical which
goes beyond the physical might have to do with possibility as
such and the basic principles of the moral and the psychological.
So the Messiah's love of enemy and non-resistance might be
a general principle that should direct even our attitudes.
But perhaps the metaphysical worlds of Derrida and of Jesus Christ
differ enormously for the Messiah whom Derrida rejects became
flesh that "all flesh might see the salvation of the Lord" (Luke 3:6)
That quotation in Luke does come from Isaiah 40:3–5, but
there the context does not present the immortality of all flesh.
In *The Gift of Death* on pages 69 and 71 Derrida treats loving
animals and his main idea is that when I rescue a cat
and am responsible for its well-being I am letting billions of others
suffer so I am sacrificing them even as I love one or a few.
So the Christian believes Jesus by becoming flesh and dying
on the cross for all flesh has ultimately saved all flesh.
All humans and all loving creatures will be rescued.
So as Derrida shows us how far Jewish love goes in
preparing the way for *agape* we can see here that *hesed*
and *ahava* will be sensitive to the impossibility of loving all.
But Christians can believe in a metaphysics of eternal love for all.

Agape and *Hesed*

II,8 Levinas' *Praeparatio Evangelica*

II,8.1 With the Third Without the Trinity

First, for Levinas, there is the other and secondly there is myself. The face of the other calls me to be a host to widows, orphans and aliens and a hostage as the suffering servant even to my enemy. This double hospitality with its love of *hesed* and *ahava* makes up the essence of Jewish ethics and precedes any ethics of justice. Ethics for Levinas means that I should acknowledge you as an irreducible person whether or not you acknowledge me, simply because it is my moral duty to do so; as in love, one resigns oneself to the possibility of not being loved in return. However, even as I serve another with altruism and no egoism so another other might love and help me as he or she watches me even in my plight as I offer my cheek to the smiter.
We have already seen how Levinas' notion of the third lets him show Derrida that pure giving is not impossible for I can receive returns in my giving from a third that still lets me give purely. So Levinas makes clear how in Jewish love there is the notion of a triadic and not only a dyadic love and we have to ask how this is preparation for the love between Father, Son and Holy Spirit. How essential to Jewish love and ethics is the third and is this clear in the Hebrew Bible and does the notion of Trinitarian love fulfill it? As Levinas begins to treat the third party he does quote Isaiah

> Peace, peace to the neighbor and the one far off (Isaiah 59:19)

The main point for Derrida and Levinas as they seek to understand Jewish love and ethics is the notion of asymmetrical or non-reciprocal giving in which I give out of love and expect nothing in return. Having a third who sees me and the other and sees me giving to the other and then gives to me seems to keep giving pure for Levinas. The third seems to make asymmetrical giving possible by bringing justice onto the scene and complementing love with justice. Is Levinas giving reasons why his God should be Trinitarian?

II,8.2 With the Wisdom of Love Without The Love of Wisdom

As we have seen Levinas thinks that

> Philosophy is the wisdom of love
> at the service of love. (*Otherweise than Being*, 162)

This makes him different from all those Greek influenced philosophers who see philosophy as the love of wisdom rather than the wisdom of love. Love is first and last for Levinas with its hospitality for others and the coming of the third with its justice and philosophy raises questions about right asymmetrical love in relation to justice. There must always be skepticism which questions knowledge just as it was there for Socrates and all Socratic philosophers. Philosophy for Levinas is not the same as it was for Plato. The love of wisdom for Plato had to do with a self-realization through a right formation in which I would get information and undergo a transformation and finally come to a conformity of my mind with the forms of things and the form of Being. For Levinas, on the other hand, my journey begins with a call from the other or a vocation and if I respond with love then there can be a convocation of myself, the other and the third and thus philosophy is the wisdom of love at the service of love. Levinas is trying to be true in his philosophizing to Jewish *hesed* and *ahava* and thus he does not have *agape* love of wisdom. Just as Derrida does not accept Jesus as the Messiah so Levinas does not accept him as the wisdom of God to be loved as wisdom. In *Proverbs* and *Ecclesiasticus* and the *Book of Wisdom* of the Hebrew Bible wisdom was seen as Lady Wisdom and as a created creature of playful delight, a word-breath Mediatrix and a mirror Image Radiatrix and Jesus is seen as this wisdom. So *agape* from the beginning was a love between Father, Son and Holy Spirit and the Son is that wisdom and the Holy Spirit is the Ruah Yahweh who also created with God. Levinas does not love wisdom as such but only God and persons.

Agape and *Hesed*

II,8.3 With a Postmodernity Without Modernity

As Levinas thinks about Kierkegaard and Nietzsche he does not have one good thing to say about them unlike Derrida who is as Caputo calls him a Dionysian Rabbi or a combination of Nietzsche and Levinas and who meditated greatly on Kierkegaard. But still Levinas is very much a postmodern thinker and three indications of this have to do with thinking about ethics as first philosophy, a logic of mixed opposites and interpersonal persons. We need to try to see what is special about his postmodern ethics, logic, psychology etc., and it would be good if we could relate all of this to his notion of the third and its loving justice. Derrida deconstructed *Totality and Infinity* because it still used a logic of exclusive opposites so Levinas gets beyond that when he comes to *Otherwise Than Being* and its mixed opposites. Corey Beals can help us when he writes:

> A central feature of the wisdom of love
> is the fact that it originates not
> in a war of all against all, as Hobbes
> would have it, but in the absolute
> responsibility of one for the Other...
> Politics is not harmonizing antagonistic
> forces. (*Levinas and the Wisdom of Love*, 94)

Modernity is marked by the rugged individual such that Hobbes will say "man is a wolf to man" and we need a police state. Of course, police are helpful but in Levians' Jewish ethics no man is an island and all persons are interpersonal which brings us to Levinas' notion of the third so that we are never in a simply dyadic relation of just two but love is triadic. In this way Levinas prevents an egoism for two and brings justice on the scene which lets Levinas be fully postmodern. The notion of the third takes Levinas beyond the same and the other and any exclusive opposites and beyond Derrida's hedgehog.

II,8.4 With a Holiness Without the Sacred

In his book called *Nine Talmudic Readings* Levinas wrote
about *The Sacred and the Holy* from pages 140 to 160 and he shows
what is wrong with the sacred and how the Holy is very different.
Levinas relates the sacred to sorcery and writes on page 141

> Sorcery, first cousin, perhaps even sister,
> of the sacred, is the mistress of appearance.

The sacred is always the exclusive opposite of the profane.
The sacred has to do with temple and anything outside the temple
is treated as profane as something bad and to be avoided.
On page 152 in a section entitled *The Modern World* he writes:

> Nothing is identical to itself any longer.
> That is what sorcery is: the modern world.

So if there is only me and you, if there is only totality and infinity
then there will be exclusive opposites such that the totality might
be profane and the infinity might be the sacred but this is appearance.
As soon as we get the third we can begin to see that all is Holy.
If we get the wisdom of love we will be able to love everyone as Holy.
Just as Levinas will have a postmodernity without modernity so
he will have a holy without the sacred because the sacred deceives.
Modernity stresses a dyadic relation in which two individuals meet
and can have an egoism for two or even become enemies to each other.
But once we see that the me of the "*me voici*" and you are even
defined in such a way that we are related to a third then justice
can come on the scene and every other can be valued as holy or
as having an equal kind of dignity with every other human person.
So Levinas is opposed to the notion of the sacred because it is
always defined as opposed to the profane which is not holy.
Levinas ends the essay with a paragraph about Jewish Tradition.
The holiness the Jewish tradition seeks comes to it from
the living God and it teaches them to avoid the sacred which is
the source of many abominations in its negating of so much.

Agape and *Hesed*

II,8.5 With an Ethics Without Ontology

Just as Levinas works out a theory about the wisdom of love that serves love and shows how that wisdom of love serves without being a love of wisdom so his ethics works without ontology. For him ethics is not a theory or a moral code but it has to do with my responsibility for you and the justice between all of us. Ontology as Levinas treats it has to do with a theory of Being and our understanding of it especially as for Heidegger. For Levinas there is already ethics as soon as the face of the other calls me to a responsible love and that ethics gets the new dimension of justice as soon as the third gets me to ask questions. As Levinas says on page 128 of *Otherwise Than Being*:

> The fact that the other, my neighbor,
> is also a third party with respect to another,
> who is also a neighbor, is the birth of
> thought, consciousness, justice and philosophy.

Philosophy for Levinas has to do with understanding the philosophies of history and showing how Jewish ethics and wisdom is different from them but might learn from them. As we think about Levinas explaining the Jewish tradition of love and justice we can see how he prepares the way for Christian love but does not have ontology the way Christians might from Augustine, to Aquinas to Kierkegaard and Nietzsche. Augustine said that the Gospel of John is like Neo-Platonism until we get to the point that the word is said to become flesh. Plotinus the great Platonic mystic whom Augustine combined with his Christianity saw us moving up from the world of the many, changing things to the Life principle through purgation. Then through illumination he saw us reaching the realm of light. Then through unification he saw us becoming one with Being. Augustine's *agape* could embrace that ontology and Levinas shows how *hesed* and *ahava* prepare for *agape* but are not there.

II,8.6 With an Authority Without Force

Corey Beals in his book *Levinas and the Wisdom of Love* discusses
the authority of the other who calls me to love and serve her.
He writes on page 90:

> Indeed, in *Otherwise Than Being*, we find that
> this authority is not only called 'The Good'
> but that "no one is enslaved to the Good" (11).
> Furthermore, despite the asymmetry of my being
> "for the Other" it is "without alienation" (OB, 114)

What the wisdom of love lets Levinas make clear about our world
of love is that I am not forced to love another but I do it freely.
It is not as if the authority of the other that calls me has power over me
but rather I respond with a generous freedom not because I have to.
Levinas does say that my

> responsibility for another is...
> impossible with a good violence. (*Otherwise than Being*, 43)

So the authority of widows, orphans and aliens can call me to
violate myself in a way and the suffering servant clearly does that.
Levinas even writes:

> The Good reabsorbs, or redeems,
> the violence of non-freedom. (Ibid., 123)

So we really do see the logic of mixed opposites at work here.
The authority of the Other in a way is the violence of non-freedom
and then in another way it does call me to freely love and serve.
It is the wisdom of love that lets us make such distinctions.
Of course, the suffering servant is violated but Levinas says
that the Good redeems the violence of this non-freedom so that it
becomes a good violence and this does prepare for the Good News.
Jesus, the Suffering Servant, died for all of us and by loving
his enemies he even redeemed them by suffering for them.
So whenever Christians suffer because of another it is good
if they offer up their suffering and being violated with Jesus.

II,8.7 With a Peace Without Price

The very title of *Otherwise Than Being* is meant to indicate how Levinas develops an ethics without ontology and that has to do with a primary peace that is connected with the Good that does good. In the Jewish world it is God who has taken the initiative to make a covenant with us that we might be able to love those in need. The responsible Jew may have to pay quite a price to bring peace and welfare to widows, orphans and aliens and when it comes to the suffering servant he may have to pay with his life to do good. As he tries to bring peace and reconciliation to his enemies no price will be too high for him to pay as he responds responsibly. This idea of being a peace maker at any price or without price is a key moment of preparing for Jesus, the suffering servant. Isaiah with his four suffering servant poems was thinking about the Jewish people as such being a suffering servant for enemies. But in the Synoptic Gospels it is first Mark's Gospel that tells the story and give the meaning of the suffering of Jesus. Jesus with the logic of mixed opposites said: "Peace, my peace I give unto you." But then he also said: "I come not to give you peace, but the sword." and Levinas prepares the way for all of this. Jesus as a Jew had an ethical religious view that we should build up a world of peace by loving others even if it costs greatly. But he also knew that as others try to follow him they might alienate even their mother and father or brothers and sisters or wife or children and thus bring a sword between loved ones. Levinas' ethics of unconditional, asymmetrical love serves others even if it violates me but once we get to an ethics of justice which the third reveals the third will want peace also for me. So with Levinas we get a combination of two opposed ideals. The ethics of love calls me to suffer for the Infinite Other. The ethics of justice that comes with the third wants justice for me. He prepares the way for Jesus who is violated to lessen violence.

II,8.8 With a Manifestation of Infinity Without Manifestation

Throughout *Otherwise Than Being* Levinas discusses his notion
of glory on such pages as 12, 58, 93, 94, 142, 146, 158 and 164.
On page 12 he writes:

> In the measure that responsibilities
> are taken on they multiply . . .
> The debt increases in the measures
> that it is paid. This diverging perhaps,
> deserves the name glory.

Glory for him is the manifesting of the unmanifest in its unmanifestness.
As I respond to the other his or her infinity begins to manifest
itself to me and it calls forth more loving responsibility from me.
The weight of my responsibility that increases as I respond to
the other begins to show its infinity and that weight is glory.
Levinas in his Jewish religion was always aware of the Glory of God.
God in his infinity is glorious and Levinas begins to see that
infinity and that glory in widows, orphans and aliens who are like God.
The more the infinitely good God becomes manifest the more
it is evident that he is unmanifest and so also with humans.
The Jewish duty love of *hesed* and the felt love of *ahava* insofar
as God reveals them to the Jews reveal the Glory of God and
inspire his people to want to give glory to God in the form of prayer.
The wisdom that arises out of loving and lets us love even better
is connected with this glory which is a debt that keeps increasing.
Our task in this life is to love better and better and to grow in
wisdom which lets us see the big picture of God's loving plan.
As Levinas puts it on page 148:

> Glorification is saying, that is, a sign
> given to the other, peace announced to the other,
> responsibility for the other.

This Jewish notion of glory prepares us to give glory to the
Father, Son and Holy Spirit as it was, is now and ever shall be.

Agape and *Hesed*

II,8,9 With a Transcendence Without Imminence

As we approach the Glory of God's infinity he becomes more
and more transcendent in the mystery of his otherness.
On page 147 of *Otherwise Than Being* Levinas writes:

> The detachment of the Infinite from the thought
> that seeks to thematize it and the language
> that tries to hold it in the said is what
> we have called *illeity*.

Levinas' only Jewish God is transcendent and not imminent.
So is the Infinity of other persons so that we know them less and less.
All of his reveals the great truth that Scotus brought out
with his metaphysics of haecceity and Ockham with his
epistemology of nominalism to which all postmodernists adhere.
As Kierkegaard already showed each individual is so singular
in its uniqueness that no universal idea can express it completely.
But with the coming of Jesus, the Son of God, a new type of
imminence came on the scene so that we can know God
ever so much better and also other persons even in their glory,
with God becoming imminent in the incarnation of his Son.
Levinas' genius in expressing the Jewish notion of the third also
becomes evident as the Trinity revealed by Jesus becomes manifest.
Jesus' revealing of the Father, Son and Holy Spirit does become
manifest as the three persons in the one God and personhood
is now revealed such that all persons are equal in dignity, each
is unique and they all depend on each other as persons in relation.
This idea as Levinas suggests it should be is also applied
to human persons and this becomes the foundation of western
metaphysics, physics, psychology politics and economics.
God and other persons are still transcendent in their unique
complexity and they, as Levinas says, become ever more
transcendent as they become more and more imminent.
Jewish ethical religion as Levinas shows is a *Praeparatio Evangelica*.

II,9 Levinas and Derrida Enlighten Us Concerning *Agape*

II,9.1 For Levinas Loves the Jewish Love of Hesed and Ahava

The Hebrew Bible is so beautiful in its unfolding of *Ahava*
and *hesed* and Levinas has a great appreciation for all of this.
His idea that the wisdom of love is to serve love is a very Jewish
idea expressed wonderfully by him and taking the Jewish tradition
another giant step along the way in its 4000-year-old history.
Levinas helps us greatly appreciate the Jewish love that
more than other love is a preparation for Jesus' *agape*.
On page 67 of his book, *Levinas and the Wisdom of Love*,
Corey Beals has a chart in which he shows how ethics
has priority over ontology and that becomes clear in seeing how
my responsibility is prior and my freedom is secondary just
as living for others is more important than living for myself.
By learning from Levinas about the Jewish loving responsibility
we can see how *agape* grew out of responsible *hesed* and loving *ahava*.
As a child Levinas began to learn of such beautiful
images as Isaiah's 49:15-16:

> Can a woman forget her baby at the breast,
> feel no pity for the child she had borne?
> Even if these were to forget
> I shall not forget you.
> Look, I have engraved you
> on the palms of my hands.

Levinas grew up learning to love God with the *ahava* of
his whole heart, mind and soul and he grew up learning
to love the *hesed* that was promised to David and that
was loved by Isaiah who pictures it here so beautifully.
It is wonderful to learn reverence from Levinas, the great
thinker of Jewish reverence, and thereby to come to appreciate
how Jewish love was such a beautiful preparation for *agape*.
Levinas knows the great wisdom tradition of Israel and its loves.

Agape and *Hesed*

II, 9.2 And Expresses its Beauty, Goodness, Truth, and Holiness.

What Levinas makes clear in his ethics of first philosophy is how
the Jewish people want to love the helpless just as God loves them.
Hesed is that duty love in which the stronger takes care of
the weaker just as Yahweh promised to assist David's house.
Thus Levinas takes an *hesedic* responsibility for widows,
orphans and aliens and speaks to our postmodern culture
of a goodness that was fist revealed to the Jews so that we can
see the beauty and truth of this holy ethics which serves others.
He goes to the prophecy of Isaiah and develops in his own thought
the notion of the Suffering Servant who loves even his persecutors.
No wonder of it that this beautiful ideal was lived out by Jesus.
And Levinas has a great feel for the glory that this reveals.
For glory is the manifesting of the unmanifest even in its unmanifestness,
for God is always beyond us even though we can understand him
better and better as we see the two Jewish loves being lived out.
Levinas explains the *hesed* for widows, orphans and aliens and
the great *ahava* that God has for us and that we can have for
others if we really come to love God with his own *ahava*.
Levinas' philosophy helps us understand just how glorious
this Jewish *hesed* and *ahava* can be that are such a wonderful
preparation for the *agape* that Jesus lived out and taught us.
Jesus took this Jewish love and brought it to its fulfillment
by showing how it is to be a universal, unconditional love
for all of God's children that all flesh might see the Lord's salvation.
In his Jewish way Levinas has gone beyond the modern way of
isolating individual persons and has shown their vital connection.
No Jew is an island for they are all part of the loving community.
The more they are marginalized, the more they should be loved.
Levinas wants to let the duty love of *hesed* develop so that it
can be the felt love of *ahava* as I do my duty to others with
my whole heart, mind and soul in loving my neighbour as myself.

II, 9.3   And Derrida's Aporia Reveals the Mystery of Revelation.

Paul Ricoeur is a phenomenological and hermeneutical philosopher reflecting after Gadamer made a case for a conflict of interpretations. And Nietzsche had already made a case for perspectivism and that each interpretation sees a different set of perspectives of something. Derrida as a Jewish philosopher could resonate with all of this and hence as he thought of ethics as first philosophy he stressed with Socrates that every interpretation can be halted by a roadblock. The *Poros* has to do with the road or pathway of a theory and Socrates as a skeptic showed how each theory can be questioned. As Derrida looks at the Hebrew Bible and his Jewish tradition he finds that revelation is very much a conflict of interpretation. Wherever you find the Jew you always find four answers to any question for there will always be something like prophets, priests, kings and sages or Pharisees, Sadducees, Essenes and Zionists just as will be the case in interpreting *hesed* or *ahava*. When we study the scholars of *hesed* we will find that Nelson Glueck argues that *hesed* always has to do with a covenant. Then several scholars will argue that it does not have to do with a covenant for that belongs to the Mosaic covenant theology and should not be read into the Davidic Promise theology of *hesed*. Then some scholars will show just how in history the notion of *hesed* became connected with the notion of covenant so that some *hesed* is connected with covenant and some *hesed* is not. Then some scholars will argue that the connection is not valid. Derrida's very philosophy of an aporetic ethics seeks to understand this conflict of interpretations and his example of the hedgehog responding to the cry of the other and crossing the busy highway excellently reveals various possibilities. As Kierkegaard would say from a viewpoint of *agape* truth is objective uncertainty held fast in the appropriation process of the most passionate inwardness and the hedgehog has that.

Agape and *Hesed*

II, 9.4 And Redoes the Approach to Western Philosophy.

As Derrida's hedgehog begins to cross the highway in response to
the cry of the other his heart has reasons that his mind knows not.
He cannot know with his mind what will happen and he may
get killed, but out of love even like that of the Suffering Servant he
is eager to do all he can to respond to whatever the other demands.
Once Derrida brings the ethics of Jewish love to Greek philosophy
and makes that primary in his own brilliant way he will
deconstruct demonstrations by disseminating definitions and
differancing distinctions as he brings a double dissymmetry
to the dialectical responding to any objections that come his way.
With his hedgehog and through his philosophy Derrida's philosophy
follows the lead of his Jewish ethical love and improves desires
by making of them a donation and debts are forgiven with
a Divine Redemption like that of Yahweh towards David's house.
Derrida even reworks the depth psychology of Freud, Jung
and Adler by improving delirium with the right dream work.
Derrida with Nietzsche knows the worth of Amor Fati or loving
our destiny even with a dancing over all of life's density.
Derrida with his Jewish love reworks the love of wisdom
and the wisdom of love from the Greeks with their *storge, eros,
philia* and *agape* up through Augustine's *Confessions* with
his own Circumfessions as he even rethinks his circumcision.
He builds out of Kierkegaard, Nietzsche, Hopkins and with Kristeva
and Irigaray and Cixous in developing his Messianicity.
With them, except for Cixous, he will not believe in a Messiah
but he does prepare brilliantly for the Messiah with his
belief in *hesed* and *ahava* and his application of that to poetry,
literature and philosophy as he always seeks to be poetic.
After all, the hedgehog appears in *Che Cos 'e La Poesia* as
Derrida brings out the kind of leap of love that poetry always
tried to not only express but to encourage in all loving hearts.

II, 9.5 So even though Derrida and Levinas have a Messianicity.
The very notion of the Messiah is deeply connected with *hesed*.
As a young boy David, the Sheepherder, was anointed and told
that god would look after him and favor him and as the anointed
he was the Messiah and then he was given the promise of *hesed*.
In his book *Difficult Freedom*, on page 89, Levinas writes:

> Messianism is the role both of an historic people
> and my role as bearer of the suffering of all.
> Not one who arrives at the end of history,
> the Messiah is everyone who says "me"
> "send me" here and now.

The Jewish people are a messianic people in that they suffer at
the hands of others and can be the Suffering Servant for others.
Also each Jewish person should say "*me voiçi,*" "here is me,"
responding to the call of the poor, of widows, orphans and aliens.
So the Jewish people and each Jew should be an anointed one
with a vocation to serve others and thus Messianism means that
ethically it is the Jewish responsibility for there to be many Messiahs.
For Levinas Messianism has to do with a pure giving in which I
am willing to sacrifice myself for others and to bear the suffering of all.
It would seem that Jesus did this perfectly but Levinas does not
seem to take up the case of that Jew and so like Derrrida he does
have a Messianism without the Messiah who introduces *agape*.
From what we see here it would seem that Levinas' philosophy is
most of all about *hesed* and its responsibility especially to care for
my inferiors and those who persecute us and me as inferiors.
So it seems that Derrida and Levinas are quite agreed upon
the task of messianicity and the denial of Jesus as true Messiah.
They seem to have a kind of Jewish humanism in which they will
see Jews as brothers and sisters and the rest of humankind as
humans whom they should respect and suffer for in a Messianic
way but they do not see all persons as their brothers and sisters.

Agape and *Hesed*

II, 9.6 Without Jesus, the Messiah, and his Agape.

Nietzsche also saw himself as an anti-Christ as did Levinas and Derrida who do not accept Jesus as the Christ which is the Greek translation for the Hebrew word Messiah. Derrida and Levinas both write a great deal about Nietzsche and Caputo pictures Derrida as a Dionysian Rabbi or a mix of Levinas, the Apollonian Rabbi, and Nietzsche the Dionysian. But neither of them can get to the heart of Nietzsche's positive philosophy which is to be an anti-Christ as Luther understood the judging Christ of atonement justice theology in order to make room for the all loving child-like Jesus of Incarnation love theology. Nietzsche sees the *agape* of Jesus as humankind's highest affirmation in that it says "Yes and Amen" to all of existence with a love that wills the eternal return of each existing being with *amor fati*. Whereas Nietzsche can take seriously every religion and philosophy Levinas and Derrida cannot for they cannot really study Jesus with an unhindered interest and they cannot see the Jesus of Nietzsche. The Gospels are good Jewish writing with a conflict of interpretation going on between the four of them and even within each as we will see when we come to Matthew's Gospel and its many voices. Levinas and Derrida find it difficult to really study Jesus Christ the Messiah and his new love of *agape* because if they did they would have to become Christina Jews if they were really sincere in affirming and living out the best love possible. Levinas' concept of the Messiah as the historic people and the one who suffers for all and the one who says: "Send me, now" beautifully expresses the Jewish depths of the *ahava* that loves God with one's whole heart, mind and soul and of the *hesed* which will love other humans with the responsibility that Yahweh had for David. Derrida too has a great feel for both loves as his image of the hedgehog shows but when it comes to Jesus is Levinas like the Pharisees of old and is Derrida like an Essene or Zionist?

II, 9.7 Their Hesed and Ahava Prepares for that Agape.

Kierkegaard and Nietzsche are recognized as the founders of
the existential postmodern movement and they both develop
a religious ethics of *agape* as first philosophy so that the God-man
is the center of Kierkegaard's philosophy as he is for Nietzsche.
Once again when Levinas looks at Kierkegaard he is only critical
of him and cannot appreciate Kierkegaard's double movement leap.
of faith that lets him renew the ethical with a universal love for all.
Derrida is more positive toward Kierkegaard but again when he treats
Fear and Trembling in his *The Gift of Death* he can appreciate the
Knight of Infinite Resignation but he neglects the Knight of Faith.
Perhaps *hesed* and *ahava* and the religious ethics of the Hebrew
Bible and the Jewish tradition are so wonderful that they have
spent their lives loving them and cannot imagine anything better.
But Jewish philosophers like Edith Stein and Henri Bergson felt
that they were completely fulfilled as Jews by becoming Catholics.
In a book on Edith Stein by Henry Bordeaux the sixth chapter
is entitled "Her Love For Her People" and the seventh is called
"Universal Love" and in responding to the call of Love she met the
God of Love and was able to be martyred in a death camp for Love.
It is hard to understand how God works and maybe he has not
called Levinas and Derrida to love Jesus as the Messiah but
rather to let them witness to just how far Jewish *hesed* and *ahava*
can go and keep going without moving onto the next phase of *agape*.
In some mysterious way the philosophies of Levinas and Derrida
might be preparing for *agape* in a way never quite yet done.
Edith Stein and Levinas were both brilliant students of Husserl,
that Jewish philosopher who became Lutheran, and they both grew
and grew in the duty love, the felt love, of their Jewish tradition
but Edith was called to Mt. Carmel to fulfill Elijah the prophet.
By being called by Jesus the Messiah and by answering his call
Edith was able to understand the three persons in one God.

Agape and *Hesed*

II, 9.8 So that God can be Agapeic Hesed and Ahava.

Once Edith Stein and Henri Bergson moved from their world of *hesed* and *ahava* to the fulfilment of that in the world of *agape* they were able to fully understand and appreciate personhood. In modernity it is interesting to notice that Spinoza did not develop his ethics out of the notion of personhood which was central to all like Locke and Kant even though they lack the notion of persons in relation which was there from Nicaea in 325.
By her conversion Edith Stein is able to get
a strong philosophy with Max Scheler of *Ordo Amoris*, the right order of love, and build her ethics on the traditional notion of personhood. So Levinas and Derrida have done a great service to our postmodern age by developing their ethical philosophies of *hesed* and *ahava* and thus leading us right up to *agape* and its implications. Once Jesus the Messiah revealed a new notion of God as the three persons of the Blessed Trinity we in the West were able to work out the notion that all three persons are God and thus have equal dignity even though each is unique and the three persons are interpersonal so that being persons in relation lets them be persons. As we saw in our first book on *Agape and Personhood* that notion of personhood was applied to human persons and has become the basis for ethics and politics and the whole culture of the West. Derrida and Levinas by denying that Jesus is the Messiah deprive themselves of God as Love, as the Love between the three persons of the one God and thus they do not have the basis for a fully personal ethics going out to the equal dignity of all persons.
We will now have to see how both *hesed* and *ahava* go into *agape* and how the notion of love and personal growth has both of those Jewish elements within it or we will not really understand it. Jesus is the obedient Son of the Father who became flesh out of obedience and suffered and died for us out of loving obedience. We can see his *ahava* for the Father and us but how about *hesed*?

II, 9.9 And we can have Gratitude for the Salvation of All.

If we believe in the *agape* that Jesus taught us then as we
practice it better and better we will grow in greater gratitude.
Love is the giving of gifts and the God of Love has given us the
gift of creation and of all that exists and then he has given us
the gift of redemption through the Messiah and he has given us
a new promise that comes out of the Hebrew Bible concerning
the salvation of all flesh and our love can play a role in that.
The Jews all through their biblical history have a wonderful
sense of gratitude for all that God has done out of love for us
and especially for his chosen people and this is their *ahava*.
God has loved us with *ahava* and we should love him
with that same sort of love that lets us praise and adore him.
Hesed was connected for them with salvation for Yahweh
promised to David that he would save his dynasty and
by the time we get to the Messiah, Jesus, he will be seen as
the savior of all flesh ad his very name, Jesus, means savior.
There are many books on *hesed* that help us understand all
that belongs to it and which help us understand its history.
But it is a strange thing that not nearly so much is written
on the concept of *ahava* in the Hebrew Bible and why this is
we will have to try to understand for it will give us some clues
about the notion of *agape* as it rises out of *hesed* and *ahava*.
It would seem that *ahava* is the central type of love that is like
the natural loves and yet is special in God's revelation to his people.
It would sure help if the Jewish scholars would write books
on *ahava* and show us how Jewish *ahava* is so special.
But we will get the help we can and try our best to see
how these two elements are in *agape* as his gift love and saving love.
Do Levinas and Derrida primarily work with *hesed* love
that goes out in responsibility especially to the poor and needy?
As we go along we will have to see if they have also a strong *ahava*.

Through *Hesed* and *Ahava*

III,7 *Hesed* and *Ahava* in Hosea

III,7.1 Can we Compare, Contrast, and Relate them?

As we try to understand the Jewish loves of *hesed* and *ahava* that prepared the way for *agape* the prophet Hosea might help us. His writing is all about love, the betrayal of love, the hardships of love and the glory of love that in spite of all comes to reconciliation. This prophecy is glorious in that it manifests God in his two kinds of love which Hosea reveals by acting out the drama of God's *hesed* and *avaha* with his people and explaining it at the same time. The prophecy begins with the marriage of Hosea and its symbolism. Chapter 1:2 tells us:

> Yahweh said to Hosea, "Go, marry a whore,
> and get children with a whore,
> for the country itself has become nothing
> but a whore by abandoning Yahweh.

Hosea marries Gomer and has three children with her and the second child is a daughter and at chapter 1:6 we read

> Yahweh then said to him, call her Lo-Ruhamah,
> for I shall show no more pity for the house
> of Israel, I shall never forgive them again.

The word here for pity is *hesed* so while Yahweh will keep his covenant of *hesed* with the House of Judah he will not keep it with the Northern Kingdom who broke away from the dynasty of David and its everlasting *hesed* and went after other Gods. Throughout chapter two the word *ahavah* is used as the unfaithful wife of Yahweh says at chapter 2:7, 14, 15

> I shall chase after my lovers
> they will assure me my keep,
> my wool, my flax, my oil and my drinks.

So *ahava* is like the love we find in *The Song of Songs* and *hesed* is not very close to *ahava* for while it includes "love" its connotations are much broader than those of *ahava*.

III,7.2 Yahweh's Ahava for Israel

At the beginning of chapter 3 we are given a second account
of Hosea's marriage:

> Yahweh said to me, "Go again, love a woman
> who loves another man, an adulterous,
> and love her as Yahweh loves the Israelites
> although they turn to other gods.

In the beginning with Israel there was *ahava* for God loved his
chosen people and they loved him as did the lovers in *The Song of Songs*.
But then Israel began to fail in her *ahava* for Yahweh and she
worshipped the Golden Calf and committed many other acts of adultery.
Then God came to David and loved him and his dynasty with *hesed*.
But the Northern tribes of Israel even disregarded that *hesed* and its
restoration of *ahava* and they broke away from the Kingdom of David.
But in 3:4–5 we read:

> The Israelites will have to spend a long time
> without King or leader, without sacrifice
> or sacred pillar . . . but after that,
> the Israelites will return and again seek Yahweh
> their God and David their King, and turn
> trembling to Yahweh for his bounty
> in the final days.

This gives us the big picture for the Northern Kingdom is destroyed
by the Assyrians even though Jerusalem is not and the people
of the ten tribes are scattered to different lands by the Assyrians.
So Jereboam and Ahab and the other Northern Kings had neither
ahava nor *hesed* for Yahweh and they were conquered and ruined.
But Hosea is here telling us that Yahweh, their God, and David
their King will continue to be bound together in *hesed* and in the
distant future, even the scattered Israelites will come back.
So Yahweh's *ahava* for Israel is so strong that she will
be forgiven in the long run and be saved by Davidic *hesed*.

Agape and *Hesed*

III,7.3 And her Responsible *Hesed* to Him

As Hosea proceeds he continues to help us understand how *hesed* and *ahava* are different and yet how they are related. At Hosea 4:1 we read:

> Hear the word of Yahweh, O Israelites,
> for Yahweh has a controversy with
> the inhabitants of the land:
> for there is no *emet* and there is no *hesed*
> and there is no knowledge of God in the land.

Hosea tells us that Yahweh is bringing a lawsuit against the Israelites. When they left the Kingdom of David and started their own they became irresponsible to Yahweh and *hesed* for *hesed* is is a relation of responsibility of God and Israel for each other. Israel had no loyalty, no responsibility to God and to their fellow Jews and thus they failed to know God and his *ahava* and his healing *hesed*. *Ahava* for the Jews is connected with the Mosaic Covenant theology and its strict justice and the Israelites failed to keep the covenant. They sinned against God and against their own people and Hosea at once spells that out in 4:2–3

> Only perjury and lying, murder, theft,
> adultery and violence, bloodshed after bloodshed,
> this is why the country is in mourning
> and all its citizens pining away.

So in justice they will be punished for every one of their crimes. Hosea can see the approaching catastrophe as Assyria is coming to be such a power and Israel even wants to ally herself with other nations and their gods and for all this they will be punished. Hosea sees that they are about to be destroyed and is explaining to them that this only makes sense as a punishment for their lack of responsibility which *hesed* and *ahava* both imply. Already they did not know God when they broke away from the United Kingdom and they continue to know him less and less.

III,7.4 And His Responsible Hesed for her

Yahweh started out loving his people with *ahava* but they were
not faithful to him so he established a new love of *hesed* with David.
Yahweh in his responsibility of love for his people showed mercy
and said that even though he had treated King Saul with justice
which was still within the realm of *ahava* he would treat David and
his with an everlasting merciful love by forgiving them their sins.
David and his would still be punished with the rods of men for there
is a natural punishment that will be meted out to any injustice.
Thus at Hosea 10:12 we read

> Sow saving justice for yourselves,
> reap a harvest of faithful love (*hesed*)
> break up your fallow ground:
> it is time to seek out Yahweh until
> he comes to rain saving justice down on you.

So here within the context of *hesed* and God's responsible love for
his people we come to know that God loves with a saving justice.
In the lawsuit against his people God has found them guilty
and yet Hosea is revealing a new aspect of God in that he has
a justice that can save insofar as *hesed* goes beyond *ahava*.
If his fallen people will be responsible to God and to each other
they can sow a seed upon which God will send rain and it will
sprout forth with this new miraculous unheard of saving justice.
This saving justice is supernatural in that it goes beyond the
natural law of a justice that will punish anyone who is unjust.
The love theology of the Davidic promise goes beyond the justice
theology of the Mosaic covenant even to the point that those who
break from David and the covenant of *hesed* will be able to return.
This may take a long time for the scattered tribes of Israel may
not want to recognize the son of David who is the savior.
But Hosea is telling us that God's love is stronger than his anger
even though the sword of his justice will rage through her cities.

Agape and *Hesed*

III,7.5 But she Goes a Whoring with a False Ahava

The book of Hosea has a three stage plan which is almost like the aesthetic, the ethical and the religious for it treats

- I. The Marriage of Hosea and its Symbolism (1:2–3)
- II. The Crimes and Punishment of Israel (4:1—14:1)
- III. The Repentance and Reconciliation of Israel (14:2–10)

At 4:15 we read

> Though you, Israel, play the whore,
> there is no need for Judah to sin too.

Both the Kingdom of Judah and the Kingdom of Israel were tempted to make alliances with Assyria or Egypt because Assyria was such a threatening power and after a three-year siege Samaria fell. According to Sargan's annals he deported 27,290 Israelites into Persia and repopulated Israel with people from Syria and Elam. However, Judah and Jerusalem were miraculously spared and the Davidic Kingdom continued on in accord with God promise of *hesed*. Thus Hosea as he is making his warnings says at the beginning of chapter 12:

> Ephraim besieges me with lying,
> the house of Israel with duplicity.
> (But Judah still is on God's side,
> he is faithful to the Holy one.)

So when Jereboam broke away from the United Kingdom in about 930 he and the tribes of Israel were no longer loyal to their God. They despised God's *ahava* as we read in Hosea 11:1–2

> When Israel was a child I loved him,
> and I called my son out of Egypt.
> But the more I called,
> the further they went away from me
> they offered sacrifice to Baal
> and burnt incense to idols.

III,7.6 But God's Davidic Hesed will Save her

So *Ahava* throughout Hosea primarily refers to the love between husband and wife when that love is spontaneous and faithful but it also is used to refer to the love between a father and his son. God called Israel his child out of Egypt and their *ahava* is further described at Hosea 11:4

> But they did not know
> that I was the one caring for them
> that I was leading them with human ties
> with leading-strings of love,
> that, with them, I was like someone
> lifting an infant to his cheek,
> and that I bent down to feed him.

Ahava is here described as a very beautiful parent-child relation between God and his people but they did not really understand God. Once *hesed* is promised to his people they can come to know God much better for the knowledge of God is a major part of *hesed*. The people do need to know God in order to be faithful to his love and in being faithful they come to better know him as the God of love. God's deep *ahava* is revealed to Israel at the end of Hosea's prophecy. At 14:5–6 we read

> I shall cure them of their disloyalty,
> I shall love them with all my heart,
> for my anger has turned away from them.
> I shall fall like dew on Israel,
> he will bloom like the lily.

The word for God's love here is *ahava* so this should help us better understand the interplay between *hesed* and *ahava* for *hesed* can save the Davidic dynasty which includes all the Jewish people even when many of them break away and betray *hesed* by leaving David. But what being faithful to *hesed* can also do is let God's *ahava* add to that *hesed* so that God not only has *hesed* but more *ahava*.

Agape and *Hesed*

III,7.7 For even Though Israel Betray Ahava

A man and a wife come together with the kind of *ahava* that we see in *The Song of Songs* and God wanted this love with his people. But his chosen people did not love him with their whole heart, mind and soul and so he established a relation of *hesed* with the family of David and all the tribes of his beloved Israel. But then Israel broke away from David and was no longer responsible to God with the ethical responsibility of *hesed* for the chosen people and the united Kingdom of God and so Hosea says at Hosea 6:6

> For I delight in *hesed* not sacrifice
> and in knowledge of God
> rather than burnt offerings.

Hosea points out how Israel betrayed this *hesed* by breaking apart from the United Kingdom but then Hosea goes further and shows how Israel also betrayed the *ahava* for God that God commanded and the metaphor of the Gomer marriage shows this. There will be punishment for the monarchy of Israel will fail as Hosea says at 13:9–11

> Israel, you have destroyed yourself
> though in me lies your help.
> Your king, where is he now, to save you,
> or the governors in all your cities?—
> whom you once pleaded for, saying,
> "Give me a King and princes!"
> In my anger I gave you a King
> and in my wrath I have taken him away.

God and his people in the delight and desire of *ahava* are like young lovers getting married but Yahweh's people betrayed the marriage and unethically forsook him like a false wife. God repaired the marriage with his *hesed* but then his people betrayed that *hesed* and thus the *ahava* it healed.

III,7.8 And then Betray Hesed

In Hosea the time line of the interplay between *ahava* and *hesed* is beginning to become clear for there is (1) *ahava* initiated by Yahweh and responded to by his people. (2) Then there is the betrayal of the *ahava* for each other by the chosen beloved. (3) Then God gives the promise of *hesed* and his everlasting merciful love. (4) But Israel betrays that *hesed* by breaking away from David (5) and furthermore she betrays any *ahava* for God by sacrificing to other gods like Baal and Ashtarte. Thus Israel does not know God and appreciate God's forgiveness of her with his everlasting merciful love and the final part of Hosea's prophecy shows that God will take her back just as Hosea was willing to take Gomer back no matter what. Israel belonged to the Kingdom of David and even though she breaks away she still belongs so God's *hesed* is there for her even though she may not know and just keep betraying it. The first three chapters of Hosea's prophecy are a good introduction for the marriage of Hosea and its symbolism tell the story of love, of crime and punishment and of repentance and reconciliation. Even though the tribes of Israel with their capital city of Samaria are conquered, destroyed and dispersed as the wandering tribes of Israel they will come back to David's God. At Hosea 2:16 we read

> But look, I am going to seduce her
> and lead her into the desert
> and speak to her heart.

Israel has betrayed the *hesed* that is meant to help *ahava* live. But it is the very nature of God's *hesed* to forgive and thus even though Israel will be punished with the rods of men she will be loved by the God of David and Jews will be able to come back to the *ahava* and *hesed* of David even as that becomes the *agape* of Jesus which lets the name of Abraham be a blessing for all.

Agape and *Hesed*

III,7.9 *Yahweh's Hesed will Bring her Back to Ahava*

The *ahava* of *The Song of Songs* shows us what it would be like
if we really obeyed the commandment to love our God with our
whole heart mind and soul and the responsibility of *hesed*
shows us what it would be like to love our neighbor as ourself.
If we could do our duty to our neighbor with the delight and desire
of *ahava* it would be because God's *hesed* shows us how to do that.
Hosea 12:7 tells the Israelites:

> So turn back with God's help
> maintain faithful love and loyalty
> and always put your trust in your God.

Here Hosea speaks of *hesed* for Yahweh will help Israel even
though she has been scattered among the nations if she will be
but loyal to him and if she trusts him he will help her to love
him with all her heart and to also her neighbors even non-Jews.
With the dispersal the 27,290 Israelites had new neighbors and
this could even help *agape* and the love of them to come on the scene.
God's *ahava* is stronger than his vengeance as Hosea says
at Hosea 11:3–4

> I myself taught Ephraim to walk,
> I myself took them by the arm,
> but they did not know
> that I was the one caring for them,
> that I was leading them with human ties,
> with leading strings of love.

"I drew them with the bonds of love" with the bonds of *ahava*.
As in *The Song of Songs* his banner over me is love and this
ahava between God and his people and between everyone
of his people and each other is the main point of the Hebrew Bible.
God has a merciful *hesed* and his people may not know this.
But he is leading them and all of mankind with the bonds of love.
This is the story of mankind that love will conquer all.

III,8 How do *Hesed* and *Ahava* Relate in the Psalms?

III,8.1 Is Hesed Primarily God's love for Man? (Psalm 5)

Larue (p. 32 of Glueck, *Hesed in the Bible*) quotes E. M. Good on page 30:

> In most of the Bible *hesed* symbolizes
> God's love for man and *ahavah* man's
> love for God, but Hosea reverses this pattern
> by expressing Yahweh's love as *ahavah*
> and human reciprocal love as *hesed*.

We can explore this helpful idea by thinking about those psalms where both *hesed* and *ahavah* are used in close proximity and see if we can better understand how they relate to each other. Psalm 5 is a morning prayer in which the speaker is exposed to danger from treacherous foes and he trusts in God to protect him. At Psalm 5:8 we read:

> But as for me, in the abundance of
> Thy lovingkindness will I come
> into Thy house.

This lovingkindness in which he trusts is God's *hesed* and he prays that God will continue to be gracious to him always. Then in Psalm 5:12 he continues to say

> So shall all those that take refuge
> in Thee rejoice, they shall ever
> shout for joy, and Thou shalt
> shelter them; Let them also that
> love Thy name exult in Thee

In the Soncino Book of The Psalms with Hebrew text and English translation, the commentator writes (p. 12), concerning the words *that love The Name*, that "those who pay allegiance to God and are faithful to his will," and the word for love here is *ahava* and this helps us see what *ahava* is. Larue (in Glueck, *Hesed in the Bible*, 32) says that according to Good in this psalm *hesed* is God's love for us and *ahava* is our love for God, and all of this makes good sense.

Agape and *Hesed*

III,8.2 Is Ahava Primarily Man's Love for God (Psalm 33)

God did promise *hesed* to David and all of his so that this everlasting merciful love is primarily Yahweh's love for man and God did command us to love him with *ahava* and our neighbor as ourself. With this felt love such as we find it in *The Song of Songs*. Psalm 33:5 has both of the words within it:

> He loveth righteousness and justice;
> The earth is full of the lovingkindness
> of the Lord.

This Psalm is a song of deliverance and celebrates a national rather than a personal victory and the word for he *loveth* righteousness and justice is *ahavah* so that when the Jews love God with *ahavah* by being righteous and just he loves them. He loves their *ahavah* for him with *ahavah* but then we are told that the *hesed* of the Lord fills the earth with lovingkindness. So God loves the Jews with *hesed* which even fills the earth. Then they love him with righteousness and justice which in Hebrew ethics are the foundations of a stable order of society. Thus God loves them first with his *hesed* and his *hesed* demands that they practice *hesed* toward the other members of the Jewish community, especially widows, orphans and aliens and when they love him with *ahava* and take responsibility for others with *hesed* just as God does for them then he loves them with *ahava*. So now we have a question as we rethink what we saw in Hosea. If God does love his people there with *ahava* is it like his *ahava* in this psalm that comes after our *hesed* to others and thus our *ahava* for him so that there is similarity in Hosea and the Psalms? Maybe, to be more exact, we should say that God loves justice and righteousness with *ahavah* and not really his people with *ahava*. So let's look back at Hosea and see if there is a reversal or not.

III,8.3 Even Though Hosea Reverses this Pattern

To understand Hosea we need to think of the Jewish past and the
Jewish future as he saw it and it did begin with Yahweh's *ahava*
for his people from whom he commanded a reciprocal *ahava*.
But, to use Hosea's images Israel went chasing after other lovers.
Then Yahweh loved David and his people with *hesed* and he
promised them to have this merciful love for them foever.
But the Northern Kingdom broke away from the United Kingdom
and thus rejected even Yahweh's *hesed* as well as his *ahavah*.
Now at Hosea's time Israel is about to be punished by the rods of men.
They can see that Assyria is about to destroy them.
Thus, Hosea begins to look to the future of the Israelites who
will be conquered and scattered and he stresses in that key
passage that we noticed before at Hosea 3:4–5:

> The Israelites will have to spend a long time
> without King or leader, without sacrifice
> or sacred pillar . . . but after that,
> the Israelites will return and again seek Yahweh
> their God and David their King, and turn
> trembling to Yahweh for his bounty
> in the final days.

So until they return to David, even in the time after Jesus
they will not know God's *hesed* for them and thus Hosea does
not stress God's love for his people as *hesed* but as *ahava*.
But they are lacking in *ahavah* for God by not recognizing
the Davidic dynasty and the *hesed* that has even become *agape*.
So it is only when they return to *hesed* and love God's *hesed*
that they will properly love God with the *ahava* that they lack.
So it is understandable why Hosea has this double reversal
insofar as he is speaking to the Israelites and their double
failure to practice true love either in terms of *ahava* or *hesed*.
It is only when they again love God's *hesed* that they will love him.

Agape and Hesed

III,8.4 Hesed is Primarily God's Love for us (Psalm 51)

The great penitential cry of Psalm 51 perhaps of David when Nathan the prophet came unto him after he had gone to Bathsheba begins in verse 3 appealing to God's *hesed*;

> Be gracious unto me, O God,
> according to Thy mercy;
> According to the multitude of Thy
> compassions blot out my transgressions.

This forgiveness and everlasting mercy is exactly what Yahweh promised to David but there is something a little strange here and that is that God is called *Elohim* whereas the God of *hesed* and David's God is Yahweh so maybe this is not a psalm of David. On page 4 of Glueck, *Hesed* in the Bible, Larue writes:

> *Hesed*, Bowen notes, appears in the Psalter
> over 100 times generally with reference to
> times of personal or national affliction.

He then divides the psalms into about seven different groups and shows several perspectives of God's *hesed* to which they appeal. All through these more than 100 psalms God's merciful love for us sinners is stressed as they pray for God's *hesed* so it ends by arguing that God will be delighted in our acts of *ahava* for him.

> Then wilt thou delight in the sacrifices
> of righteousness, in burnt-offering
> and whole offering;

The psalms are mostly a prayer to God for his *hesed* to us. But they do recognize that God wants *ahava* from us and that we should have *ahava* for our neighbor as for ourself. Psalm 51:12 shows that we need God's help to love him:

> Create in me a clean heart, O God;
> and renew a steadfast spirit within me.

I need to appeal to God's *hesed* that he might give me *ahava* for him.

III,8.5 And we must Love our Neighbor with Hesed (Psalm 69)

Psalm 69 is a prayer of the persecuted in which a devout servant of God is undergoing cruel treatment and feels that his sufferings are due to his religious loyalty as was the case with Jeremiah. It may have been a psalm that was composed during the Babylonian captivity and it does cry out for vengeance on the persecutors. Psalm 69:25 says:

> Pour out thine indignation upon them
> and let the fierceness of thine anger
> overtake them.

These persecutors are not Jews but a foreign enemy and so they deserve no *hesed* or *ahava* since they are not true neighbors. From verses 14 to 17 the Psalmist prays for God's *hesed*:

> O God, in the abundance of Thy mercy
> answer me with the truth of Thy salvation ...
> Answer me, O Lord, for thy mercy is good;
> according to the multitude of Thy compassion
> turn thou unto me.

So again *hesed* is God's love for man and this notion is consistent throughout the Psalms which pray for God's compassion. But the psalm does end with *ahavah* at Psalm 69:36–37

> For God will save Zion, and build the cities
> of Judah; and they shall abide there,
> and have it in possession.
> The seed also of His servants shall
> inherit it; and they that love His name
> shall dwell therein.

Those who love the Name of God with *ahava* shall dwell in Judah. This Psalmist prays that God will protect him and his people with *hesed* and then the holy people will love God with *ahava*. The true neighbors who are God's people must be just to each other with *hesed* even though these Babylonian enemies need not be loved.

Agape and *Hesed*

III,8.6 But Ahava must be our Primary Love for God (Psalm 117)

In the Soncino *The Psalms* (p. 388) the commentator says

> The shortest of the Psalms is one of the grandest.

It has only two verses, one on *ahavah* and one on *hesed* and that is really the essence of all the psalms.

1. O praise the Lord, all ye nations;
   Laud Him, all ye peoples.

2. For His mercy is great toward us;
   And the truth of the Lord
   endureth forever. Hallelujah.

Ahavah for God consists of praise, love, worship and adoration. This psalm looks forward to the day when all peoples and nations will fulfill the great commandment and love God with a total *ahavah* and then it tells how this can happen in terms of the Davidic promise of *hesed* for Yahweh's merciful *hesed* is so great to David's house that someday all the peoples of the earth will belong to the house of David. This tiniest of psalms already tells how *hesed* will become *agape* and let all peoples love God with an *agape* that fulfills *ahavah*. We should have *ahavah* for God because God is deserving of our love because of his mercy or his *hesed* for us and the truth that God will always love us with *hesed* is a truth enduring forever. In the Soncino edition (p. 333) the commentator says:

> Its insertion in the Psalter is a witness
> to the universal aspiration of Judaism.
> The mission of Israel remains unfulfilled
> until the hope voiced in this Psalm
> becomes a reality.

All nations and peoples are meant to see the fulfillment of the promise made to Abraham so that they can all be blessed by the name of Yahweh and this is an aspiration of the Jews even though they are not eager to be missionaries to all peoples.

III,8.7 And we must Love our Neighbor with Ahava (Psalm 119)

Now we move from the shortest psalm (117) to the longest (119).
For each letter of the Hebrew Alphabet this psalm has eight verses
and it is all about Torah as a way of life or it is about love for law.
There are about a dozen references to *ahava* in the psalm and about
a half dozen references to *hesed* as it treats loving the command to love.
Verses 47 and 48 read:

> And I will delight myself in Thy commandments
> which I have loved.
> I will lift up my hands also unto
> Thy commandments, which I have loved;
> and I will meditate in Thy statutes.

The great commandments say:

> Love the Lord your God, with your
> whole heart, mind and soul,
> and your neighbor as yourself.

We are commanded to love God, ourself and our neighbor with
ahavah and now this psalm goes further and loves the commandment.
The Jewish people have been given a commandment to love with
ahavah and what could be more lovely and loveable than the command.
Verses 75 and 76 read:

> I know, O Lord, that Thy judgments are righteous,
> and that in faithfulness Thou hast afflicted me.
> Let, I pray Thee, Thy loving kindness be ready
> to comfort me according to Thy promise.

So throughout the psalms we get this balance of God's *hesed* for
us that we might be able to do his will and love him with *ahavah*.
This is the great revelation that God has made to his chosen people.
A very important way to love God is to really love our neighbor.
If we do not keep the second commandment of *ahava* for our
neighbor then we do not keep the first of *ahava* for God.
This psalm shows us that to keep the command we have to love it.

Agape and *Hesed*

III,8.8 *And Come to See God's Ahava for us (Psalm 119)*

From verses 124 to 126 we read:

> Deal with Thy servant according unto Thy mercy,
> and teach me Thy statutes.
> I am Thy servant, give me understanding;
> That I may know Thy testimonies.
> It is time for the Lord to work;
> They have made void Thy law.
> Therefore I love Thy commandments
> above gold, yea, above fine gold.

Once again this begins with *hesed* and ends with *ahavah* and the psalmist prays that God in his *hesed* will help him and his to understand the law and love all of the Ten Commandments. Many are not following the law and are making the psalmist and many others to suffer and he prays that they will be punished. He already understands God and his *hesed* quite well in that when people do not follow the Ten Commandments "It is time for the Lord to work" and let them be punished with the rods of men. That is the way the law of *hesed* works for even though it is love it is still a law for God's primary love implies a secondary justice. We can come to see and understand God's *ahavah* for us even as we understand the justice of his *hesed* for God in his *ahavah* has given us the commandments to practice *ahava* and if we do not follow those commands then we will suffer the consequences. Many peoples might have something like the Ten Commandments. It is well known that the world religions have the golden rule. But, the Jews were the first to see God's *ahavah* and then his *hesed*. They were the first to see how the God of loving *ahava* gave the double command of *ahava* and the psalmist loves this command even more than fine gold for its glory is richer than anything. In revealing the law of *ahava* God is making himself more manifest as a God of love than he ever did before.

III,8.9 Which He Shows us with His Hesed (Psalm 119)

Once again *ahava* and *hesed* are put together in one verse and explained in terms of each other in Psalm 119:159:

> O see how I love Thy precepts;
> Quicken me, O Lord, according
> to Thy lovingkindness.

Once again we see an *ahava* for God and his precepts and once again *hesed* is translated as the lovingkindness of the Lord. The term lovingkindness is a good translation of *hesed* and it does help us to see the notion of God's mercy even for us sinners. Also he tells us here how the precepts of the Lord are loved by him even though many of the faithless do not observe the Lord's word. He prays that God will quicken him with his lovingkindness. To quicken means to make more lively so he is praying that God with his *hesed* will quicken his *ahava* and make his faith and love more faithful and more loving for he sees that if he is to practice *ahava* it can only be done with God's helpful and quickening *hesed*. The psalmist is dependent on God for everything good: his life, his love, his understanding and even for his ability to pray. And what he concentrates on in the praise of his prayer is loving God's law for that is a great gift that God has given to the Jews. At verse 157 he writes:

> Many are my persecutors and mine adversaries;
> Yet I have not turned aside from thy testimonies.

Perhaps, even though they are his neighbors, he does not love them as he loves himself and even turn the other cheek for them. He loves the land of the Ten Commandments but has his *ahava* gotten as far as loving his enemies especially his neighbors? At verse 163 he writes:

> I hate and abhor falsehood
> Thy law do I love.

Has the law of love not yet become clear that we should not hate?

Agape and *Hesed*

III,9 How do *Hesed* and *Ahava* Lead up to *Agape*?

III,9.1 Do the Jews have Four Opinions on Everything?

Within the Bible there are different views about *hesed* and its
major traits such as reciprocity, universality and covenant.
Revelation for Jews proceeds through a conflict of interpretations.
Within the Pentateuch there are the voices of the Yahwist and Elohist,
the Dueteronomist and the Priests all working at truth together.
There are prophets, priests, Kings and sages trying to clarify God's
revelation as are Pharisees, Sadducees, Essenses and Zealots.
Just as Glueck and the many *hesed* scholars debate whether or not
hesed is a reciprocal relation so do Buber, Levinas and Derrida.
Buber like Glueck argues that the I-thou relation is mutual
whereas Levinas and Derrida insists that ethics as first philosophy
with its responsibility to and for others cannot be reciprocal.
There are Orthodox, conservative, liberal and secular Jews and
the secular Jew might be as serious about the ethics of *hesed*
between all people and the maintenance of *ahava* as would the orthodox.
When we come to the New Testament there are the four Gospels and
each of them stresses different aspects of the same Christian *agape*.
The New Testament writers were Jewish and when we explore Matthew
we will have to ask if he has various voices himself developing
the truth of *agape* for different times and situations and audiences.
So we have to determine what the essence of *agape* is and then see
how far *hesed* and *ahava* proceed in reaching that essence and
its major properties and attributes so that we can adequately
appreciate how well Jewish revelation prepares the way for *agape*.
Of course, determining the meaning and history of *hesed* and *ahava*
and their relation is difficult in itself as we have just seen.
So now we have to work with the three of these complicated concepts.
As Wallis points out on page 103 the Septuagint for the most
part translates *ahava* as *agape* so his few words can help
us a great deal in beginning our exploration of the three loves.

III,9.2 The Septuagint Usually Translates Ahava as Agape.

On page 103 Wallis points out that the basic meaning of *ahava* is
to be sharply distinguished from *racham* or mercy and compassion
and *dodh* or the knowledge of God so that,

> [c]onsequently, the Hebrew of the *OT* has filled the concept
> of *ahava* with an entirely special meaning.

This could mean that *ahava* is sharply distinguished form *hesed*.
For *hesed* does include mercy and a knowledge of God whereas
ahava which is the commanded love for God and neighbor
does not imply mercy or any special knowledge of God in his mercy.
Wallis goes on to write:

> That the *LXX* uses the very *agapao* as a translation
> for *ahabh* in an overwhelming majority of cases
> also favors this assumption.

That *ahava* is very different from *hesed* which is not translated
as *agape* but as goodness, mercy, kindness, piety and kindness.
Wallis says that in prebiblical Greek

> the difference between the meaning of *erao*
> *phileo,* and *agapao* is pale and fluid.
> *Agapao* means "to be content with something.

Wallis's main point about *ahava* being translated as *agape*
in *The Septuagint*, in these quotations from page 103, is that

> *Agapao* acquired its classical meaning
> initially through translation from the Hebrew.

So all that *ahava* meant in the Hebrew Bible *agape* came to mean
in *The Septuagint* and thus we have to see what *ahava-agape*
meant in *The Septuagint* and then what it came to mean for Matthew.
Willis does point out that sometimes in *The Septuagint ahava*
is translated as *philia* especially in the wisdom literature and
especially in *Proverbs* when the love of wisdom is called *philia*.
Of course, that is very natural for the love of wisdom for
the Greeks was philosophy which could hardly be disregarded.

Agape and *Hesed*

III,9.3 But how New is the Meaning of Agape in Matthew?

So the term *agape* did get a new meaning for the Jews in *The Septuagint* and it came to get another new meaning with Jesus. It is our task to be clear about love for the Jew and then see how Matthew, the Jew, saw Jewish love as a preparation for the love that Jesus taught with his *agape* that was *ahava* and *hesed*. To begin we must see that Matthew has a new notion of God as the Father, the Son and the Holy Spirit and this will imply a clear new universal love for all the human children of God. On page 57 Glueck writes that

> *hesed* ... is the proper conduct of all men toward one another. On the one hand, mankind is regarded as one large family, and on the other, as children of one heavenly Father.

Most scholars disagree with Glueck and and think that the covenant of *hesed* applies only to the Jewish people. As we try to distinguish the differences between *hesed* and *ahava* in Matthew we will try to see if the universality of *agape* flows more out of either our duty love or our felt love. In terms of the *ahava* that we are commanded to have for our neighbor Matthew does show that that now goes out to all humans. So the *agape* of Matthew will be a new unconditional, universal love for the family of man and insofar as the New Testament is a New Covenant it will extend out trying to convert all to love. So with the *agape* of Jesus in Matthew we do see a qualitative leap into the new rather than just a qualitative buildup of the *hesed* and *ahava* of the Jews which were qualitative leaps in their time. God's revelation to the Jews in the *ahava* of the Mosaic covenant and the *hesed* of the Davidic Promise let them see a loving personal God unlike any known to humankind by experience. Does Matthew see God as revealed by Moses, David and Jesus?

III,9.4 And How does Matthew Relate Hesed to Agape?

If *The Septuagist* related *ahava* to *agape* within the Jewish context
is there any strong relating of *hesed* to *agape* in *The Septuagint*.
In the Glueck book on page 10 Felix Asensio's investigation
of Greek and Latin translations of *hesed* is considered and in
the Septuagint *hesed* is often translated as *eleos* or mercy.
Hesed is usually translated in terms of beneficence and goodness,
or justice or grace in bringing out the conduct beyond feeling.
So *hesed* is not usually related to *agape* in the Septuagint.
However, on page 18 of the Glueck book, Dom Rembert Sorg who
studies *hesed* in the psalms writes:

> *Hesed* appears to correspond to the Greek *agape*
> and Latin *caritas* as contrasted to *eros* and *amor*,
> but the English terms "love" or "charity" are
> unsatisfactory translations for they include
> features of love not included in *hesed*.

So Sorg thinks that the *agape* of Matthew and *The New Testament*
is most of all a translation of *hesed* even though the Septuagint
translated *ahava* as *agape* and Sorg excludes those from *hesed*.
As we come to Matthew we will have to explore his *agape*
to see if it is primarily *hesed* or *ahavah* or a mix of the two.
Does *The Septuagint* have an *agape* that is not the *agape* of Matthew?
First we need to think about the many voices in his Good News.
Are there different kinds of *agape* in the different voices he uses?
The notion of Christ or the Messiah is obviously related to David
and perhaps the promise of *hesed* to all of David's dynasty
that now with Jesus will expand to include all humans.
Does that perhaps imply that Jesus *might* in some way
emphasize a love of *ahava* that goes out to save all people?

Agape and *Hesed*

III,9.5 A Preview of Matthew's Agape

Just to begin thinking about Matthew's understanding of *agape* so that we can better relate it to *hesed* and *ahava* we might begin with nine points:

1. *Agape* fulfills the Law and the Prophets
2. *Agape* loves the Kingdom and righteousness
3. *Agape* does not separate the weeds from the wheat.
4. *Agape* gives Peter authority.
5. Is *Agape* more gracious to some than others?
6. *Agape* is vigilant until the *parousia*.
7. *Agape* is responsible for the whole world.
8. *Agape* is to baptize in the name of the trinity.
9. *Agape* believes in the Lord's continued presence.

While the first point might relate more strongly to *ahava* do not the next eight seem to have more to do with fulfilling *hesed*? For Matthew the main part of the Law that Jesus came to fulfill is the double commandment of *ahava* in which we should love the Lord our God with our whole heart, mind and soul and our neighbor as ourself who will now come to include everyone. But as soon as we come to the Kingdom are we not treating the Kingdom of David and Christ as the Messiah or anointed king? And is not righteousness one of the main aspects of our *hesed*? Now with the Christ there will no longer be Gentile weeds and Jewish wheat and all sinners should become reconciled and Christ's kingly authority is passed on to Peter and his sucessors. *Agape* should now go out as *hesed's* gracious mercy to the new kingdom of all the Father's family and there should be a new *ahava* that loves all persons who have equal dignity. The end of the earthly temporal kingdom that will be fulfilled by the coming of the heavenly eternal kingdom does see the Lord's continued presence even after his ascension as bringing about the need for an *hesedic* responsibility for all and for always.

III,9.6 A Preview of Matthew's Many Voices

As we study *agape* in Matthew as the fulfillment of *hesed*
and *ahava* it will also help if we listen to what we might call
the many voices of Matthew for with Luke he does use the three
early voices of the Q community and he does use Mark's outline.
Like Luke he will also have his own Infancy Narrative but his
already contains his own very Jewish approach to that event.
His Gospel like the Torah or Penteteuch is made up of five
well worked out sections that have to do with the new Kingdom.
So as we study his view of *agape* as fulfillment of *hesed* and *ahava*
we might again notice his many voices in

1. His Infancy Narrative
2. His use of Q 1–3
3. His use of Mark's synoptic outline in
4. The proclaiming of the Kingdom
5. The preaching of the Kingdom
6. The Mystery of the Kingdom of heaven
7. The church as first fruit of the kingdom
8. The Approaching Advent of the Kingdom of heaven
9. The Passion and The Resurrection

Matthew does see Jesus as the new Moses and thus his Gospel
as the new Torah or Law and that could relate to the Law of *ahava*.
But, insofar as his Gospel is primarily concerned with the
coming of the kingdom it would seem to have to do with *hesed*.
Does Matthew's Gospel relate *hesed* and *ahava* in a special
way in the New *agape* that was not there even in the Septuagint?
Is there a special new aspect of glory connected with this *agape*
of Jesus the Christ that will manifest something new about God?
Will the *kabod* and the *Shekinah* of God become seen in a
qualitatively new way in the *agape* that reveals the three
persons in the one God and eventually a new way to view all persons?
Will this *doxa* or glory of Matthew reveal the glory of *agape*?

Agape and *Hesed*

III,9.7 Does the Christ Expand a Davidic Hesed?

As Matthew works out the *agape*ic fulfillment of *hesed* and *ahava* in terms of a further insight into God and his glory and in terms of the universality of love through space he also emphasizes very much the notion of an everlasting love between everyone. *Hesed* is often translated as an everlasting merciful love and in *The Song of Songs ahava* was seen to be as strong as death. Matthew's notion of the heavenly kingdom is about eternal life and our eternal love with God and with all the angels and saints. When we think of Jews who take *hesed* seriously it seems that they could have come to be like the Sadducees and the Pharisees. The Phariseic type came to believe that there would be a life after death for the pious who live according to the law of *hesed*. The Sadduceic type did not believe in life after death and thus an everlasting merciful *hesed* for them was only here and now. The central notion throughout Matthew's Gospel is that of the Kingdom which Christ, the King, and the offspring of David, is revealing to us as an expansion of *hesed* for everyone. So while the Jews could have four opinions about life after death, for the Essenes and the Zionists could have their view too, Matthew shows that for the Christian there is a new faith that brings the conflict of interpretations to an end with belief in eternity. It would seem that the *agape* of Matthew is mostly an expansion of *hesed*, however, he does structure his Gospel into an Introduction, a Body with five parts and a conclusion and the Body does have to do with the Mosaic Pentateuch and so *ahava* is also important. But *hesed* as Yahweh's everlasting merciful love for David's dynasty is central and Matthew's Christ extends David's dynasty to all the people of the earth and the everlasting becomes the eternal. Matthew's Gospel ends with the great commission to go out and baptize all people in the name of the Father, the Son and the Holy Spirit. The Trinity's *agape* lets *hesed* become universal and everlasting.

III,9.8 And Does Jesus Expand a Mosaic Ahava?

At Matthew 22:34–40 we can see how the *agape* of Jesus expands the Mosaic *ahava* for he answers the Pharisees who ask him which is the greatest commandment of the Law by saying:

> You must love the Lord your God
> with all your Heart, will all your soul,
> and with all your mind. This is the greatest
> and the first commandment. The second
> resembles it: You must love your neighbor
> as yourself. On these two commandments
> hang the whole Law, and the Prophets also.

The word used for love here is *agape* and in this case it is a translation of *ahava* and Jesus gives it a new importance by saying that the whole Law and the Prophets hang on it. So Jesus is expanding the notion of *ahava* with his new concept of God as Father, Son and Holy Spirit, his new concept of neighbor that universally includes every person and his new concept of heaven it which this love will go on eternally and forever. All that Jesus teaches in his *Sermon on the Mount* and through out his three years of teaching will have to do with this lesson that makes *agape* and this *ahava* the foundation of all. As we now go to Matthew we will study his *agape* which fulfills the Law and the Prophets for he says at Matt 5:17

> Do not image that I have come
> to abolish the Law or the Prophets.
> I have not come to abolish but
> to complete them.

Matthew thinks deeply about the *agape* that Jesus taught and he wants most of all to explain it to the Jews who should be able to appreciate it most of all because it is so Jewish. It seems mysterious that Matthew's Christ Jesus did not use two words for love and we will have to see if it has two meanings.

Agape and *Hesed*

III,9.9 Are There Four Ways of Doing the Expanding?

In order to try to understand Matthew's *agape* as well as possible we should see if we can make a case that there were four views about *hesed* and four about *ahava* as the Yahwist, the Elohist, the Dueteronomist and the Priests put together the Law and as it was interpreted by the Prophets. If these Jewish opinions are there in a conflict of interpretations about Love then Jesus would probably fulfill it. Will the conflict of interpretations about *hesed* and *ahava* be there in Matthew so that if we attend to them we will be able to understand *agape* in many of its mysterious nuances. Matthew's Gospel is placed first in *The New Testament* as if it were written first but it does rely upon Mark's Gospel. However, Matthew does use the book of Q which was put together by the Christian community in Galilee before Mark. So in some ways Matthew's Gospel precedes Mark's and the Q scholars show three stages of the Q story of Jesus and there is a great conflict between these even concerning love. To bring all this out and not overlook it will make us think deeply into opinions about the *agape* of Jesus and these could be related to opinions about *hesed* and about *ahava*. Also we will at times complicate things even more by attending to some of the stories in Luke that are different from those in Matthew. In this way by doing comparative and contrasting exegesis we will be able to think more deeply into *agape* and its *hesed* and its *ahava*. Of course, we will look at Luke in great detail in another meditation upon *agape* but just to consider some noticeable differences can help us not to overlook the many conflicting voices that let Jewish revelation take place and then to think about how that works in Christian revelation. Of course, we might also consider that there might be four Jewish opinions concerning how well the Jesus of Matthew really fulfills *hesed* and *ahava* in *agape* but can Jews look deeply at such things?

Through Matthew's *Agape*

IV, 7   And *Eros* Righteous

IV, 7.1 Eros too can be Self-Centered

When two lovers stand face to face enraptured in each other they
could be self-sacrificial for each other like a parent for a child.
But in natural *eros* there is also a self-love for if my beloved
shows interest in another I could feel threatened and be jealous.
Eros is such that I want my beloved to love me and no one else and
I can be exceedingly happy when I am the only focus of her *eros*.
In many ways I have to be a self-loving egoist and perfect myself
in the ways that I, with the help of others, see as best for me.
Each of us has to take good care of ourselves and spend our life
doing what we think is best for our family, friends and beloved.
That is only natural but Jesus came to reveal a supernatural love
which gives one's life even for the enemy and it would seem that
he might be more opposed to eros than any other natural love.
To bring righteousness into the hearts of humans that they
might enter the Kingdom of the Father he loved the little
children with affection and loved his disciples as friends.
After Jesus spoke about divorce and adultery and fornication he was
asked what he thought about marriage and at Matt 19:10–12 he said,

> It is not everyone who can accept what
> I have said, but only those to whom
> it is granted. There are eunuchs born
> that way from their mother's womb, there
> are eunuchs made so by men and there
> are eunuchs who have made themselves
> that way for the sake of the Kingdom of heaven.
> Let anyone accept this who can.

A eunuch is a celibate and Jesus tells us that some are born
without much of a sex drive and some have been forced
by others to be celibate but Jesus and his disciples can
choose to be celibate for the sake of the Kingdom of love.

Agape and *Hesed*

IV, 7.2   As Was the Case with King David

From this we can see that there are three vocations according to Jesus for there can be two types of lay person, either the married or the single, and then there is the celibate religious life. Jesus says it is not for everyone to be his disciple and be celibate but he says: "Let anyone accept this who can." St. Paul said basically the same thing and from St. Augustine to Luther we see the struggle of persons wanting to do this. Finally after years of trying Augustine was gifted with celibacy. Luther never could achieve it and following him all modern clergy have no longer tried to live like Jesus and St. Paul. So a key difference between modernity and postmodernity is the network of the three great secret things, "sex, death and religion" and postmodernists like Kierkegaard, Hopkins and Nietzsche were celibate and geniuses of sublimated sexuality's creativity. Jesus' approach to the mystery of the Kingdom and the mystery of the three great secret things has a deep down relation as his *agape* relates to *eros* in its frequent need for reconciliation. To ponder this and better see how Jesus' *agape* fulfills Davidic *hesed* we might think of David and all the difficulties that arose from his adultery and yet how God loved this great sinner. As Jesus tells us he came to love and save sinners. King David's sex life and its many terrible results are vividly described in *The Court History* in *First and Second Samuel* and in *The First Book Of Kings* and the problems are unbelievable. When it came to sex and *eros* King David knew little of righteousness and yet God promised him his everlasting love. But, David and his were terribly punished by the rods of men. Our point here is to see how sinful erotic love can be and yet how the *agape* of Jesus can save those who suffer from the sin by making relations righteous in reconciliation. Not many are sinners like David but there are erotic sinners.

IV, 7.3   And it Can Cause Great Family Hatred

David married King Saul's daughter, Michal, but that never
worked out and then he married Abigail, the wife of Nabal.
He married also Ahninoam and of these marriages were born
Amnon, his first born, and Absalom and his sister, Tamar,
and the Prophet Nathan seems to have guided Bathsheba.
Solomon was born of that marriage and then the trouble started.
Amnon went through a wild relation with his half-sister,
Tamar, loving her, then raping her and then hating her.
She went crazy and her brother Absalom killed Amnon.
Absalom tries to get the Kingdom which has been promised to
Solomon and Absalom gets killed and David mourns him.
Then Adonijah, another of David's sons, attempts intrigue
against Solomon and like so many of David's get killed.
David has to contend with the dangers of wealth, sex, and power.
To combat these dangers Jesus recommends poverty, celibacy,
and obedience as an answer for David's family woes.
David greatly loved each of his wives and each of his children.
What he wanted most of all was reconciliation with each of
them and between each of them and this is what Jesus provides.
This has to do with the mystery of the Kingdom and the mystery
of the three great secret things for his new religious views
on sex have to do with his new religious views on death.
David was promised an everlasting merciful love and
the Kingdom is all about a new view of the everlasting.
Before the time of Jesus celibacy was only appreciated by
mystical types like Plato and in the time of David there was
instead a great emphasis on polygamy for those of wealth.
None of the priests, prophets, kings and sages and none of
the Rabbis recommended celibacy but it can bring us to
rethink sexuality and celibates like Jesus can help sinners
like David for their loving action speaks louder than words.

Agape and *Hesed*

IV, 7.4 But Jesus' Agape can Redeem Eros.

As Jesus begins this discussion about sex, marriage and family life he responds to the Pharisees at the beginning of Matthew chapter 19 who ask him about divorce by saying,

> Have you not read that the creator from
> the beginning made them male and female
> and that he said: "This is why a man
> must leave father and mother, and cling to
> his wife, and the two become one body?"
> They are no longer two, therefore, but
> one body. So then, what God has united,
> man must not divide.

With Jesus marriage becomes a sacred sacrament instituted by him to give grace to wife, husband, children and to all. In erotic love within the context of the sacrament or matrimony there can be a self-opening of one's own person to another. Lovers can abandon themselves to each other in a commitment until death do us part and feel their love to be stronger than death. As David made love to his wives he too loved each one of them. He wanted everlasting love with each but all went terribly wrong. Many of his wives and children were at war with one another. One son raped his half-sister and some of them killed each other. Deep in his heart David longed for reconciliation between each and it seemed that it could never be, but the *agape* of Jesus allows for precisely that, for the punishment of the rods of men can end. And the everlasting *hesed* become *agape* lets there be a purgatory in which the reconciliation process can take place until all are ready to love each other and God forever in the new Kingdom. The greatest story ever told can have a happy ending for all. Even a great sinner like David can still be the beloved of God. Until Jesus came with his love and preached the mystery of the Kingdom of heaven it was never clear how this could be.

IV, 7.5   For Self-sacrificing Celibacy can take Us

Now we come to the mystery of celibacy as we try to understand
how it can help make *eros* righteous and bring reconciliation.
As we go back to Matt 6:33–34 and recall what Jesus
said about righteousness we can begin to get help.

> Set your hearts on his Kingdom first,
> and on his righteousness, and all
> these other things will be given you as well.
> So do not worry about tomorrow:
> tomorrow will take care of itself.
> Each day has enough trouble of its own.

If we continue to think about King David we can see that each
day did have enough trouble of its own for him and for his.
But Jesus is simple like a child and wants his disciples
to be that way too in order to help those who are troubled.
That is the essence of *agape* to live altruistically for others.
That is why Jesus says at Matt 19:12:

> And there are eunuchs who have made themselves
> that way for the sake of the Kingdom of heaven.
> Let anyone accept this who can.

For many, many people *eros* is the most powerful force in
the universe and God made us that way that the human race
might continue for if it were not so powerful we might avoid
it and all the trouble that sex and family life can bring us.
But, it is Jesus' task to make *agape* primary in our lives
and to give *eros* a righteous direction with *agapeic* guidance.
If Jesus' disciples will be celibate like him and channel the
power of their eros in an *agape*ic direction then all those who
meet them might begin to give *their eros* an *agapeic* direction.
Actions do speak louder than words and the righteous actions
of the disciples can be a yeast for all those who listen to them.
Self-sacrificing celibate *agape* can open us to the mysterious.

Agape and *Hesed*

IV, 7.6   Into the Mystery of the Three Great Secret Things

All great art has to do with the three great secret things of sex, death and religion and first of all Jesus introduced a new religion of *agape*ic love for all persons, especially enemies. The first great mystery of the Kingdom of heaven has to do with death and according to Matthew we are all going to live forever either in heaven or in the hell-fire that Q2 stresses. To really understand the secrecy of sex we might think about the sex life of David and see what Jesus, the son of David, and also the Lord of David (see Matt 23:41–43), can teach us of what would become of David whom it would seem might go to hell when sent there by the apocalyptic Son of man and Christ. Already God promised him his everlasting merciful *hesed* and Jesus' *agape* cannot disregard but must fulfill that. But what is the glory of sex that David and Amnon and others in the David story experience as David beheld Bathsheba and Amnon looked upon Tamar and went out of their minds with love? Sex does have its great secrets and women keep their beautiful breasts and bodies until they reveal them as did Bathsheba. When that happens David knows that there is secret after secret yet to be revealed and his desire to partake of those secrets makes him feel as if he is seeking the infinite and the eternal. Biblically you never know a person until you know them sexually and the unexpected happened when Amnon came to know Tamar so that he felt he had gone to hell rather than into heaven's heights. If people get consumed by sex it can lead to their destruction. And this is the point of the David stories but Jesus brings hope not only that all of David's can be reconciled but that sex can become sacramentally more and more beautiful as it did for all the women who loved Jesus in a pure and celibate way. Not only did the apostles become celibate that they might help Jesus lead all sorts to heaven but so did his many women.

IV, 7.7   And the Women Loved the Celibate Jesus

The first Glorious Mystery is the Resurrection for when Jesus
arose from the dead he showed that love could last forever.
Eros' deepest secret is that it wants a love stronger than death.
And as we look at the conclusion of Matthew's Good News
this is precisely what we find for as Jesus rises from
the dead he promises us that we too will live and love forever.
The great mysteries of sex and death come together here
in this greatest of religious mysteries that Jesus has triumphed.
On Holy Thursday at the last supper a woman according to
Matthew anointed Jesus by lovingly pouring ointment on him.
Then we are told at Matt 27:55 that at his death,

> Many women were there, watching from
> a distance, the same women who had
> followed Jesus from Galilee and looked
> after him. Among them were Mary of Magdala,
> Mary the mother of James and Joseph,
> and the mother of Zebedees' sons.

Because Jesus was celibate any woman could celibately love
him with an *agape*ic love and even their husbands would not
object for they could love him too with *agape*ic friendship.
At the last supper, at the death, at the burial and at the
the resurrection the women play a prominent role and
their love for Jesus and his for them gloriously stands out.
They live together in a righteous *eros* and their *eros* will
have secret elements that are even stronger than an *eros*
that has never known sublimation or of Jesus' *agape*.
When Jesus appears to the women Matthew says at 28:9–10,

> And there, coming to meet them, was Jesus.
> "Greeting," he said. And the women came
> up to him and, falling down before him,
> clasped his feet.

IV, 7.8   For His Agape can Heal Broken Erotic Hearts

The women who fell on their knees and lovingly grasped
the feet of Jesus were looking deeply into the mystery of love.
They knew he had the answer for all of our woes and they
knew the power of his love even before the Resurrection.
Now this unbelievable miracle put them on their knees before
him forever and they knew that heaven would be like this forever.
As we have seen with the David stories *eros* can break our hearts.
These women had their hearts broken when he was killed.
But, when the angel of the Lord told Mary of Magdala and the other
Mary who went to visit the sepulcher that he was risen
we read at Matt 28:8,

> Filled with awe and great joy the women
> came quickly away from the tomb and
> ran to tell the disciples.

They were filled with awe because they were beginning to get
a glimpse of how Jesus not only conquered death but how
he was also providing a remedy for every heart broken by *eros*.
If everyone could live forever and come to know of Jesus' love
then there would be time when all broken hearted lovers
could be reconciled and thus bring righteousness at last to *eros*.
Even before these women met Jesus they believed in God
and they beheld in awesome wonder all the beings his hands had made.
But now that every living being that had ever lived could live on
with Jesus in their own glorified body as he was now in his
was just so astounding that their minds could never grasp it.
But their hearts did get a glimpse of what the mystery of the
Kingdom was all about and as Jesus introduced it when he was born
now that he was risen from the dead the women began to behold it.
No wonder of it that they were filled with great wonder and joy.
The first glorious mystery of the resurrection truly was glorious
and it did begin to manifest what the unmanifest Kingdom could be.

IV, 7.9   With His Reconciliation of which Matthew Writes

As the David stories tell us reconciliation often seems impossible.
There was nothing more that David wanted for all of his.
Yahweh promised him his everlasting merciful love and yet
how could that ever happen as his loved ones died hating each other?
And as we saw at Matt 5:23 Jesus does demand reconciliation:

> If you are bringing your gift to the altar
> and there remember that your brother has
> something against you, go and be reconciled
> with your brother first, and then come back
> and present your offering.

But now with the resurrection of the dead and an eternal life
it is possible eventually to get this reconciliation between everyone.
We will not get into the Kingdom of heaven until we are reconciled
with all because heaven is a lovely world without any enmity.
David and all of his had a lot of hell on earth or what we might call
purgatory on earth for purgatory is this process of reconciliation.
We can pray for the poor souls that they might be reconciled
and they can help us because we need to be reconciled with each other.
The ladies who loved Jesus were apostles to the apostles as they
were told by Jesus to go to the eleven and tell them that
they should meet with him in Galilee and they loved him
with a love and now an understanding of him that was special.
As they went to the eleven they even thought of poor Judas
and even though he had hanged himself in despair they
knew that he too would be reconciled in the Kingdom of heaven.
Jesus had commanded reconciliation and the ladies who
loved him knew that all would obey him eventually and that
the righteousness he loved and died for would come for all.
Deep in their heart they prayed "Oh my Jesus, forgive us
our sins and lead all to heaven especially those like Judas."

IV, 8 And Friendship Righteousness

IV, 8.1 *Friendship too can be Self-centered*

Aristotle defined friendship as two people standing side by side
appreciating the world together and he saw them as eating
a peck of salt together as they worked together on a common project.
Aristotle saw himself as being friends with Plato as they worked
together at the love of wisdom, contemplation and seeking the truth.
But Aristotle saw friendship as limited to a few for most
people are acquaintances who do not spend their life together
working at a common task for most of us have different ways of life.
That the friend is for Aristotle the other half of my soul
shows that friendship is not an altruistic love for all.
Aristotle saw the friend as the other half of my soul and
that shows the self-centeredness of friendship which excludes others.
When we think of friendship as Aristotle so well defined it we
can see that it, like the other natural loves, is lacking in righteousness.
The masses of people as Aristotle would see it would not be
capable of friendship for they would not have a dedicated life
which they could share with another of the same kind of dedication.
But once Jesus' *agape* brings us to see that all persons have
an equal dignity we can see what it takes to make friendship right.
We should be friendly to all and try to appreciate the vision of each
for their vision can contribute to ours and we can help them.
Jesus went to simple persons like fishermen to be his friends
and the women who loved him with their *agape*ic *eros* were also
friends with him for they too wanted to help with his mission.
He wanted to stand side by side with everyone and share with
them the vision of the Kingdom of heaven in all its mystery.
Friendship, unlike *eros*, is not one of the three great secret things
but friends study together the mystery of those secret things.
Jesus is revealing that the Father, Son and Holy Spirit are
agape and their *agape* is more like friendship than *eros* or affection.

IV, 8.2 But David and Jonathan

The Hebrew Bible has many stories of friendship but the greatest
is that of Jonathan and David which begins at 1 Samuel 18,
after David replied, "The son of your servant, Jesse
of Bethlehem," when Saul asks him whose son he is.

> After David had finished talking to Saul,
> Jonathan's soul became closely bound to David's
> and Jonathan came to love him as his own soul.
> Jonathan made a pact with David to love him
> as his own soul; he took off the cloak
> he was wearing and gave it to David,
> and his armor too, even his sword,
> his bow and his belt.

David killed Goliath and he was a wondrous warrior and
the people of the United Kingdom came to love him more
than King Saul and Saul's son, Jonathan, also recognized
that David was the Lord's beloved and took David as his friend.
As it turned out Jonathan was in effect saying that if God
has chosen David to be king instead of himself that was God's will.
This language of the Bible sounds almost like Aristotle's in
describing friends as the other half of each other's soul.
This passage shows us the beauty of friendship and what
Jesus wants his disciples to do is to love everyone they meet
even as Jonathan here loves David with this friendly commitment.
This friendship of Jonathan has an abandonment that seems
to be as strong and as passionate as that of erotic lovers.
Jonathan gave David his cloak, his armor, his sword,
his bow and his belt and these are symbolic of Jonathan's
commitment to David even as his new king instead of himself.
Jonathan made a pact with David and as husband and wife
might give each other a wedding ring so Jonathan is giving
an outward sign of his friendship and loyalty to David.

Agape and *Hesed*

IV, 8.3 Wanted it to Reconcile their Families

Beginning at 1 Samuel 18:7 King Saul sees David
as a threat and is trying to kill him.
When they came back from a battle the women would
come out to greet them dancing and singing:

> Saul has killed his thousands
> and David his tens of thousands.

And jealousy began to stir in Saul and it grew stronger and
stronger and he saw that the people wanted David as king.
Jonathan would never become king if David became king
but Jonathan could see that David was graced and he was
himself graced enough to appreciate and side with his friend.
Jonathan initiated a friendship that he hoped would reconcile his
family with that of David and David greatly appreciated Jonathan's
good intentions and the excellent person that he knew Jonathan was.
Often Saul tried to have David killed and his daughter, Michal,
whom he gave to David as a wife, protected David and several times
Jonathan protected David from his own father's attempt at murder.
Before Saul was king each of the tribes of Israel and Judah had
their own rulers and Saul was the first ruler of the United Kingdom.
But now the people of Judah broke away and made David
their king so Saul saw the usurpation right before his own eyes.
Finally Saul and Jonathan were both killed and
2 Samuel 1:26 has a lament of David for Saul and Jonathan:

> O Jonathan in your death I am stricken,
> I am desolate for you, Jonathan, my brother,
> very dear to me you were,
> your love to me more wonderful
> than the love of a woman.

David knew the secret loveliness of *eros* with Bathsheba
and many other adorable women and yet he says that his
friendship with Jonathan was more wonderful than his *eros*.

IV, 8.4   And Jesus' Agape makes that Possible

It is hard to imagine a friendship more beautiful and noble
than that of Jonathan and David and yet it ended in lament.
And what a lament it was! David's love for Jonathan was
more wonderful than the love of a woman and how beautiful
was the love of Bathsheba for David and David for Bathsheba!
Bathsheba could feel the masculine power and beauty in every cell
of David's body and her female being ached with love for him.
Likewise as David first beheld Bathsheba his heart was
on fire with desire to be with that lovely female female.
As she gave him her further secrets month by month and
year by year in little death after little death he wanted nothing
more than to be in ecstatic trance and glory with her forever.
And yet he says that his friendship with Jonathan was even more
wonderful so even more strongly he wanted that to be forever.
Yahweh did promise David his everlasting merciful love and
that somehow meant that David and his could be in love forever.
And yet David's family had more hatred than any kind of love.
And now Jonathan was dead and gone forever so what did God
mean by an everlasting love that would outlast any punishment?
The *agape* of Matthew's Jesus provides the answer to this question.
The love of Jesus culminates in his resurrection and the glorious
mystery of his body ascending into heaven and with faith and
hope we can all trust that forever we will be able to be there too.
David and Bathsheba and all his loves will be there too in a
reconciled love where they can love each other's unique bodies
forever in a totally satisfying celibacy of ever further knowing.
And as Jesus will be there in friendship with all his disciples
so will David and Jonathan get to be there in that number.
In the *agape* that makes their friendship righteous these souls
will be able to expand together forever as they get to share in
friendship all that ever was and all that ever will be without end.

Agape and *Hesed*

IV, 8.5   For his Disciples were Friends

David and Jonathan's special friendship did exclude others
for Jonathan's father, King Saul, was David's enemy and by being
friends with David Jonathan was working against his own father.
David and Jonathan had a friendship for two and no one else could
know the regal attitude, moods, feelings, thoughts, words and deeds
that they shared together as they tried to understand their lives.
But throughout Matthew's Gospel Jesus reveals to us the mysteries
of a Kingdom in which all will begin to dwell in a new friendship.
In the Kingdom of heaven throughout eternity we will be able to know
each other better and better as friends and all enmity will have been
purged away as *agape* will let us love each other forever with
affection, friendship, and *eros* in a new *agapeic ahava* for neighbor.
So at the end of Matthew's Gospel in the Great Commission we read:

> Go, therefore, make disciples of all nations;
> baptize them in the name of the Father
> and of the Son and of the Holy Spirit,
> and teach them to observe all the commands
> I gave you. And know that I am with you
> always; yes, to the end of time.

Then at the end of time we will be with him and each other in love
throughout all of eternity for that is the meaning of the Kingdom.
The disciples became friends with each other and with Jesus as
they became celibate and left all behind to follow him.
Now they are to go out and begin the great task of making of
everyone on earth a disciple who will live in a society of friends.
He tells them to teach them all the commands he has given them and
all those will be kept if they but love the Lord their God with
their whole heart, mind and soul and love their neighbor as they
love themselves and now it is seen that everyone is their neighbor.
It is this task of making disciples and friends of all that
is the meaning of the promise given to David of everlasting love.

IV, 8.6 Working with an Angelic Celibacy for All

One of the secrets of sex is that at its best it does commit
lovers to each other and no other and that is why Jesus said
that you already commit adultery if you so much as desire another.
Celibacy is the commitment to have sex with none so that you
can be open to love all in a new *agape*ic friendship of standing
side by side with everyone and seeking salvation for all.
Jesus did have a new *agape*ic *eros* with those ladies who in their
celibacy could love him in his uniqueness and even as a man
but most of all his disciples, both men and women, are in a new
*agape*ic friendship with him and each other that seeks to have that
*agape*ic friendship and affection for all the people of all the nations.
It will take a long time to bring this about and that is why
Jesus will be with his disciples, both men and women, until
the end of time as through his Holy Spirit he helps them with this.
As time is going on the reconciling can take place in purgatory
so that David can become reconciled with Saul and his
and with Bathsheba's husband whom he has killed.
What Jesus promises us in this new mysterious kingdom
is how to forgive others as they forgive us so that as the process
of purgation works itself out David will not be making his
own to suffer because of his failure to love in a righteous way.
The *agape* of Jesus is so altruistic that it loves the enemy
even more than itself and especially in a childlike innocence
and in self-sacrificing celibacy it can reconcile with the enemy.
If the disciples will really be disciples and follow Jesus in
his celibate love a friendship will flourish that reconciles all.
This is the mercy that David believed in when God promised him
his love and it is the mercy that Jesus makes clear and fulfills.
In poverty, celibacy and obedience the disciples will be able
to show a new way to those caught up in the desire for wealth,
pleasure and power for they will show the way of Jesus to them.

Agape and *Hesed*

IV, 8.7 And Righteously Obeying Him

David was promised that his dynasty and Kingdom would last forever. But he could never have guessed in the slightest what that dynasty and Kingdom would come to mean when Jesus the Christ began to proclaim and preach the mystery of that fulfilled Kingdom. The main point about this Kingdom of heaven, which is the guiding theme through Matthew's Gospel, is that everyone will have an eternal life and time to become reconciled with everyone. If persons just obey Jesus and live righteous lives the Kingdom of heaven will be theirs and in being with God the Father, Son and Holy Spirit forever they will be able to love all of theirs as well. To obey Jesus and live righteously we really only need to do one thing and that is love righteously as did he and that is we need to love others and even our enemies more than we love self. So what David will come to see in his eternal life is that Jesus revealed nine new dimensions of his own everlasting Kingdom.

1. It will be an eternal Kingdom.
2. The chosen people will include all people.
3. It will be a Kingdom of altruistic love.
4. Even of enemies who are to be loved more than self.
5. And it will be for childlike believers.
6. And the closest disciples here on earth will be celibate.
7. That they might devote their life to bringing the Kingdom to all.
8. And purgatory will give us all a chance at reconciliation.
9. So that David will be able to be reconciled with all of his.

Agape as Jesus revealed it is: 1) an eternal love, 2) a universal love, 3) an altruistic love, 4) an unconditional love, 5) a childlike love, 6) a celibate love, 7) a missionary love, 8) a purgatorial love, and 9) a love that so loves love that it promises heaven to all. As the disciples followed Jesus and worked more and more for the mysterious Kingdom of heaven they often failed to obey him as did Peter and yet *agape* reveals Peter as a saintly sinner.

IV, 8.8 By going out to baptize all the nations

It is the very nature of love that it wants to share with others.
Affection, eros, friendship and *ahava* each tend to be exclusivistic.
But the *agape* that Jesus introduced was entirely unheard of
for he wanted to make those loves righteous by opening them to all.
Jesus is the son and Lord of David and *agape* grew directly
out of *hesed* and fulfills *hesed* but *agape* is so different as
can be seen when we look at the attitude of David to the enemy.
King David was loved by his people primarily for killing the enemy.
As we know he got his start with Goliath and the gruesome
is at the heart of the David stories for we know how the people
loved him when he cut off the head of the giant with his own sword.
Basically the David stories have to do with killing the enemy and
with building up his harem often, of course, for political reasons
so that he is exactly the opposite of Jesus who loves his enemies
and recommends celibacy so that love might be taken to all enemies.
When you think of the three religions of the Book: Judaism, Islam
and Christianity it is as if Islam bypasses Christianity and goes back
to the very faith and spirit of Judaism at the time of David.
Mohammed built up a harem much like David's and the history
of Islam is a history of victory after victory over the enemy so that
you could say that the Moslems were very successful followers
of David and never paid the slightest attention to the *agapeic* revolution.
Islam would go out and try to make all nations Islamic but
that is not at all like celibate missionaries going out to take
the message of *agape* to all so that they might ask for baptism.
In some strange ways Christianity with its *agape*ic ideal which
we see in Matthew's gospel is more like Buddhism than even
Judaism or Islam for Matthew glorifies love and peace rather
than the kind of warlike process that even King David displayed.
The women danced and sang because David killed tens
of thousands and David loved killing thousands and for his women.

Agape and *Hesed*

IV, 8.9   And Bring them all Reconciliation

As we reflect upon postmodern approaches to Jesus' message
we can see that Luther and Calvin stressed the atonement justice
theology of Q2 and did not believe in the incarnation love theology
of Q1 and they are with Matthew in stressing righteousness.
The implication of their theology is that King David himself whom
the Lord loved would go to hell and not heaven for he never did
get reconciled with God or within his family or with his people.
Being consistent with their justice theology Luther and Calvin both
saw no good scriptural reason to believe in purgatory and hence
as Calvin maintained most people are destined for hell.
But if you believe that Jesus became man and died for us
because he loved us then the possibility for reconciliation for David
and for many lesser sinners seems to be a logical outcome.
Believing that God is a loving God as Jesus revealed him to be
could still let righteousness have its place but in the long run love
would win out and that is the logic of love that implies purgatory.
Persons who are still not righteous cannot enter the Kingdom
of heaven but the loving childlike Jesus can still save each of us.
We have the hope that we will be graced to forgive those who
trespass against us and that they will all someday forgive us.
As the postmodernists Kierkegaard and Nietzsche thought about
their modern Lutheran heritage they both stressed in their own way
the God-man and his works of love and the childlike Jesus.
As we conclude we will consider in detail the thought of
Levinas and Derrida and see how different it is from that of
Kierkegaard and Nietzsche when it comes to *ahava, hesed* and *agape*.
Matthew's gospel proclaims the Kingdom that has the nine
elements that we have begun to spell out and the question arises
will Derrida or Levinas believe in any of those traits of *agape*?
They want to get beyond modernity but how far can they go
without accepting the Messiah and his good news of love for all?

IV, 9 And Septuagint *Agape* Righteousness

IV, 9.1 *By Fulfilling Ahava with Eternity*

The Kingdom of heaven which is the focus of Matthew's gospel
puts a new kind of emphasis on the eternal life of every person.
Jesus' new love of *agape* and the reconciliation it demands gives
his disciples a new faith and hope that they will be able to
love each other with our heavenly Father throughout all eternity.
The Jewish people before Jesus did have notions of the everlasting.
Hesed is an everlasting merciful love but that could not mean
throughout all of time and the Sadducees could take it that way.
Psalm 138 ends with David singing:

> Though I live surrounded by trouble
> you keep me alive-to my enemies fury!
> You stretch your hand out and save me.
> Your right hand will do everything for me.
> Yahweh, your love is everlasting,
> do not abandon us whom you have made.

Yahweh's *hesed* is everlasting and Yahweh is an everlasting God
but David did not think of a life after death in which he
would be reconciled with all of his wives and children and
especially not with enemies who included many of his dear ones.
Lovers naturally want to be with each other forever and the
Pharisees did believe in a life after death but Jesus with his
resurrection gave life after death a new meaning unheard of before.
That David and Bathsheba and Jonathan and all of David's could
be happy together forever in heaven never occurred to anyone.
So the *agape* of Jesus is going to let us love God and our
neighbor and all of our loved ones and even our enemies
forever and thus it fulfills *ahava* in an undreamed of way.
All of our relations will have to be righteous in order that
we might achieve the reconciliation that can let the Kingdom
of heaven be, and with purgatory that will become possible.

Agape and *Hesed*

IV, 9.2 By Fulfilling Ahava with Universality

The great love command of *ahava* to love our neighbor as we
love ourself is the Golden Rule for all religions for we should
all treat others as we would like to be treated with kindness.
But to love all foreigners was not dreamed of for as we
have seen in the David stories most neighboring peoples
were enemies and there was fury not love between them.
So in this respect too Jesus' *agape* was a revolutionary idea.
Not only does the *agape* of Jesus extend throughout all
of time into eternity but it is meant to extend through all space.
Matthew's Jesus not only teaches us that all persons are our
neighbor but he teaches us that we are all brothers and sisters.
When speaking of reconciliation he says that if your brother has
anything against you go and be reconciled first with him.
The *Our Father* shows that we are all children of the same Father.
In the Kingdom of heaven we will be one people and one family.
However, *agape* will preserve not only family affection but it will
preserve *eros* in that we will each have eternity to get to
known and love each unique other even as male and female.
Agape will also preserve and fulfill *ahava* even in so far as
it was translated in the Septuagint as *agape* but an *agape*
that is not yet Jesus' *agape* as Matthew's good news makes clear.
Mary Magdalene and the other women who loved Jesus will get
to continue loving him in their own way throughout eternity.
But all the women who have ever lived will get to love him
and be loved by him and he will say each of their names in
a unique and special way even though there will be billions.
It is our gift and task to start building up the Kingdom of
heaven here on earth by loving all humans as our neighbors.
But to do that we should also love them as our brothers and
sisters, as our friends and even as our beloved for while there
is no marriage in heaven we will be in our glorified body.

IV, 9.3 By Fulfilling Ahava with Altruism

The *ahava* which God revealed to the Hebrew people did have
altruistic elements for in loving our neighbor as ourself
there is an equal balance of altruism and of egoism.
Levinas brings out the altruism of caring for widows, orphans
and aliens and he stresses the altruism of the Suffering Servant.
Matthew's Jesus teaches an *agape* that is primarily altruistic
and thus he transforms and fulfills the altruism of *ahava*.
Insofar as Matthew uses Mark's synoptic outline he treats
of an altruistic *ahava* for in the first half of Mark's gospel
Jesus is taking care of widows, orphans, aliens and the needy
in Galilee then in the second half he goes up to Jerusalem
to become the Suffering Servant who dies for those killing him.
The Jesus of Q1 in his Sermon on the Mount is totally
altruistic in loving the enemy and in not resisting any evil.
Matthew teaches us of a Kingdom in which Jesus is altruistic
and in which Jesus teaches that God the Father is also altruistic
in loving humankind so much that he sends his Son to us.
The disciples who came to love Jesus had a difficult time in
learning how to understand his altruistic *agape* and thus
Peter went through several stages of resisting what Jesus said
about dying for others and he resisted those who were taking Jesus.
When Jesus went through the anxiety of his Agony in the Garden
none of the disciples prayed with him as they went to sleep.
By loving Jesus more and more the disciples came to
practice his altruistic love more and more and that helped
them to better understand not only Jesus but also God the Father.
As we listen to the teaching of Jesus about his universal and
eternal love we begin to understand its altruism and as we
try to imitate him and practice that love we come to understand
it and him better even as we discover how difficult it is.
Understanding leads to practice and practice leads to understanding.

Agape and *Hesed*

IV, 9.4 *By Fulfilling Ahava with Unconditionality*

The Hebrew people were called to an unconditional love for Yahweh. They were to be his people and he was to be their only God. They were also called to unconditionally love their neighbor. The Ten Commandments clarified how they were to practice this law. When Jesus called Peter, Andrew, James, John, and his disciples he called them to a new kind of unconditional love in which they were to give their lives that all might enter his Kingdom of love. In Matthew's Gospel we see how the disciples, both men and women, loved Jesus and from them we see how we must love. Throughout all ages since we have been able to think about him and seek him, to talk with him and to feel his nearness to us. You can see how the Jews who had unconditional love for God would think that Jesus and his disciples were blaspheming against the true God since they did not believe in the Son of God. Holy Jews loved their God unconditionally and if they did not believe that Jesus and his *agape* fulfilled Yahweh and his *ahava* then you can see why they felt it their duty to get rid of Jesus. This new unconditional love of *agape* does go beyond *ahava* in all the nine ways we are reflecting upon in this last chapter. *Ahava* as an unconditional love of the Jew for Yahweh does not believe in an eternal, universal, altruistic, unconditional love for everyone including the enemy that will go out with a childlike, celibate, missionary love to teach all about loving love. Judaism is an ethnic religion which believes that the Jews are God's chosen people and that you do not go out trying to convert non-Jews into being Jews for that is not God's will. The disciples of Jesus were given the gifts of faith, hope and love and that love committed them to an unconditional love for Jesus and for all persons as they totally surrendered to Jesus. In the 23rd Psalm you see how David was totally committed to his Good Shepherd and so should every Christian be to Jesus.

IV, 9.5 By Fulfilling Ahava with Childlikeness

We first meet Matthew's Jesus as the baby Jesus, the Son of God
and the child of Mary and how many loved this sweet baby Jesus?
So many great artists have painted him and Christmas cards
show him to us in ever new ways and Christmas is his day.
Matthew's Jesus tells his disciples that if they want to follow him
they must become like little children with total trust in the Father.
This image of the child is the highpoint of Nietzsche's *Zarathustra*.
In the world of *ahava* and Judaism no great prophet, priest, King
or sage is ever primarily seen as childlike and so again this
trait of *agape* that the lover must be childlike is a transformation.
The *agape* that promises that all persons who ever loved are the
children of God and that Jesus has come to save them demands
a childlike trust and hope in love for it is an unimaginable story.
This greatest story ever told will not even be considered by
scientific adults who are not happy, carefree, childlike, believers.
God's affirmation of love for all persons has become known
only with Jesus and in loving Jesus as a child we can come
to believe in him and his salvation for everyone forever more.
This Kingdom of heaven is absolutely mysterious and
only the childlike can believe in it with a playful, questioning love.
This Jesus not only promises all persons eternal salvation
but he tells us he must suffer and die for it and so must we.
Then he tells us that he will be resurrected from the dead
and so will we and all loving beings throughout all of time.
God's birth, God's suffering and death, God's resurrection
and God's eternal altruistic love are strange beyond knowledge.
And yet like little children we are called to believe in such
an unconditional, altruistic, universal, eternal love and
to spend our lives helping Jesus to bring this story about.
It takes a childlike spirit to believe that each of us can play
a role in helping Jesus to bring about this Kingdom for all.

Agape and *Hesed*

IV, 9.6 By Fulfilling Ahava with Celibacy

As we see in Matt 19:10–12 Jesus' disciples can have
three types of vocation: there can be those who are married.
those who are single and those who are called to celibacy.
As Jesus says:

> There are eunuchs who have made
> themselves that way for the sake of
> the Kingdom of heaven.
> Let anyone accept this who can.

Celibacy is another special way persons can imitate
Jesus in his unconditional love for his Father and his Kingdom.
The disciples who were Jews would not have known of celibacy
as a way of unconditionally dedicating one's life to serving God.
Abraham, David and Solomon were polygamists but it does seem
that monotheism implies monogamy and by the time we get
to Hosea and the *Song of Songs ahava* points in that direction
with an *eros* that brings one man and one woman together in
a union that excludes any adultery until does us part.
A man and a woman can discover a love of total surrender
to each other and it can let them love Jesus with total surrender.
The sacrament of matrimony can bless a couple in holy wedlock
so that they lock themselves together and throw away the key.
All of this holy love could naturally be understood by the
Jewish people and Jesus' Jewish disciples but this new idea
of following Jesus with celibacy is a new aspect of *agape*.
The disciples, priests, nuns and religious are called
to a life of poverty, celibacy and obedience in which they are
to dedicate themselves completely in the spirit of the Jesus of Q1
to bringing the good news of the Kingdom of heaven to all people.
They are to love Jesus and his church just as a married man
would love his wife and family or a woman would love her husband
and children for celibacy is to free them for missionary love.

IV, 9.7 By Fulfilling Ahava with Missionary Love

As we have said *ahava* is an ethnic love that does not seek to go out and convert other people to it because God chooses his own. But once Jesus revealed *agape* with its eternal dimensions and universal intent it was only natural for Jesus to say:

> Go therefore, make disciples of all the nations;
> baptize them in the name of the Father and
> of the Son and of the Holy Spirit, and teach
> them to observe all the commands I gave you.
> And know that I am with you always;
> Yes, to the end of time.

The Jews would be very upset with Jesus and his disciples for trying to convert them from their *ahava* to this new *agape* for all. They would no longer be the special chosen people now that all are the chosen people so even if you have a messianicity without the Messiah as does Derrida your messianicity is still without these nine traits of *agape* which is also rejected..
The Jews would see Jesus and his disciples as proselytizing and they would see that as a negative activity for according to them it could only be a step backwards rather than a step forward. In a way the people of *ahava* have a great superiority complex and they think they are the best and in accord with this self-image they are high achievers in acquiring wealth, in successful family living and in excelling in so many of the arts and sciences.
But Jesus teaches that all humans are God's chosen loved ones and that everyone has a great dignity and his goal is to take his message and let all the nations know how the Father loves them. *Agape's* universality demands a missionary activity that all persons might come to know of *agape*, of how they are loved, and of how they should love all others even as God loved his David. The missionary wants to let everyone pray: "Oh, how goodness and kindness pursue me, every day of my life" (Ps 23:6–23).

Agape and *Hesed*

IV, 9.8 By Fulfilling Ahava with Purgatorial Love

The notion of purgatory helps make sense of the *agape*
in Matthew's Gospel for it does make reconciliation possible.
If no one is fit for the Kingdom of heaven until they are
reconciled with everyone then purgatory makes that possible.
Q1 presents a Jesus who loves and forgives all while Q2
presents a Christ who judges and sends many into hell.
Purgatory can be seen as this hell fire which cleanses sinners.
So we can pray for the blessed dead and they can pray for us.
In a communion of saints we can all suffer and help
each other to get the reconciliation that takes us into the Kingdom.
So the Jesus of Q1 is the ultimate Jesus who will forgive all
sinners, love enemies and bring all into the Kingdom of heaven.
The Christ of Q2 who is the rewarder punisher judge makes
that happy eternity for all possible by sending sinners to purgatory.
There Mary and all the Angels and Saints can intercede for us
until we are ready to be with them and while we are still here
on earth so we also can help relieve the poor souls in purgatory.
On the final day we will each be joined with our glorified bodies
and be with Jesus, Mary, Joseph and God the Father, Son and
Holy Spirit together loving and knowing each other forever more.
Just as many Jews thought there was no life after death, but
some did, so also there could be a possible purgatory or not.
In 2nd Maccabees Mrs. Maccabees prays with her living sons
for their brothers who have been killed and this praying for
the dead is the first implication connecting *ahava* and purgatory.
If we love our neighbors we can pray for them when they are dead.
It is this idea of loving the dead and helping them that *agape*
fulfills *ahava* and that Holy Mother Church has always
fostered in her Church's Year of Grace as we pray for sinners
and the forgiveness of sin and a life everlasting for everyone.
Purgatory is a reconciliation process for persons and for ideas.

IV, 9.9 By Fulfilling Ahava with the Loving of Love

What the Jesus of Matthew's good news teaches most of all is
that love is the highest value and greatest reality in the universe.
Jesus teaches us that we can all love God and each other in
the Kingdom of heaven forever and that that will totally fulfill us.
There are many kinds of different love: affection, friendship,
eros, ahava, hesed, bhakti, karuna, jen, rahim, etc.
And *agape* can fulfill all these loves as they can each bring out
different dimensions of *agape* for each is eternally loveable.
What Jesus teaches is that we should love above all and
if we do then we will properly love God and each other forever.
As we will later study in the first letter of John, "God is *agape*."
The Father, the Son and the Holy Spirit are their love for each other.
The Holy Spirit is the love between the Father and the Son and
creation began when they altruistically shared their love with others.
As we read in the Priestly Creation Story of Genesis I
whatever God created was good and he created the male and
the female humans in his own image and likeness for we
were created in the likeness of the *agape* Jesus revealed.
When *ahava* was revealed to the Jewish people by Moses
they came to see that the focal point of their life should be
to love God with their whole heart, mind and soul and their
neighbor as themselves and the Ten Commandments clarified this.
When *hesed* was revealed to David he knew of God's everlasting
merciful love for him and his dynasty and just as *ahava*
was the center for all Jewish life so *hesed* was that for Judah.
Jesus teaches us that we should unconditionally dedicate
our lives to developing *agape* for *agape* and if we do that
we will fulfill each of our loves that all want an eternal love.
Agape for *agape* believes and hopes in an eternal, universal,
altruistic, unconditional, childlike *agape* that might even
become celibate to be missionary that all might love Love.

Bibliography

Beals, Corey. *Levinas and the Wisdom of Love*. Waco, TX: Baylor University Press, 2007.
Cohen., A., ed. *The Psalms Hebrew Text & English Translation with an Introduction and Commentary by A. Cohen*. London: Soncino, 1958.
Derrida, Jacques. "Che Cos è la Poesia?" In *A Derrida Reader: Between the Blinds*, edited with an introduction and notes by Peggy Kamuf, 223–37. New York: Columbia University Press, 1991.
———. *The Force of Law: Mystical Foundation of Authority*. Translated by Mary Quaintance. In *Deconstruction and the Possibility of Justice*, edited by Drucilla Cornell et al., 68–91. New York: Routledge, 1992.
———. *The Gift of Death*. Translated by David Wills. Chicago: University of Chicago Press, 1992.
———. *Given Time: 1. Counterfeit Money*. Translated by Peggy Kamuf. Chicago: University of Chicago Press, 1991.
———. *Glas*. Translated by John P. Leavey Jr. and Richard Rand. Lincoln: University of Nebraska Press, 1986
———. *Violence and Metaphysics: An Essay on the Thought of Emmanuel Levinas in Writing and Difference*. Translated by Alan Bass. Chicago: University of Chicago Press, 1978.
Glueck, Nelson. *Hesed in the Bible*. Translated by Alfred Gottschalk. Cincinnati: Hebrew Union College Press, 1967.
Levinas, Emmanuel. *Difficult Freedom: Essays on Judaism*. Translated by S. Hand. London: Athlone, 1990.
———. *Entre nous: Essais sur le penser-à- l'autre*. Paris: Grasset, 1991
———. *Nine Talmudic Readings*. Translated by A. Aronowicz. Bloomington: Indiana University Press, 1990.
———. *Otherwise than Being or Beyond Essence*. Translated by Alphonse Lingis. The Hague: Nijhoff, 1981.
———. *Proper Names*. Translated by Michael B. Smith. Standford, CA: Standford University Press, 1996.
———. *Totality and Infinity: An Essay on Exteriority*. Translated by Alphonse Lingis. The Hague: Nijhoff, 1980.
Peperzak, Adriaan T., ed. *Ethics as First Philosophy: The Significance of Emmanuel Levinas for Philosophy, Literature and Religion*. New York: Routledge, 1995.
Sakenfeld, Katharine Doob. *The Meaning of Hesed in the Hebrew Bible: A New Inquiry*. Missoula, MT: Scholars, 1978.
Wallis, Gerhard. "The Meaning of Ahava in the Hebrew Bible." In *Theological Dictionary of the Old Testament*, edited by G. Johannes Botterweck and Helmer Ringgren, 1:99–118. Grand Rapids: Eerdmans, 1974.

www.ingramcontent.com/pod-product-compliance
Lightning Source LLC
Chambersburg PA
CBHW071147300426
44113CB00009B/1116